French Fiction in the Mitterrand Years

OXFORD STUDIES IN MODERN EUROPEAN CULTURE

GENERAL EDITORS

Elizabeth Fallaize, Robin Fiddian and Katrin Kohl

Oxford Studies in Modern European Culture is a new series conceived as a response to the changing modes of study of European literature and culture in many universities. Designed to combine focus with breadth, each title in the series will present a range of texts or films in dialogue with their historical and cultural contexts—not simply as a reflection of history but engaged in a mediation with history, conceived in broad terms as cultural, social and political history. Flexible, interdisciplinary approaches are encouraged together with the use of texts outside the traditional canon alongside more familiar works. In order to make the volumes accessible not only to students of modern languages but also to those studying the history or politics of modern Europe, all quotations are offered in both the original language and in English.

French Fiction in the Mitterrand Years

Memory, Narrative, Desire

Colin Davis and **Elizabeth Fallaize**

OXFORD
UNIVERSITY PRESS

OXFORD
UNIVERSITY PRESS

Great Clarendon Street, Oxford OX2 6DP
Oxford University Press is a department of the University of Oxford.
It furthers the University's objective of excellence in research, scholarship,
and education by publishing worldwide in

Oxford New York

Athens Auckland Bangkok Bogotá Buenos Aires Calcutta
Cape Town Chennai Dar es Salaam Delhi Florence Hong Kong Istanbul
Karachi Kuala Lumpur Madrid Melbourne Mexico City Mumbai
Nairobi Paris São Paulo Singapore Taipei Tokyo Toronto Warsaw

and associated companies in Berlin Ibadan

Oxford is a registered trade mark of Oxford University Press
in the UK and certain other countries

Published in the United States
by Oxford University Press Inc., New York

British Library Cataloguing in Publication Data
Data available

Library of Congress Cataloging in Publication Data
Data available

ISBN 0-19-815956-0
ISBN 0-19-815955-2 (Pbk.)

1 3 5 7 9 10 8 6 4 2

Typeset by Graphicraft Limited, Hong Kong
Printed in Great Britain
on acid-free paper by
Biddles Ltd, Guildford and King's Lynn

Acknowledgements

We would like to thank Alex Hughes, Julia Waters, Sarah Kay, and Alan Grafen for help and advice in the preparation of this book, as well as the students who have discussed and sometimes dissented from the views we develop here. Chapters 1, 4, and 5 were initially drafted by Elizabeth Fallaize, and Chapters 2, 3, 6, and the Conclusion by Colin Davis; we each drafted one half of the Introduction. The book in its final form is the joint work of both authors.

Contents

Introduction

Reports of the demise of the French novel have so far proved to be premature. The competition of other media, especially film and television, has so far not been as fatal as some have anticipated. In fact many authors have found productive accommodations with these media, cashing the cheques for film scripts or filmed versions of their novels, publicizing their latest works through television and the press, borrowing and adapting images, themes, and structures from popular culture in their literary works. Patrick Modiano is a case in point: his novels often play upon the reader's familiarity with popular culture, especially detective fiction; and he has been actively involved in film-making, having co-written a film script (*Lacombe Lucien*, co-written and directed by Louis Malle), allowed his work to be filmed (*Villa Triste*), and he has even acted on screen himself, playing Catherine Deneuve's ex-husband in Raul Ruiz's *Généalogies d'un crime*. If, as has frequently been alleged, fiction is in crisis, then it is a crisis which has been going on for centuries; it is the condition of the novel's continuity and the source of its vitality. And if there is no Proust or Balzac today, then neither was there a Proust living in 1840 or a Balzac in 1910. It is not for us to decide, and it is certainly not our intention in this book to attempt to predict, which of the writers of more recent decades will still be considered worth reading in fifty years' time. The aim of the current book is to analyse some of the most important and interesting directions in recent French fiction through detailed discussions of a selection of texts, all published during François Mitterrand's period as President of the Fifth Republic (1981–95).

The Mitterrand years

French writers living under the fourteen-year presidency of François Mitterrand were living through a period of sharp change in political and intellectual climate. The very existence of a Socialist President of the Fifth Republic, following on from Charles de Gaulle, Georges Pompidou, and Valéry Giscard d'Estaing, in itself appeared a new and radical departure from the past, quickly confirmed by the triumph of the Socialist and Communist Parties in the legislative elections which Mitterrand called within weeks of his own victory. In the euphoria of the street parties, the traditionally close relationship between intellectuals and the left in France fed the sense that one of their own was at last installed in the Elysée, and that he had both the means and the will to bring about radical reforms.

However, as economic circumstances worsened, as the regime adopted an increasingly pragmatic approach, as the early reforms passed into memory and Mitterrand found himself in an awkward yet ultimately manageable marriage with the right, the picture became more confused. A new consensus style of politics was emerging; the left showed itself willing and able to manage a market economy, give or take a few nationalizations, the Communist Party lost both its place in government and much of its influence, and the old alliance of intellectuals with the left appeared irrelevant. By July 1983 the government was complaining in *Le Monde* that French intellectuals had fallen silent.[1] The connections between culture and revolution were no longer in evidence, grand theory in politics was no longer the order of the day, and writers, as we shall see, turned their attention away from theory and on to other issues, including a concern with France's role in a past preceding the Mitterrand era.

Mitterrand himself was not of course responsible for these shifts, although his own political style, blending tactical oscillations with a sense of history, fitted well with the mood and turn of events. Mitterrand was in power almost as long as Napoleon; we can only guess at the place in twentieth-century French history that hindsight will allocate to him, but the term 'the Mitterrand years' can already stand as a kind of shorthand for an era which had moved on sharply from the prosperous political and intellectual confidence of the 1960s and early 1970s, and from an idealized notion of union between intellectuals and the left. The change that had been anticipated by the left and the intelligentsia at the time of Mitterrand's election had soon been aborted, but a significant ideological shift, even abandonment, had nevertheless occurred. We will now examine in the rest of this introduction the political, intellectual, and cultural contexts of the years in which the texts with which we are concerned were produced and which they helped to form.

Political framework

Mitterrand was elected in 1981 on a Socialist platform: in the French context this meant, as Alistair Cole notes, alliance with the Communist Party,

---

[1] See Max Gallo, 'Le silence des intellectuels de gauche', in *Le Monde*, 26 July 1983.

Keynesian reflationist economic policies, nationalizations, and support for traditional industrial sectors.[2] The first two years were indeed devoted to a reformist push which included nationalizing five key industrial groups and thirty-six private banks and financial institutions; the introduction of important decentralizing reforms designed to transfer powers away from the government in Paris and bring a greater degree of autonomy to local authorities in the provinces; the legitimization of the role of trade unions in the firm, and a series of welfare reforms enabled in part by the introduction of a wealth tax, in 1982. A Ministry for Women's Rights was created, and the death penalty was abolished in September 1981, a cause strongly connected with left-wing campaigns and, in particular, with the name of Albert Camus.

However, by 1984 adverse economic conditions and a rise in unemployment had brought about a change of direction. Reflation had given way to devaluation of the franc; the coal and shipbuilding industries were cut to the bone and an austerity programme combining pay and price freezes had been introduced. The Communists, whose support Mitterrand had needed in 1981, withdrew from government, and, when the legislative elections took place once again in March 1986, Mitterrand lost his Socialist assembly and was presented with a new right-wing set of partners. This 'cohabitation', as it came to be known, between a President of one political persuasion and a legislative assembly of another, was unprecedented in the Fifth Republic, and it was widely supposed that the constitution would be unable to stand the strain.

In the event the constitution proved robust and Mitterrand worked for two years with the leader of the victorious right-wing coalition, Jacques Chirac, as Prime Minister. Chirac launched a privatization programme, including some of the groups which had been nationalized in 1981, and abolished the wealth tax. Plans to extend the principle of selection in universities met head-on opposition and had to be dropped; similarly, a law planned to restrict immigration proved unpopular and never reached the statute books. Despite a programme of economic liberalism, unemployment remained obstinately high; this failure, combined with the unpopularity of some of the proposed legislative measures, led to a decline in the right's fortunes and a recovery in Mitterrand's popularity. He was re-elected to the presidency in 1988 against Chirac and Raymond Barre, having transformed himself from an interventionist Socialist leader into a statesman-like figure above the maelstrom of everyday politics.

[2] Alistair Cole, *French Politics and Society* (Hemel Hempstead: Prentice Hall, 1998), 36.

His second term saw a muted repetition of the pattern of government which had marked his first: it began with a legislative assembly in which the Socialist Party had the most seats but no overall majority; Mitterrand appointed a series of Socialist Prime Ministers whose room for manœuvre was severely restricted by continuing high rates of unemployment. In 1993 another electoral swing took place, the right coalition won a large majority, and Mitterrand began on a second period of cohabitation, this time with Edouard Balladur as Prime Minister. Throughout his second term Mitterrand tried to maintain his role as statesman by focusing on foreign policy and the issue of European integration, rather than on domestic policy, but his personal standing slipped badly and he increasingly came to be seen as a weak and untrustworthy figure, playing a greatly reduced role. In 1995, Jacques Chirac succeeded him as President—this replacement of Mitterrand by his old rival and ex-Prime Minister mirrored the pattern of shifts and substitutions between parties and personalities, appearing in first one guise, and then another, so characteristic of the period. Mitterrand died less than a year after leaving office, on 8 January 1996.

Trials and Tribulations

The Mitterrand years had more than their share of crises, scandals, and traumatic events. In 1985 the government was forced to admit that French secret-service agents had sunk the Greenpeace ship *Rainbow Warrior*, involved in protests against French nuclear testing in the Pacific in 1985, to worldwide indignation. The year 1992 saw the trial of four doctors at the National Blood Transfusion Centre, three of whom were found guilty of supplying blood which they knew carried a high risk of being infected by the AIDS virus. Victims were outraged that no more serious charge was brought and, although it was clear that the decision not to use an American process for destroying the virus but to wait until a French one was ready had been taken at a high level, the relevant ministers managed to escape trial. It was not until well after the Mitterrand administration had ended, in 1999, that three ministers, including Laurent Fabius, eventually came to trial, again on minor charges.

More agonizing still for the national consciousness was the series of trials for crimes against humanity relating to the Vichy period, and the mood of self-examination of French complicity in Nazi crimes. Claude Lanzmann's film *Shoah* (1985), undertaking a lengthy and painful series of interviews with both survivors and participants in the Holocaust, underlined the apparent ordinariness of many of the participants in the organized destruction.[3] Louis Malle's *Au revoir les enfants* (1987), though very different in style, also narrates the fate of a group of Jewish boys denounced to the Gestapo by a school orderly. Klaus Barbie, the SS officer in charge of the Gestapo in Lyon from November 1942 to August 1944 was put on trial in France in May 1987 and defended by a French lawyer, Jacques Vergès. The whole of the first day of the trial was taken up with the reading of the list of crimes of which Barbie was accused and eventually found guilty.

Paul Touvier, a French collaborator, was tried and found guilty in 1994, whilst René Bousquet, who had been tried and acquitted in 1949, was charged afresh with crimes against humanity in 1991, when new information came to light showing that he had directed the infamous round-up of Jews by the French police at the 'Vél d'Hiv', a cycling stadium in Paris, in July 1942. Bousquet was assassinated in 1993, before he got to trial, but in 1994 it emerged that Mitterrand had tried to protect him and a whey-faced President had to submit to being interviewed on television about his own wartime record and his relations with Bousquet. Mitterrand had marked his entry into office with the laying of a red rose on the tomb of Jean Moulin, a Resistance hero who had died under torture after being betrayed to the Gestapo. In the following years not only Mitterrand's own Resistance record but even that of Moulin became subject to questioning. The image of a heroic wartime France solidly resisting the Nazis was no longer viable.

Racism, immigration, and the question of what relationship France should have with its Muslim population were also troubling issues of the period, and continue to be so. The issue of multi-culturalism versus assimilation is particularly thorny in France and was focused with acuity in 1989 by the affair of the Muslim headscarf, in which three schoolgirls were forbidden to wear the traditional scarf to school. Many left-wing voices, including the weekly magazine *Le Nouvel Observateur*, were raised in favour of the ban, in line with the French secular Republican tradition. The mass anti-racist movement SOS Racisme, founded in the mid-1980s and led by the young activist Harlem Désir, initially defended the girls' right to signal their cultural identity, but, when the debate resurfaced in 1994, under Chirac, they changed sides, fearing a rise in Muslim fundamentalism. When the Socialists first came into office they halted aided repatriation, favoured by the previous government, and offered an

---

[3] The film lasts more than nine hours and was shown in two parts. See Emma Wilson's thoughtful discussion of the film as testimony in her *French Cinema since 1950*. Personal Histories (London: Duckworth, 1999), 85–8.

amnesty covering over a hundred thousand illegal foreign workers. By 1989 Mitterrand was speaking on television of a threshold of tolerance for immigrants within French society which had now been crossed; no doubt he was mindful of electoral support for the National Front and its leader Jean-Marie Le Pen, who had made a significant showing in the 1988 Presidential election.

A series of terrorist attacks on Paris during the period 1985–7 increased suspicion of immigrant communities. In the first two weeks of September 1986, after a series of explosions, visas were imposed for all foreigners except EC nationals, and the police were authorized to check identity documents at will. Most large stores searched customers before permitting entry, and an atmosphere of tight security was in evidence in public buildings. The origins of the attacks were far from clear, but Mitterrand's attempts to play a role in the Middle East, and the holding of terrorists in French prisons were undoubtedly factors.

La Haine, a film made by Mathieu Kassovitz released in 1995, at the end of the Mitterrand period, in many ways encapsulated the explosive tensions in French society. Made in a black-and-white documentary style, it follows the lives of a group of three young men on a bleak housing estate in the aftermath of riots. Although the group is itself interracial, the film culminates with the shooting of a white police officer by one of the black youths. The alienating nature of the urban environment, the police brutality to which the youths are subjected, the chasm depicted in the film between the lives of its protagonists and those who live in the *beaux quartiers*, all combine to make the final act of violence seem completely inevitable.

The President of Culture

One of Mitterrand's early decisions in office was his personal choice of a sculpture by Daniel Buren to fill the courtyard of the historic Palais Royal, built by Richelieu on the right bank of the Seine, close to the Louvre. The sculpture, consisting of a series of truncated columns vertically striped in black and white, matching the spacing of the existing colonnades, and the striped blinds of the first-floor windows, proved controversial largely because of the way it juxtaposed the boldness of a modern sculptural project and a key historical site. Opponents wanted to preserve the site but Buren and his supporters argued that contemporary art should be in an open dialogue with the past, bringing it to life for the modern spectator.[4] Mitterrand's choice is emblematic both of his own concern with France's history, and its relation to the present, and of his commitment to an ambitious programme of modern architecture.

The programme of 'grands projets' was announced in the second year of Mitterrand's first term and eventually came to include the extension of the Louvre museum, the removal of the Finance Ministry to a huge new building at Bercy, the creation of a new opera-house at the Bastille, the construction of a Grande Arche in the new Défense area, mirroring the Arc de Triomphe in the Place de la Concorde, and the building of a new National Library. Other projects inherited from the previous regime included the park at la Villette, for which the whole blueprint was radically modified, and the Institute of the Arab World.

What was the thinking behind this grand programme? David Looseley identifies a number of intertwined aims. On the one hand, there was the desire to reassert and redefine a national culture, bolstering Paris's shaky status as a cultural capital of the world, and generally restoring French self-confidence. But the projects were also intended as beacons of Socialist cultural policy, especially in so far as they represented a renewal of the urban environment and could serve as embodiments of democracy at work. Thus the new National Library was planned on a scale which would not only provide a resource for specialist research, as the old library had done, but also enable the general public to access a vast range of books and audio-visual materials. The choice of location at Tolbiac was designed to provide the focus for the renewal of an entire *quartier* on the left bank of the Seine. The location of the new opera-house at the Bastille had obvious revolutionary symbolism and it was also conceived as an opening up of an art form generally felt to be élitist to a much wider public. Scientific culture was to be brought to the masses through the park at la Villette, built in the former abattoirs zone of Paris, in which science and art, the city and nature, leisure and learning would combine.

Perhaps the most striking project of all, and one which has met with considerable success, was the extension and renovation of the Louvre. The Ministry of Finance had occupied a whole wing of the Louvre since the nineteenth century, preventing many of the museum's riches from reaching exhibition. The plan to move the Ministry out to an entirely new site at Bercy, to renovate the wing for the museum, and to build new reception facilities, was intended to revitalize the Louvre, suffering from a crisis in falling numbers of visitors, giving it the space for much-needed

[4] The discussion of Buren's sculpture and much of the following section on the 'grands projets' draws extensively on David Looseley's book *The Politics of Fun* (Oxford: Berg, 1995).

support facilities and attracting a new wider public. Mitterrand commissioned the Chinese-American architect Ieoh Ming Pei to carry out the transformation of the Louvre, a controversial decision not only because Mitterrand decided on his own without holding the usual competition, but because Pei's proposal included the construction of a large glass pyramid in the Cour Napoléon, through which visitors would enter the museum. Like the Buren columns, Pei's glass pyramid sets up a relationship with a historical monument, literally making the museum more transparent and leading visitors into a large forum with a wide array of facilities designed to draw the public into contact with the collections.

The state's cultural concerns were not of course limited to the 'grands projets'. After the Socialist triumph in the legislative assemblies of 1981, Jack Lang became the highly visible Minister of Culture, and although he had to leave office in March 1986, he returned in June 1988 to March 1993. Lang was keen to support the French film industry, perceived in many quarters in France as having fallen victim to domination by Hollywood, and one of his first gestures was to refuse to attend the annual festival of American cinema in Deauville. This may well appear to have been the gesture of a King Canute, but echoed French anxieties about the proliferation of American fast food, films, television series, and, of course, language, at the expense of traditional French culture. State subsidies for French films encouraged the production of what came to be called heritage films, which became closely associated with Socialist film policy.[5]

A number of these films were reworkings of canonical literary texts, such as Zola's *Germinal*, Flaubert's *Madame Bovary*, and Proust's *Un Amour de Swann*, whilst *Camille Claudel* (Bruno Nuytten, 1988), examining the relationship of dramatist Paul Claudel's sister with the sculptor Rodin, drew on the worlds of both French literature and sculpture. Claude Berri's *Jean de Florette* and *Manon des sources*, based on novels by Marcel Pagnol and lyrically celebrating the countryside of Provence, were also given state support and in 1986 drew more than six million and four million viewers respectively. The assertion of France's literary and cultural past is evident in these films, but their relationship to the present was less clear and they are open to the criticism of being exercises in nostalgia.[6] One film which the Socialists financed, and which succeeded in relating to the present in ways which the regime would have preferred it not to, was Wajda's Franco-Polish co-production *Danton* (1982). Not only did the film portray the iconic Republican figure Robespierre as a tyrant, but

---

[5]   See Guy Austin's chapter 'Socialist Film Policy and the Heritage Film', in Mairi Maclean (ed.), *The Mitterrand Years* (Basingstoke: Macmillan, 1998), 276–86.

[6]   See Phil Powrie, *French Cinema in the 1980s* (Oxford: OUP, 1997), 18.

connections were made in the film's reception between Robespierre and Jaruzelski, the Polish leader of the 1981 military coup which had outlawed Solidarity, and whom Mitterrand's regime had refused to try to oust.

Other types of film did also receive state funding, such as Luc Besson's *Subway* (1985), representative of the new 'cinéma du look' genre, privileging visual style, and Mehdi Charef's 'beur' film *Le Thé au harem d'Archimède* (1985).[7] However, as Guy Austin points out, none of the officially financed films achieved the box-office success of low-budget popular comedy films such as Coline Serreau's *Trois hommes et un couffin* (1985), which plays with the idea of three men taking on a maternal role, and Etienne Chatiliez's *La Vie est un long fleuve tranquille* (1987), a film made by a former director of television advertisements which revolves around the deliberate swapping at birth of two babies from polarized class backgrounds.[8] Finally Jean-Marie Poiré's *Les Visiteurs* (1993), another popular comedy film, attracted over 13 million viewers in the last year of Lang's regime, more than twice as many as the hugely expensive and officially supported *Germinal*, made by Claude Berri and also released in 1993. The dialogue with French history and culture of the past favoured by the Socialist regime seems to have worked rather more successfully in the realm of architecture than in the more popular cultural form of the cinema.

Literary and intellectual contexts

Although the diversity of literary works published under the Mitterrand presidency resists any unifying overview, there is already a degree of consensus about some of the significant trends which can be observed. Almost all commentators agree on at least one point, namely that recent fiction is—openly or covertly, to positive or negative effect—produced under the shadow of the so-called *nouveau roman*, which was at the centre of French literary debate during the 1950s and into the 1960s. The *nouveau roman* was itself to some extent a reaction against what its practitioners saw as the moral earnestness of immediate post-war literature, encapsulated in Jean-Paul Sartre's call for literary commitment in his essay 'Qu'est-ce que la littérature?' (1947). With greater distance from the war and the moral questions it posed, some avant-garde writers wanted to explore more experimental forms of writing. The term *nouveau roman*

---

[7] 'Beur' means second generation North African immigrants living in France.

[8] Austin, 'Socialist Film Policy', 282.

was adopted to draw together a group of writers (of whom Nathalie Sarraute, Alain Robbe-Grillet, Claude Simon, and Michel Butor are the best known) with little in common other than that most of them were published by the Editions de Minuit. Some characteristic features may nevertheless be identified: formal experimentation; disappearance of stable, easily distinguished characters as centre of the novel, accompanied by the refusal of received notions of psychological coherence; disruptions of chronological sequence; elusive, untrustworthy, or inconsistent narrators.[9] The aim of these features was to develop forms of literature capable of reproducing and conveying changing perceptions of the world. Explicitly rejecting committed literature and what they regarded as the outdated, ossified forms of realist fiction, they set out to thwart their readers' expectations of coherence in plot and characterization. They tended to attribute (often wrongly) to the realist novelists of the nineteenth century a naïve faith in the power of language to encapsulate reality. The traditional novel, it was argued, clarifies and simplifies the world by implying that it can be impartially viewed, understood, and judged. New linguistic, psychological, and epistemological theories required new narrative strategies: if language is opaque, ordering our experience of the world rather than reflecting it, if identity is fragmented, elusive, constantly in flux, and if the world is never knowable except partially and unreliably, then fiction should also be opaque, disordered, and confusing. In general, the *nouveaux romanciers* are linked by a preoccupation with the nature, limits, and function of narrative. As the author and theorist Jean Ricardou famously put it, literature is no longer 'l'écriture d'une aventure', but rather 'l'aventure d'une écriture'.[10] The texts turn in on themselves and their own narrative procedures; the act of writing becomes the ultimate subject of the novel.[11]

So the *nouveau roman* constitutes an invigorating challenge to its readers' expectations. Unfortunately it proved to be *too* challenging for many of its potential readers, who preferred to be entertained rather than subverted at every turn. From its earliest years, the *nouveau roman* was accused of being formalistic and even terroristic, self-regarding, over-theoretical, creatively sterile, or just straightforwardly dull. But there is no

---

[9] A longer list of elements characteristically found in the *nouveau roman* is given in William Thompson, 'Introduction—The Contemporary Novel in France: A Generation of Writing and Criticism', in William Thompson (ed.), *The Contemporary Novel in France* (Gainesville, Fla.: University Press of Florida, 1995), 9.

[10] 'the writing of an adventure'; 'the adventure of a writing'. Jean Ricardou, *Pour une théorie du nouveau roman* (Paris: Seuil, 1971), 32.

[11] This paragraph draws on material from Colin Davis, 'French Literature since 1940', in Valerie Worth-Stylianou (ed.), *Cassell Guide to Literature in French* (London: Cassell, 1996), 185–6.

doubt that it set the parameters by which subsequent writers would understand their own literary projects. Some, such as Philippe Sollers and the authors grouped around the journal *Tel Quel*, sought to radicalize the *nouveau roman*, still too tied in their view to the generic constraints of the novel; others (and on the whole the most commercially successful authors), such as Patrick Modiano and Michel Tournier, rejected more or less vehemently the techniques—though not always the subversive aims—of the literary avant-garde. The crucial point, however, is that even the rejection of the *nouveau roman* does not entail a simple step backwards into some fantasized lost world of literary innocence. Repudiation is also recognition of the importance of what is repudiated; and for good or ill, the *nouveau roman* established itself as a decisive, defining feature of post-war French literature.

However, by the time Mitterrand became President in 1981, the *nouveau roman* was well past its heyday, and for some writers it could already be confined to the past; its key concerns had not so much vanished from the literary scene as migrated and mutated into a variety of sometimes unrecognizable forms. Of the authors questioned in 1989 by *La Quinzaine littéraire* about their literary influences, some acknowledged the importance of the *nouveau roman* whereas others professed a complete lack of interest in it.[12] In the intellectual scene also, significant changes were taking place. The lively debates provoked by existentialism and structuralism from the 1940s to the late 1960s were pretty much consigned to the past; Marxism had lost its place as the dominant political philosophy of the post-war period; poststructuralist thinkers such as Derrida, Lyotard, Deleuze, Kristeva, Cixous, Foucault, Irigaray, Barthes, Bourdieu, and Lacan had been causing controversy in France for some time and were slowly becoming better known in the English-speaking world. Post-structuralism was characteristically wary of any attempt to tie down thought or experience to stable norms or fixed paradigms; desire, for example, was theorized as free-flowing, transgressive, and multiform rather than channelled through the matrix of compulsory heterosexuality or tied to the rigid, repressive structures of the Freudian Oedipus complex. In the United States the term *postmodern* was already being used to describe the contemporary situation. The word acquired wider currency in France after the publication of Lyotard's *La Condition postmoderne* in 1979. On the opening page of *La Condition postmoderne*, Lyotard characterizes the postmodern condition as 'l'incrédulité à l'égard des métarécits',[13] that is,

---

12 See 'Où va la littérature française?', *La Quinzaine littéraire*, 532 (16–31 May 1989).
13 'incredulity towards metanarratives'. Jean-François Lyotard, *La Condition postmoderne. Rapport sur le savoir* (Paris: Minuit, 1979), 7.

it entails a collapse of belief in grand overarching narratives (such as Christianity, or Marxism, or faith in progress) which make sense out of the chaos of history. Terry Eagleton gives a concise account of postmodernity (the period) and postmodernism (the movement):

> **Postmodernity is a style of thought which is suspicious of classical notions of truth, reason, identity and objectivity, of the idea of universal progress or emancipation, of single frameworks, grand narratives or ultimate grounds of explanation. Against these Enlightenment norms, it sees the world as contingent, ungrounded, diverse, unstable, indeterminate, a set of disunified cultures or interpretations which breed a degree of scepticism about the objectivity of truth, history and norms, the givenness of natures and the coherence of identities. [. . .] Postmodernism is a style of culture which reflects something of this epochal change, in a depthless, decentred, ungrounded, self-reflexive, playful, derivative, eclectic, pluralistic art which blurs the boundaries between 'high' and 'popular' culture, as well as between art and everyday experience.**[14]

Sarraute had characterized the period of the *nouveau roman* as 'l'ère du soupçon';[15] in the 1980s, the philosopher Gilles Lipovetsky characterized the postmodern world as 'l'ère du vide',[16] describing a situation of generalized disenchantment with politics as with art: 'plus aucune idéologie n'est capable d'enflammer les foules, la société postmoderne n'a plus d'idole ni de tabou, plus d'image glorieuse d'elle-même, plus de projet historique mobilisateur, c'est désormais le vide qui nous régit, un vide pourtant sans tragique ni apocalypse.'[17] Whether it is to be deplored (as by Eagleton) or celebrated (as it sometimes appears to be by Lyotard, though inconsistently), the notion of postmodernity has proved to be one of the most influential grids through which the recent and current situations of Western societies may be understood; and we shall see in subsequent chapters how different authors have negotiated the absence of shared norms and standards, the rejection of sense-making paradigms, the cultivation of singularities rather than universals, and the rootlessness of the postmodern condition.

The *nouveaux romanciers* sometimes presented their project as a radical break with the past. Postmodernism, on the other hand, entails a thorough scepticism towards such apocalyptic rhetoric; for the postmodernist, 'originality'—in as far as the term retains any meaning— involves doing something fresh with given materials, inventing a new

---

[14] Terry Eagleton, *The Illusions of Postmodernism* (Oxford: Blackwell, 1996), p. vii.
[15] 'the age of suspicion'.   [16] 'the age of the void'.
[17] 'no longer is any ideology capable of enflaming the crowds, postmodern society no longer has idols or taboos, no glorious image of itself, no motivating historical project, from now on it is the void which governs us, but it is a void without tragedy or apocalypse.' Gilles Lipovetsky, *L'Ère du vide. Essais sur l'individualisme contemporain* (Paris: Gallimard, 1983 and 1993; Folio edn.), 16.

relation with the past, rather than hoping to start again as if from zero. In fact, one of the distinguishing features of fiction after the decline in direct influence of the *nouveau roman* has been its readiness to return to what seemed to have been lost. However, this return cannot be a simple regression, since what is revisited is necessarily seen with different eyes. In particular, three returns are worth sketching at this stage, since they inform much of the analysis of the following chapters: the return to history, the return of the subject, and the return of storytelling.

1. The return to history. In this case, the convergence of literary-historical and socio-political factors can be seen most clearly. The literary avant-garde of the 1950s and 1960s had explored the self-generating nature of textuality sometimes at the expense of its representational capabilities; but the events of May 1968 and the resignation of De Gaulle in 1969 gave renewed impetus to the reassessment of history through fiction.[18] Throughout the 1970s, French intellectuals and writers took a critical look at France's recent past, especially its involvement in the Second World War. Two films, Marcel Ophüls's *Le Chagrin et la pitié* (1971) and Louis Malle's *Lacombe Lucien* (1974) broached the issue of Collaboration and thus contributed to the climate of soul-searching which continued up until the Barbie trial of 1987 and beyond. The early novels of Modiano, *La Place de l'étoile* (1968), *Ronde de nuit* (1969), and *Les Boulevards de ceinture* (1972), and Michel Tournier's *Le Roi des aulnes* (1970) also painted a much darker picture of the war years than a broad French public had previously wanted to see.[19] By the 1980s, the principle that fiction is bound up with history was firmly re-established; and this was no longer conceived as necessarily retrograde or naïve, betraying a facile belief in the representational powers of language. In this book, Chapters 1 and 3 on Duras and Semprun in particular show how a highly sophisticated literary practice may be bound up with a reflection on France's colonial past or the Holocaust respectively.

2. The return of the subject. A self-conscious, self-aware human subject, locatable within an individual 'self', has been assumed to be the ground of intention, and thus of artistic endeavour, for much of European history. But from the 1950s through to the 1970s, the literary practices of the avant-garde and the philosophical positions of structuralists and poststructuralists were hostile to such a concept of subjectivity, and they tended to dismiss the subject as an ideological illusion, or a pawn of

---

[18] On this topic, see Margaret Atack, *May '68 in French Fiction and Film. Rethinking Society, Rethinking Representation* (Oxford: OUP, 1999).

[19] On the more general trend of the so-called 'mode rétro' and the reassessment of the war years, see Alan Morris, *Collaboration and Resistance Reviewed. Writers and the 'Mode Rétro' in Post-Gaullist France* (New York: Berg, 1992).

history, or a product of impersonal signifying structures, or a meta-physical error. In 1968 Barthes announced the 'death of the Author' as a literary counterpart to Foucault's provocative declaration of the 'death of Man'; only seven years later, however, he published *Roland Barthes par Roland Barthes*, a partly autobiographical text in which the Author seems to return from the dead.[20] Even the *nouveaux romanciers* Robbe-Grillet and Sarraute turned to autobiography, albeit in the attenuated form of what rapidly became known as *la nouvelle autobiographie*.[21] Of course such writers were too sophisticated simply to regress to a pre-structuralist view of the subject. In particular, they were influenced by the view, put forward by psychoanalysts such as Lacan and Kristeva, that the most crucial property of the subject was that it was unconscious, and thus beyond our reach. Instead of returning to self-conscious subjectivity accessible through observing one's own thoughts, writers of the Mitterrand years explore an unconscious subjectivity sensed only obliquely through our anxieties and desires. Attempts to grasp it must admit the hypothetical, indeed fictional, nature of their enterprise. On the inside front cover of *Roland Barthes par Roland Barthes*, Barthes declared that his own subjectivity was fictionalized by the very act of writing about it: 'Tout ceci doit être considéré comme dit par un personnage de roman.'[22] The critic, novelist, and autobiographer Serge Doubrovsky coined the term *autofiction* to describe the generically problematic status of a practice of writing which is fully neither fiction nor autobiography, but which combines both.[23] However fractured, fictional, illusory, or elusive the subject might be, the questions of subjectivity, of the relationship between author and narrator, or author and text, were restored as valid topics for literary investigation, especially in relation to the central issues of identity, memory, and desire. In the current book this is reflected in particular in the chapters on Duras, Guibert, and Ernaux.

3. The return of storytelling. In the heady days when fiction was radically subverting our deepest convictions, frustrating our expectations and desires, and restructuring the way we perceive the world around us, it was sometimes easy to forget that reading and writing were also supposed to be sources of pleasure. One of the salient features of more recent fiction

---

[20] See Roland Barthes, 'La Mort de l'auteur', reprinted in *Le Bruissement de la langue* (Paris: Seuil, 1984), 61–7, and *Roland Barthes par Roland Barthes* (Paris: Seuil, 1975).

[21] See Alain Robbe-Grillet's trilogy *Le Miroir qui revient, Angélique ou l'enchantement*, and *La Mort de Corinthe* (Paris: Minuit, 1984, 1988, 1994), and Nathalie Sarraute, *Enfance* (Paris: Gallimard, 1983). On the 'nouvelle autobiographie', see Raylene Ramsay, *The French New Autobiographies. Sarraute, Duras, and Robbe-Grillet* (Gainesville, Fla.: University Press of Florida, 1996).

[22] 'All this should be regarded as if it were spoken by a fictional character.'

[23] See Serge Doubrovsky, *Autobiographiques. De Corneille à Sartre* (Paris: PUF, 1988), 69.

has been the rediscovery of the pleasure of writing and, whatever the degree of sophistication of the novelist in question, the role of writer as storyteller and entertainer. This can be seen in the novels of Sébastien Japrisot, who had a background as author of crime fiction and who finally established himself as a major international novelist with the publication of *Un long dimanche de fiançailles* in 1991. His novel of 1986, *La Passion des femmes*, describes the increasingly improbable adventures of a man whose name is constantly changing, and who may or may not be an escaped convict. At the end of nearly all of the episodes, he is apparently murdered by a different woman; yet he escapes miraculously, only to be murdered again at the end of the subsequent episode. In the closing pages of the novel, with the protagonist finally and indisputably dead, a figure who identifies himself as the novelist rouses himself from his musings and returns to eat dinner with his wife and child. The text is dominated by a narrative exuberance, a sheer exhilaration in constructing and telling stories. This is ultimately brought back to earth by the revelation that stories are only stories, not to be taken too seriously, though no less enjoyable for the final anticlimax which reveals them as mere fabrications. In this book, this revaluation of storytelling can be seen in particular in Chapters 2 and 4 on Pennac and Echenoz. At a thematic level, storytelling performs the crucial function in Pennac's novels of binding together in something like a unified community a selection of listeners who otherwise have little in common; and at a textual level, Echenoz's writing sets itself up as a site where the playful dimensions of language and storytelling become ends in their own right, without the need for grand theoretical justifications. It is also significant that both Pennac and Echenoz draw on themes and structures from popular culture, such as the spy story or the family saga. Authors of fiction with serious intellectual and aesthetic ambitions no longer inevitably set themselves apart from the interests of a broad reading public. More generally, this return to storytelling is part of French literature's continuing reflection on its own role and function, a reflection which can be seen to be ongoing in all the texts discussed in the current book.

These three returns are reflected by the three terms in the subtitle to this book, narrative (the return of storytelling), memory (the return to history), and desire (the return of the subject, in the particular form of the subject of desire). In the following chapters, these issues are constantly intermingled, each enriching, complicating, and problematizing the others. Our aim is to show how, in the context sketched above, the writers whose work we discuss negotiate these key issues, meditating in their own way on the dilemmas of love, death, and storytelling which are the novelist's stock-in-trade.

Choice of texts

In 1989 an edition of the journal *L'Infini* presented the work of more than twenty of the most promising young writers of the day. During the same year, in an edition entitled 'Où va la littérature française', *La Quinzaine littéraire* gave the responses of thirty-four contemporary authors to a questionnaire about their writing. Not one of the authors chosen by *L'Infini* also appears in *La Quinzaine littéraire*.[24] The handful of volumes which have been published in recent years dedicated to French fiction 'after the *nouveau roman*', or more specifically to fiction of the 1980s, propose for the reader's attention a huge range of authors and trends (the minimalist novel or the 'roman impassible', 'la nouvelle fiction', 'la nouvelle fable', the postmodern novel, autofiction, or 'la nouvelle autobiographie'). Some names recur: of the older generation of writers still active during the Mitterrand presidency, the stature of Duras, Tournier, Robbe-Grillet, Sarraute, and Simon is firmly established; of the younger writers, Ernaux, Echenoz, Toussaint, and Redonnet are widely cited. But it is a daunting fact that there is as yet little consensus about the texts and authors which are most worth reading and studying. And this fact causes obvious problems for the selection of texts to be discussed in this book.

The only decision of principle that we took was not to consider fiction written in French by citizens of former French colonies (often referred to as francophone literature). We felt that this would introduce too many new factors and issues which it would be impossible to handle within a book such as this. A number of authors other than those discussed here were suggested to us, and we actively considered a variety of alternative texts, such as Hélène Cixous's *Le Livre de Promethea* (1983), Patrick Modiano's *Quartier perdu* (1984), Michel Tournier's *La Goutte d'or* (1985), Jean-Philippe Toussaint's *La Salle de bain* (1985), Marie Redonnet's *Rose Mélie Rose* (1987), or Serge Doubrovsky's *Le Livre brisé* (1989). In the end we settled on a group of texts which correspond to our own tastes and interests whilst also being readily available and in our view accessible to a wide range of readers. Of the six authors whose works are considered here, two were already firmly established by the beginning of the 1980s (Duras had been publishing since the 1940s, Semprun since the 1960s), two published their first books in the 1970s (Ernaux, Echenoz), and two achieved their first successes in the 1980s (Guibert, Pennac). Despite these generational differences, the authors share a number of overlapping thematic

---

[24] See 'Génération 89', *L'Infini*, 26 (Summer 1989), and 'Où va la littérature française?', *La Quinzaine littéraire*, 532 (16–31 May 1989).

and aesthetic concerns which allow us to discuss some of the key issues of recent fiction. We believe that each of the texts we have chosen is interesting and important in its own right; some readers will disagree, and it is not our business to try to anticipate or dictate what future generations might think. Duras's *L'Amant* has a strong claim to be the most successful novel of the 1980s in combining public success and aesthetic significance, finally bringing a wide audience to an author often considered difficult. But in general we are emphatically not claiming that the six texts discussed in detail are the 'six great texts' of the Mitterrand presidency. It is neither possible nor interesting to make any such claim; and it was by no means the least significant factor in our selection that all the texts discussed are quite simply works that we and (as far as we can tell) our students have enjoyed reading and studying.

1 The Story of her life: Marguerite Duras's *L'Amant* (1984)

The phenomenon of *L'Amant*

Why, in the mid-1980s, did a 70-year-old woman writer with a reputation for difficult, avant-garde texts, read by left-wing intellectuals, top the French best-seller lists and become an international star? In a variety of forms this question was posed repeatedly as sales of Marguerite Duras's *L'Amant* climbed up towards the two million mark and her text carried off the Goncourt prize, designed to reward young writers of promise.[1] In fact this was far from being the first time that Duras had caught the mood of her times: *Moderato Cantabile* (1958), a novel centring on a violent *crime passionnel* and jettisoning many traditional realist conventions had ensured her a place in the *nouveau roman* stable, the formalist literary movement spearheaded by Alain Robbe-Grillet and Nathalie Sarraute which dominated (some would say strangled) the French novel in the late 1950s and 1960s.[2] Though she took a relatively back-seat role in the grouping, she succeeded in establishing a literary reputation in this period such that her apparently radical espousal of the feminist cause in the early and mid-1970s was met with interest, and her international reputation began to grow rapidly. However, her mantle as a writer of the 'feminine', largely cast upon her by others, cut little ice in France once the women's movement began to lose its public impetus, and indeed she began to distance herself from feminism before the 1970s were over, though she remained a well-known media figure.

The advent of the Mitterrand era had a strong personal meaning for Duras. During the Second World War she had worked in a Resistance network headed by François Mitterrand, and he had been personally responsible for saving her husband from dying in Dachau. A former member of the Communist Party, Duras held strong left-wing views, though not necessarily ones that coincided with party political programmes; she campaigned hard for Mitterrand in the 1981 Presidential elections, and remained a figure closely associated with him throughout his tenure of office, visiting the Elysée Palace, recounting the story of his role in her husband's survival in *La Douleur* (1985), and publishing interviews with

[1] See e.g. Josyane Savigneau *Le Monde*, 'Duras face à l'avenir', p. 1 'Le Monde des livres', 8 Mar. 1996.
[2] See Introduction, pp. 9–13.

Mitterrand at the time of the parliamentary elections in 1986. She died only two months after him, in the spring of 1996.

Yet her association with Mitterrand, her left-wing reputation, and her feminist past, cannot account for the phenomenon of *L'Amant*. Journalists and critics disagreed over whether the book was a break with her previous writing, or essentially a reworking of her childhood in Indo-China, the source of motifs which reappear in so many of her novels, plays, and films. Most of her 1980s readers were not in a position to pronounce on this issue: they were responding to a powerfully emotional text, digging deep into the past of the woman at the centre of its narration, and into France's own colonial past, to uncover transgression, desire, separation, and death, the ecstatic and dangerous appeal of the mysterious other. The exploration of the relationship between a young poor white schoolgirl and her rich Chinese lover in the setting of 1920s Saigon evoked for French readers a colonial past pre-dating their inglorious forced withdrawal from Indo-China in 1954 after the French military defeat at Dien Bien Phu. The novel seems to have caught, or helped to create, a popular mood of desire to revisit a less problematic colonial past, a mood also evident in the popular success of Claire Denis's film *Chocolat* (1988), depicting her childhood in the French African colonies, and Wargnier's nostalgic film *Indochine* (1991).

The love affair was also of course in itself disturbing and intriguing. Was Duras really evoking a scandalous episode of her own past, as seemed to be suggested by the picture of her face accompanying the book, illustrating the narrator's description in the opening paragraphs of her ageing face 'lacéré de rides sèches et profondes, à la peau cassée' (10).[3] The question of the autobiographical basis for the text was returned to repeatedly in press interviews, and in the special hour-long television interview with Duras which Bernard Pivot conducted for the prestigious literary book show 'Apostrophes', in September 1984.[4] The notion of such a romantic and scandalous past for a public figure was in itself exciting. But the text does not deal only with the relations between 'la jeune fille' at its centre and the lover. Another, arguably just as central relationship, is the fraught tie between the girl and her mother (Pivot was keen to know if the mother had actually known of the nature of the liaison: Duras replied that she had not, though her mother had accepted money from him).[5] The figures of

---

[3] 'Scored with deep dry wrinkles, the skin cracked'.

[4] Accounts of Duras's adolescence by biographers such as Françoise Lebelley follow the broad outlines of the narrative of *L'Amant*, and identify the lover. See F. Lebelley, *Duras ou le poids d'une plume* (Paris: Grasset, 1994).

[5] In *L'Amant de la Chine du Nord* (Paris: Gallimard, 1991), a later and longer reworking of the same material, Duras writes that the mother not only knew but actually discussed the affair with her daughter.

the two brothers, and that of the girl's schoolfriend, Hélène Lagonelle, also swim sharply into focus at times, at others swirling more blurredly into the stream of desire which runs beneath the whole text, finding only one of its expressions in the relationship with the lover. Narrative modes, modes of re-enactement and of trawling the memory, thematics of displacement and otherness, madness and death, occupation of gender and racial borderlands, the tragic echoes of history in twentieth-century France—all these strands of the text will interest us as readers.

The sexual unconscious

But let us begin with the girl and the lover, and with the textual exploration of what might be termed the sexual unconscious of the relationship, that is to say, what each desires in the other, what roles each one calls upon the other to play. The lover's desire for the girl is constructed more conventionally than the girl's own feelings: she feels his gaze upon her, when they meet on the ferry, and is filled with the certitude of being desired, in a sense which she disassociates from ideas of beauty: 'Il n'y avait pas à attirer le désir. Il était dans celle qui le provoquait ou il n'existait pas. Il était déjà là dès le premier regard ou bien il n'avait jamais existé. Il était l'intelligence immédiate du rapport de sexualité ou bien il n'était rien' (28).[6] The lover thus makes his first appearance as a desiring gaze, but he is not allowed to maintain it, as the narrative veers away from him for a long stretch; when it eventually returns to his gaze, we discover him to be trembling, intimidated. He has the advantage of being older, male, and visibly wealthy, but he is Chinese and she is white. In the expensive black car in which she allows herself to be driven to Saigon, she learns that he is a sophisticate, is familiar with the cafés and nightclubs of Paris, and with 'les adorables Parisiennes' (45). When he becomes her lover she declares him to be wonderfully expert, virtually defined by his amorous skills: 'c'est ce qu'il fait dans la vie, l'amour, seulement ça. Les mains sont expertes, merveilleuses, parfaites' (54).[7] Yet he is also vulnerable, an only child whose mother is dead and whose father dominates him through the family fortune; he uses love and love-making to shore himself up against his insecurity, plunging at once into the absolute vocabulary of romantic love, giving the girl a diamond ring, and building promises of eternity. He even wishes for his father's death so that he can marry her.

[6] 'There was no need to attract desire. Either it was in the woman who aroused it or it didn't exist. Either it was there at first glance or else it never had been. It was instant knowledge of a sexual rapport or else it was nothing.'

[7] 'this is his occupation in life, love-making, nothing else. His hands are expert, marvellous, perfect.'

Her body appeals to him partly through its childish, half-developed nature; for him she is a child, his child, with whom he can play a semi-maternal role, bathing and dressing her. He is far from being always able to play the dominating seducer part which she craves; on the first occasion on which they make love he rips off her dress and throws her down on the bed to order, only to turn away in tears. He has to be comforted and the girl has to take on the mantle of seducer. His love is often agony and physical suffering, an 'amour-maladie' (love as sickness) in the Racinian tradition: 'Il gémit, il pleure. Il est dans un amour abominable' (50). When the date of her departure is eventually fixed, his suffering becomes more intense than his desire: 'Il disait: je ne peux plus te prendre, je croyais pouvoir encore, je ne peux plus. Il disait qu'il était mort' (133).[8] As her boat departs for France she feels his gaze upon her once more, even though he is invisible, paralysed with distress in the back of his car. Later the girl imagines him acceding to his father's wish to marry a Chinese girl, and being capable of making love to his wife only after a long period and by substituting the white girl for the body in his bed. His last words to her, which carry the full weight of being the final words of the text, freeze him in the role of archetypal romantic lover, as he whispers that he has always loved her, will do so until his death.

The girl, in contrast, refuses to use the language of love, denies the romantic concept of being the only and absolute beloved, and enjoys the idea that she might be one amongst many of his women. Yet the fact that the narrative is entirely constituted by the recreation of the narrator's memories means that the lover's desire for the girl is itself part of her later reconstruction; we have only her reading of his desire for her. His role as besotted sufferer and consummate lover, bearing the keys to the magic kingdom of wealth, carries the whiff of an adolescent girl's absolutist expectations, retained in the account by the older narrator.

The narrative perspective produces a more extensive exploration of the girl's desire than of the lover's, drawing on both the narrator's past and present impressions. At the time, the girl is conscious of her own desire for the lover, at first expressed as a desire for his body, his skin and the rich sumptuousness of his clothing. The appeal of his wealth is also present from their first meeting, as he stands by his luxury black limousine, and becomes important not only in allowing the girl the powerful role in relation to her mother and brothers of getting them dined out in expensive restaurants, but also, crucially, in maintaining the provisional status of their relationship, which she seeks. As the affair progresses, the girl

---

[8] 'He moans, he weeps. Wracked by love'; 'He'd say: I can't come inside you any more, I thought I could still manage it, I can't any more. He'd say he was dead.'

becomes aware of other figures creeping into her sexual imaginary: the younger brother, 'le jeune chasseur', is explicitly recognized between the lovers as a presence in her desire: 'oui, je le savais, quelquefois il était présent dans la jouissance et je le lui disais, à l'amant de Cholen, je lui parlais de son corps et de son sexe aussi, de son ineffable douceur, de son courage dans la forêt et sur les rivières aux embouchures des panthères noires' (122).[9] This highly poeticized and lightly veiled confession avoids actually naming the brother, or his relation to her. The older narrator also perceives a trace of her elder brother, also referred to indirectly: 'L'ombre d'un autre homme aussi devait passer par la chambre, celle d'un jeune assassin, mais je ne savais pas encore, rien n'en apparaissait encore à mes yeux' (122).[10] The poetic veiling occurs as the text begins to open up traditionally taboo areas in representations of love and desire: not only does the girl herself acknowledge that the desire she enacts with the lover has many origins, carrying with it echoes of desire running between herself and others, even forbidden others, but she reveals what she knows of it to the lover.

In *L'Amant de la Chine du Nord* (1991), a text published seven years after *L'Amant* which reworks much of the same material, the pivotal role of the younger brother in the narrator's sexuality is more developed and the narrator more fully realizes that 'elle avait vécu un seul amour entre le Chinois de Sadec et le petit frère d'éternité'.[11] Yet the younger brother already plays an important structural and thematic role in the earlier text, acting as a figure for the girl's feelings for the lover which she refuses to openly articulate. The most striking example of this is the positioning in the narrative of references to the younger brother's death, an event which belongs to a much later period in the narrator's life, ten years after the main events related in *L'Amant*, when she had long been in France. References to his death accumulate during the narrative, as if spelling out a future disaster, and culminate, less than twenty pages before the end, in a long account of the intense shock and pain which the narrator felt on receiving the telegram informing her of her brother's death—a distress which also mingles with the suffering she had endured a few months earlier when she lost a child. This material, deeply marked by pain and loss, immediately precedes the account of the girl's departure for France, and

---

[9] 'the young hunter'; 'yes', I knew about that, sometimes he was present in my pleasure and I'd tell him, the lover from Cholen, I'd talk to him about the other's body and about his penis as well, about his indescribable sweetness, about his courage in the forest and in the river estuaries with black panthers.'

[10] 'The shadow of another man must also have passed through the room, the shadow of a young murderer, but I didn't know that then, none of that was evident to me then.'

[11] *L'Amant de la Chine du Nord*, 201; 'she had lived a single passion with the Chinese man from Sadec and the eternal little brother.'

functions as an emblem of her unstated suffering. The figures of the lover and the younger brother become deeply entangled.

The narrator's passion for her younger brother is shown to develop in the hothouse family atmosphere between the violence of the older brother and the emotional vacuum left by the mother's apparent failure to love her younger children. But the intensity of this atmosphere is such that, as we saw above, the image of the elder brother also slips into her sexual unconscious. The elder brother's gambling, drug-taking, and social marginalization are, ironically, mirrored by the way in which the wealthy lover spends his days gambling and smoking opium. The girl draws attention to this when she refers to the lover as a millionaire layabout. In the restaurants to which the lover miserably accompanies the girl's family, the girl recognizes his fear as echoing that of her younger brother, whilst she herself both physically resembles the violent older brother and imitates his contemptuous behaviour to the lover.

The elder brother's violence is also echoed in a minor mode when the girl and the lover act out scenes of violence together in the lover's flat, which becomes an echo chamber of the family's extreme emotions. The narrator recognizes the link between the two, when she writes of the family: 'C'est là le lieu où plus tard me tenir une fois le présent quitté, à l'exclusion de tout autre lieu. Les heures que je passe dans la garçonnière de Cholen font apparaître ce lieu-là dans une lumière fraîche, nouvelle. C'est un lieu irrespirable, il côtoie la mort, un lieu de violence, de douleur, de désespoir, de déshonneur. Et tel est le lieu de Cholen' (93).[12] Outside the family, the girl's schoolfriend, Hélène Lagonelle, the only other white girl in the school, also comes to occupy a particularly mobile place in the narrator's sexual imaginary. Hélène Lagonelle is an innocent, resembling the younger brother in her incapacity to learn, and unconscious of the effect she produces when she walks naked through the school's dormitory. The narrator dwells upon the beauty of Hélène Lagonelle's white body, finally declaring herself 'exténuée du désir d'Hélène Lagonelle' (91),[13] as fantasies of violent sexual relations with her friend take hold of her. Her imagination roves from playing the role with Hélène that the lover plays with the girl herself, to a more closely identificatory stance, in which she would take Hélène to the lover, and experience pleasure vicariously through Hélène.

[12] 'That's the place where I'll be later, once the present is left behind, all other places will be excluded. The hours I spend at his place in Cholen show that other place in a stark new light. It's an intolerable place, on the edge of death, a place of violence, pain, despair, dishonour. And so is the Cholen place.'

[13] 'Worn out with desire for Hélène Lagonelle'.

The exploration of the girl's desire for the lover thus produces a whole network of transgressive desires, and makes sexuality into a core mode of being, channelling pain and pleasure, death and life. Desire is understood in the text not as object-fixated but as fluid, mobile, incorporating taboo sexualities—incest, lesbianism, violence—as much as heterosexual relations. Ever present in the background of all the girl's relations and desires, however, is a maelstrom of madness centring on the mother, sucking into its orbit almost all the figures in the girl's consciousness.

The heart of maternal darkness

Three years after the publication of *L'Amant*, Julia Kristeva, another major intellectual figure of the 1980s in France and, amongst other things, a psychoanalyst, warned that Duras's texts bring the reader so close to the brute experience of madness, that they present dangers to readers of a fragile mental disposition.[14] In *L'Amant* the madness is centred on what Kristeva calls the lugubrious gothic madness of the narrator's mother, which drives the daughter into an attempt to efface her mother and escape from the stranglehold of their mutual passionate hatred. Yet, as Kristeva suggests, the attempt is doomed as the daughter merely tightens her obsessive bond, and the mother haunts her most intimate experiences. Thus, in the lingering description in the opening pages of the text of the idiosyncratic assortment of garments which the girl is wearing on the ferry, at the moment of the first meeting with the lover, the narrator tells us that she is wearing an old silk dress of her mother's, sleeveless and heavily *décolleté*, shoes and a hat that her mother has bought her, her face is made up with face powder also belonging to her mother, and her hair is held in the plaits that her mother has taught her to brush and braid.

Interwoven into this description, so heavily laden with the maternal presence, is the first account of her mother's depressive illness. The narrator states: 'J'ai eu cette chance d'avoir une mère désespérée d'un désespoir si pur que même le bonheur de la vie, si vif soit-il, quelquefois, n'arrivait pas à l'en distraire tout à fait' (22),[15] and she describes the daily surfacing of her mother's disabling melancholia, her sudden incapacity to cope with ordinary tasks, the washing and dressing of her children,

[14] In *Soleil Noir. Dépression et mélancolie* (Paris: Gallimard, 1987), 235. A chapter entitled 'La maladie de la douleur' ('the sickness of pain') is devoted to Duras. Kristeva repeats her warning in a special issue of the *Nouvelle Revue Française* on Duras of March 1998.

[15] 'I had the luck to have a mother so desperate with such pure despair that, sometimes, even the joys of life, however intense, could not altogether distract her from it.'

sometimes even the feeding of them. The visual image of the maternally identified girl is thus undercut by an evocation of maternal failure, and both are carried forward into the account of the meeting with the lover. The mother precedes the lover in the narrative, as well as in the chronology of the daughter's passions, and is never far from the daughter's consciousness. 'Elle est à enfermer, à battre, à tuer' (32)[16] rages the narrator as she recalls her mother's lack of interest in her writing plans, her determination that her daughter will leave Indo-China, do the *agrégation* in mathematics, and not find herself in her mother's position.

The narrator's rage swings from hatred to love: 'la saleté ma mère mon amour' (scum my mother my love); both mother and daughter plan on separation but only succeed in a geographical sense. Before the narrative of the meeting with the lover has reached the moment when he approaches her, the narrator has leapt long years ahead, to the last few years of her mother's life in a château in the Loir-et-Cher, to her final realization that her mother has always been mad: 'De naissance. Dans le sang' (40).[17] Later, when the narrator evokes her first love-making in the flat, thoughts of the mother again invade repeatedly: as the girl is initiated into sexual pleasure, she experiences a triumphant sense of separation from and superiority over her mother, relegating her to a childlike status, outside the knowledge of pleasure. But this sense of separation is counterbalanced by a fear that she is only fulfilling her mother's predictions. The swinging from love to hatred, from bitter accusation to pride in her mother, continues throughout the narrative, producing often irreconcilable views of the maternal figure, at one moment presented as colluding with the liaison for financial gain, at others as punishing her violently on suspicion, as the daughter pursues the struggle to disentangle herself from a mother whose madness has filled the space of the child's dreams: 'le malheur de ma mère a occupé le lieu du rêve' (58).[18]

Mother–daughter narratives are a common thread in women's writing, often producing a highly complex and less idealized narrative than those of mother–son relationships—indeed within *L'Amant* itself the mother–daughter relation stands in stark contrast to that of the mother and elder brother, for whom the mother repeatedly sacrifices everything she owns before eventually, at her own request, being laid to rest with him in his tomb, an image of such intolerable splendour that the narrator can hardly bear to contemplate it. Duras's mother–daughter narrative in this text resembles what Adrienne Rich has called 'the heart of maternal darkness', in other words a narrative which draws on maternal

---

[16] 'She should be locked up, beaten, killed.'   [17] 'From birth. In the blood.'
[18] 'My mother's unhappiness filled the place of my dreams'.

violence and on daughterly anger.[19] In the extreme case of matrophobia, according to Rich, the daughter so dreads the deep pull towards identification with the mother that she must try to purge herself of her mother's bondage and perform radical surgery to become free. The daughter's drive in *L'Amant* towards the lover, towards social disgrace and repudiation, is one that she barely understands herself. When she says that: 'je devais le faire, [. . .] c'en était comme d'une obligation' (51), she underlines her feeling of being driven by unconscious forces; they can be read as a desperate attempt to free herself from maternal identification, even though the mix of violence and mothering she seeks from the lover, together with the certainty that she will be separated from him, essentially mirror her relationship with her mother. 'Il me traite de putain, de dégueulasse, il me dit que je suis son seul amour' (54–5),[20] records the narrator happily, duplicating her address to her mother as 'la saleté ma mère mon amour'.

The daughter admires her mother's quality of persistence, recognizes that her mother was driven to despair by her betrayal by the corrupt administration of the colony and the tragedy of the concession into which she poured all her efforts and resources for seven years of their childhood. Yet her madness is not containable, spills over into the violence of the elder brother, and fills her daughter's universe with images of the mad, the distraught, the dead, and the suicidal. The narrative contains the deaths of all four of the other family figures—father, mother, elder and younger brother—and that of the baby of the mad woman beggar, who gives away the baby to the family to look after, as well as the narrator's loss of her own baby, much later in life. The relationship between the girl and the lover is in the narrator's mind a dark doubling of the liaison between another white woman in the colony whose young lover kills himself when the woman leaves him to accompany her husband to a new posting. The narrator dwells on the disgrace the two women share, on the infamy of their 'jouissance à en mourir' (111)[21] and on the woman's despair. As the narrator comes to the account of her departure for France she remembers the story of a boy she had known at school who, at the age of 17, had walked off in the middle of a game of cards on board ship and drowned himself in the sea. This memory is linked to the temptation the girl herself feels, as she stands on board deck, listening to a Chopin piece she had never mastered, to jump overboard in her turn, suddenly no longer convinced that she had not loved the man from Cholen. All these doubling

[19] See Adrienne Rich, *Of Woman Born. Motherhood as Experience and Institution* (London: Virago, 1977), 247–80.
[20] 'I had to do it, it felt like an obligation'; 'He calls me a whore, a slut, he tells me I'm his only love.'
[21] 'pleasure to die from'.

of roles with the despairing and the suicidal return the girl each time to the fraught identification with the despair of the mother, perhaps the most strikingly and darkly mirrored in the mad beggarwoman whose children are 'tous morts ou jetés' (106)[22] and who gives up her last baby to the girl's family, before setting off on an immense and apparently senseless journey, through mosquito-infested forests, over plains and mountains, forever wandering and haunting the imagination of the narrator-writer, peopling her books.

The madness of war

Beyond the girl's family history, and the narration of episodes taking place within the colony itself, the despair of the narrative also encompasses evocations of more generalized disaster and conflagration, through a frame of reference to war, and to the Second World War in particular. 'Je vois la guerre sous les mêmes couleurs que mon enfance' (78)[23] writes the narrator, who apprehends the nature of war via her experience of her elder brother and his violation of the minds, bodies, and lives of the weak. The narrative veers back from the lovers in the flat but, barely two paragraphs later, returns to the stories of two American women living in wartime Paris during the German occupation. Marie-Claude Carpenter is curiously out of place: 'Pourquoi elle était là plutôt qu'ailleurs, pourquoi elle était aussi de si loin, de Boston, pourquoi elle était riche, pourquoi à ce point on ne savait rien d'elle, personne, rien, pourquoi ces réceptions comme forcées, pourquoi, pourquoi dans ses yeux, très loin dedans, au fond de la vue, cette particule de mort, pourquoi?' (82)[24] The 'cauchemar blanc' which the narrator traverses when she visits Marie-Claude Carpenter, suggests the absence, the nightmare displacement of war and exile, in which death lurks. The dissonance of Marie-Claude Carpenter's name is echoed by that of Betty Fernandez, 'étrangère elle aussi' (82),[25] beautiful, like Marie-Claude, and equally strangely attired. The horrors of the war, only hinted at in the portrait of Marie-Claude, are more suddenly and brutally evoked through the similarity of Betty Fernandez's greeting to that of one of her guests: 'Bonjour vous allez bien? Cela, à l'anglaise,

[22] 'all dead or thrown out'.   [23] 'I think of the war in the same way as I think of my childhood.'
[24] 'Why she was there rather than anywhere else, why she too was from so far away, from Boston, why she was rich, why no one knew anything at all about her, no one, not anything, why these social gatherings, as if they were obligatory, why, why in her eyes, far away in the depths of her sight, this fragment of death, why?'
[25] 'also a foreigner'.

sans virgule, dans un rire et durant le temps de ce rire la plaisanterie devenait la guerre elle-même ainsi que toute souffrance obligée qui découlait d'elle, la Résistance comme la Collaboration, la faim comme le froid, le martyr comme l'infamie' (85). Betty Fernandez, announces the narrator in matter of fact tone, was a collaborator—a position, the narrator adds, absolutely equivalent to her own past membership of the Communist Party, in its complete lack of judgement and its assumption that a political solution can be found to a personal problem. Betty Fernandez's perfect social grace is now inseparable, for the narrator, from all that happened during the war, including the discovery of the concentration camps.

This irruption of the question of personal and political positions taken up during and immediately after the war, together with the reference to the Holocaust, corresponds both to the mood of guilty self-examination over the events of the war, which gripped the French consciousness in the 1980s and 1990s, and to Duras's own writing preoccupations in this period. In 1985, the year following the publication of L'Amant, Marguerite Duras was to publish La Douleur, a collection of short texts which set out to throw into question the boundaries between Resistance and Collaboration and suggest that the personal realities of wartime existence cannot be seen in black-and-white terms. The collection also contains the diary form account of Duras's agonizing wait for the return of her husband from Dachau, a text heralded within L'Amant itself by the apparently casually offered account of the way in which the elder brother stole the food rations she had been storing up for her husband's return.[26] La Douleur appeared in the same year as Claude Lanzmann's long and harrowing film Shoah; both works thus served as grim prefaces to the 1987 trial of Klaus Barbie for his part in the murder and deportation of French Jews under the Vichy regime.[27]

In L'Amant the evocation of the Holocaust, and of the issues of Collaboration and Resistance, muddy the boundaries between private and public disaster; the violence and loss enacted between the girl and her lover, the girl and her mother, and between the girl and the younger brother are parallelled on a wider, cataclysmic scale. It also raises questions about the possibility of ethical judgements of individual behaviour.

---

[26] For a reading of La Douleur in the context of 1980s questioning of representations of the war years see Claire Gorrara, Women's Representations of the Occupation in Post-68 France (London: Macmillan, 1998).

[27] See the Introduction for a discussion of the questioning of France's own collaboration in wartime crimes which reached as far as Mitterrand himself.

Narrative paths

La Douleur purports to be in part a diary found by Duras long after the events recorded in it. This is by no means an unproblematic claim and the status of *L'Amant* is just as difficult to resolve, if not more so. Critical reaction at the time of publication, as already mentioned, fastened on the text as autobiography and it has since been treated as an autobiographical piece of writing in a number of critical studies of autobiography as a genre, despite the fact that the narrator states at the beginning: 'L'histoire de ma vie n'existe pas. Ça n'existe pas. Il n'y a jamais de centre. Pas de chemin, pas de ligne' (14). However there is no intrinsic reason, as Michael Sheringham writes, why the autobiographical genre cannot evolve and innovate, like any other genre: the 1980s saw the publication of several 'nouvelles autobiographies', the term being especially appropriate as two of the most notable examples, alongside Duras, were Alain Robbe-Grillet and Nathalie Sarraute, former *nouveaux romanciers*.[28] The lack of belief in a coherent narratable linear development of the self need not debar the writing of autobiography. It does, nevertheless, require different techniques, and most readers are struck by the way in which the narrative constantly fluctuates between past events and the writing present, by the switches from the narrating first person to a third person 'jeune fille', by the dislocation of conventional syntax in many sentences, the way in which the progress of the narrative depends on association and memory in the writing present, rather than on a chronological ordering of the past, and by the lingering attention paid to photographic images, both remembered and imagined.

The focus on the writing present, and on lapses and contradictions of the narrator's memory, make self-evident the fact obscured by many an autobiographer that the text bears a much stronger relation to the writer's current preoccupations and construction of the past than to a historically verifiable set of facts. The willingness of the narrator to follow the unruly path taken by her own thoughts draws the reader not into an illusory past, but into something resembling a dream experience, with all the sudden changes of locale, apparently implausible disruptions of subject and strong visual images of the uncensored mind. It is precisely this privileged admission to intensity of experience, together with the implied invitation to become the dream analyst, which is one of the strongest appeals of the text. As the story of what happened on the ferry is constantly deferred,

---

[28] 'The story of my life does not exist. There is never any centre. No path, no line.' Michael Sheringham, *French Autobiography. Devices and Desires* (Oxford: Clarendon Press, 1993), 16.

it grows in significance, drawing into its orbit a rich collection of jagged pieces of the memory which connect to it, illuminate it, and are illuminated by it. Like the branch of the Mekong river which the ferry crosses, with its current so strong that 'il emporterait tout, aussi bien des pierres, une cathédrale, une ville' (18), the relationship between the girl and the lover becomes a fast-flowing channel leading the girl imperiously towards the ocean on which she will set out in the last few pages of the narrative. Images of water and the sea frequently recur, from the girl's early fear, 'j'ai peur, j'ai peur que les câbles cèdent, que nous soyons emportés vers la mer' (18), to the moment in the lover's flat when restraints do snap and she is 'emportée vers la jouissance' represented by 'la mer, sans forme, simplement incomparable' (50), and to the instant on the boat when she contemplates throwing herself into the sea, understanding at last that she had lived through 'un amour qu'elle n'avait pas vu parce qu'il s'était perdu dans l'histoire comme l'eau dans le sable' (138).[29] Where her mother becomes overwhelmed by her failure to keep out the ocean through the wall she constructs so laboriously, the girl manages the same powerful forces by allowing them to take their course. Perhaps the narrative is above all a survival story.

Another feature of the narrative much remarked upon, and which ties it more strongly to autobiography, or at least to family history, is the use of photographs, both imagined and in existence.[30] The role of the family album in constituting an official version of family history is familiar to most of us: it is only when an event occurs that does not fit the official narrative and cannot be included that the essentially unrepresentative nature of the album strikes home. In true Orwellian style photographs may disappear from the album's pages, as family history changes, or even, now, be altered to add or remove figures. Duras's text insists on the tension between the photograph and the family narrative, both by including descriptions of the profoundly disunited family grouped together in an illusion of group identity for the camera, and, more radically, by creating her text from a highly pictorial scene, lovingly and lengthily evoked, and referred to as the photograph which was never taken:

Elle aurait pu exister, une photographie aurait pu être prise, comme une autre, ailleurs, dans d'autres circonstances. Mais elle ne l'a pas été. L'objet était trop

---

[29] 'It would carry anything away, not just stones, a cathedral, a town'; 'I'm afraid, I'm afraid that the cables might give way, that we might be carried out to sea'; 'carried away by pleasure'; 'the sea, formless, simply incomparable'; 'a love that she had not noticed because it had got lost in history like sea in the sand'.

[30] The following discussion owes much to the excellent article by Pierre Saint-Amand entitled 'La photographie de famille dans L'Amant', in Marguerite Duras. Rencontres de Cerisy, ed. Pierre Vircondelet (Montreal: Editions Ecriture, 1994), 225–40.

mince pour la provoquer. Qui aurait pu penser à ça ? [. . .] C'est pourquoi, cette image, et il ne pouvait pas en être autrement, elle n'existe pas. Elle a été omise. Elle a été oubliée. Elle n'a pas été détachée, enlevée à la somme. C'est à ce manque d'avoir été faite qu'elle doit sa vertu, celle de représenter un absolu, d'en être justement l'auteur. (16–17)[31]

This insistence on the absence of the photograph situates the whole text as resting on a lacuna; as Pierre Saint-Amand remarks, the missing photograph is an illustration of the negating gesture which Duras makes about her writing project when she writes that there cannot be a narrative of her life, because there is no centre. In one sense, the missing photograph is the missing centre. However, the absence of a historical photograph can also be said to be the ideal circumstance for the imaginative exploration which the writing self carries out. The absence becomes the 'author', as she writes above; in the absence of the photograph, the text elaborates in the written word the image of the girl on the ferry. An inversion has taken place: where a photographic image normally speaks for itself, bearing at most a laconic written label of the type 'Sadec, 1927', here the writing continually expands and takes the dominant place. This issue of the tension between photographic image and accompanying written label is one which resurfaces in a number of contemporary texts and it exemplifies ironically a trend in defining a written self in relation to a visual medium.[32]

The missing photograph would have been incongruous, potentially scandalous, certainly bursting with life and sexuality. The contrast with the other photographs of the family referred to in the text is striking. The narrator recounts her mother's determination that photographs of the family should be taken: 'Elle se plaint du prix mais elle fait quand même les frais des photos de famille. Les photos, on les regarde, on ne se regarde pas mais on regarde les photographies, chacun séparément, sans un mot de commentaire, mais on les regarde, on se voit' (115).[33] The photographs lie, evoking unity and communication where there is none. However, two

---

[31] 'It could have existed, a photograph could have been taken, like others, elsewhere, in other circumstances. But it wasn't. The event was too insignificant for that. Who could have thought of taking one? [. . .] That's why the picture, and it could not have been otherwise, does not exist. It was omitted. It was not thought of. It was never detached, picked out from the rest. And it is this lack of having been taken that makes it so valuable, allows it to represent an absolute, to be precisely its author.'

[32] Marie Redonnet's *Rose Mélie Rose* (1987) uses twelve imaginary photographs to structure her heroine's life narrative. Annie Ernaux also draws on photographs from her past, and Barthes famously comments on family photographs in his *Roland Barthes par Roland Barthes* (1975).

[33] 'She complains about the price but she pays out anyway for family photos. We look at them, the photos, we don't look at each other but we look at the photographs, each of us separately, without a word of comment, but we look at them, we see ourselves.'

other photographs are more tellingly eloquent in their representation of the mother: in one, which the narrator calls the photo of despair, the children are grouped around their mother in front of their ill-fated house in Hanoi. The children look neglected and the mother is gripped by depression. The second forms part of the mother's ritual preparation for death, the last photo for the family to cherish, retouched like a body prepared for its final viewing. Although it too is a lie, its presence in the text truthfully speaks of the narrator's struggle with her mother, her desire for her death. In their representation of despair and death, these two last photographs, at least, are in tune with the narrative.

Borderlands and indeterminacies

The ferry crossing across the Mekong river with which the narrative opens, and the ocean crossing with which it comes to a close, signal the constant crossing of frontiers and borders which the text sets up. Geographic, racial, cultural, and sexual frontiers are confronted and sometimes dissolved as the poor white girl of French parentage meets her rich Chinese lover in the ill-reputed Chinese district of Saigon, bringing with her her desires for her brothers and her white friend, Hélène Lagonelle. Writer and theorist Gloria Anzaldua, herself a product of the borderlands between the United States and Mexico, writes of a 'mestiza' (mixed) consciousness arising from borderlands in which cultures and races occupy the same territory. The *mestiza* 'flounders in uncharted seas' as languages and cultures collide, learns to operate in pluralistic mode and to flee the rigid boundaries and walls erected by fixed notions of identity, whether racial or sexual.[34]

The narrator of *L'Amant* spends her childhood in the forests, the creeks, and the pepper plantations, hunting black panthers and eating the fish and vegetables that the natives eat. Her family circle includes Dô, the family servant so devoted to the narrator's mother that she accompanies her everywhere, even unpaid, even to France. The lover claims that the girl resembles the local girls:

> **Lui, l'amant de Cholen, il croit que la croissance de la petite blanche a pâti de la chaleur trop forte. Lui aussi il est né et a grandi dans cette chaleur. Il se découvre avoir avec elle cette parenté-là. Il dit que toutes ces années passées ici, à cette intolérable latitude, ont fait qu'elle est devenue une jeune fille de ce**

---

[34] See Gloria Anzaldua, *Borderlands/La Frontera. The New Mestiza* (San Francisco: Aunt Lute Books, 1987).

pays de l'Indochine. Qu'elle a la finesse de leurs poignets, leurs cheveux drus dont on dirait qu'ils ont pris pour eux toute la force, longs comme les leurs, et surtout, cette peau, cette peau de tout le corps qui vient de l'eau de la pluie qu'on garde ici pour le bain des femmes, des enfants. (120)[35]

In Saigon she lives in a boarding-school mainly frequented by 'métisses', the mixed blood daughters of local women abandoned by their French fathers; only the girl and Hélène Lagonelle are white. Yet in the girl's imagination Hélène Lagonelle's white flesh merges across race and gender with that of the lover himself: 'Je la vois comme étant de la même chair que cette homme de Cholen' (92).[36]

The girl inhabits a borderland, in which boundaries dissolve and identities merge, and yet she is constantly called upon to compartmentalize her life. She may resemble the girls around her in the school but she receives a formal French education at the French lycée in Saigon, and she rides in the front of the local bus in the place reserved for white passengers. She has to promise her mother that she could never bring herself to make love with a Chinese man: 'Comment veux-tu, je dis, avec un Chinois, comment veux-tu que je fasse ça avec un Chinois, si laid, si malingre?' (74). She is unable to treat the lover with even a minimum of courtesy when she is with her brothers 'parce que c'est un Chinois, que ce n'est pas un blanc' (65). Instead, she writes in a phrase that evokes the horrors of war, 'il devient un endroit brûlé' (66).[37]

In the lover's room, barriers lack material substance. Lying on the bed, separated from the crowds outside by only a cotton blind, both part and not part of them, the girl has an intense sense experience of the town:

Le lit est séparé de la ville par ces persiennes à claire-voie, ce store de coton. Aucun matériau dur ne nous sépare des autres gens. Eux, ils ignorent notre existence. Nous, nous percevons quelque chose de la leur, le total de leurs voix, de leurs mouvements, comme une sirène qui lancerait une clameur brisée, triste sans écho.

Des odeurs de caramel arrivent dans la chambre, celle des cacahuètes grillées, des soupes chinoises, des viandes rôties, des herbes, du jasmin, de la poussière, de l'encens, du feu de charbon de bois, le feu se transporte ici dans

---

[35] 'The lover from Cholen believes that the little white girl's growth has suffered from the heat, that it has been too much for her. He too was born and grew up in this heat. He discovers that he has this in common with her. He says that all the years she's spent here, at this intolerable latitude, have made her turn into a girl from Indo-China. That she has their slender wrists, their hair so thick that it seems to have taken all the girls' strength, and her hair is long like theirs too, and, above all, she has their skin, all over her body, a skin that comes from the rainwater which is kept here for the women and the children to bathe in.'

[36] 'I see her as being of the same flesh as the man from Cholen.'

[37] 'A Chinese, I say, how on earth do you imagine that I could do that with a Chinese, so ugly, such a weakling?'; 'because he's Chinese, because he's not a white man'; 'He becomes a scorched place.'

des paniers, il se vend dans les rues, l'odeur de la ville est celle des villages de la brousse, de la forêt. (53)[38]

Although some of these sense impressions are specifically of the Chinese quarter, they are extended to the wider surroundings and evoked with an intensity which suggests a close identification with a country which is not in fact primarily evoked in idealized or exoticized terms. The magical luminosity of the nights in the dry season are, certainly, lovingly dwelled on, but more frequently the narrator recalls the stultifying heat, the monotony of a climate which has no springtime, the frequency of the epidemics, and the sight of the disease-ridden crowds.

Sometimes she speaks as an insider, sometimes as an outsider; the struggle which the girl has to live several lives at once echoes her mother's ambivalence. Her mother wears cotton stockings in the heat, in order to play the role of the French headmistress, but her hair is in a Chinese chignon; she retires back to France but then changes her mind and returns. The strains of keeping the compartments and contradictions going are an obvious root of her mental disturbance; but, where the mother is above all symbolized by her attempt to build a dam, to hold back the ocean, the girl becomes unwilling to categorize, make boundaries. It is in this spirit that the narrator can describe her decision to join the Communist Party as equivalent to the decision to collaborate with the German occupying forces.

Like moral judgements, gender roles also become indeterminate. The girl relishes her appearance on the ferry, the clash of the man's felt hat, itself thrown into question by its pink colour, and its ambivalent relation to her high-heeled gold lamé sandals. Here the girl appears literally to enact Judith Butler's theory of gender as performance for if, as Butler argues, gender identity, like other identities, is generated by repeated rule-bound discourses, then it is open to the individual to vary and subvert the various styles and positions which we repeat.[39] The illusion of gender identity can be exposed by parodic and subversive elements, here represented by the hat and the sandals. A similar gender and racial blurring occurs when, in an effort to find an existing image that would resemble the non-existent photograph, the narrator turns to a photo-graph of her son: 'Il est en Californie avec ses amies Erika et Elisabeth

---

[38] 'The bed is separated from the town by the latticed shutters, the cotton blind. Nothing solid separates us from the people in the street. They know nothing of our existence. We perceive something of theirs, the sum of their voices, their movements, like a siren starting up and breaking off, mournfully, with no response. Caramel smells enter the room, and smells of roasted peanuts, chinese soups, roast meats, herbs, jasmin, dust, incense, charcoal fires, fire is carried in baskets here, it's sold in the street, the smell of the town is the smell of the bush villages, of the forest.'

[39] See Judith Butler, *Gender Trouble. Feminism and the Subversion of Identity* (London: Routledge, 1990).

Lennard. Il est maigre, tellement, on dirait un Ougandais blanc lui aussi' (21). Far from clarifying the image of the girl on the ferry, this sudden entry into the picture of the narrator's son complicates all the categories already in place: Indo-China becomes California, female becomes male (but framed by two females), French becomes Ugandan. The girl on the ferry has not yet met her lover but she has already become a mother. And yet, because of a similarity of expression, of non-coincidence with his own appearance—'Il se veut donner une image déjetée de jeune vagabond' (21)—the narrator is able to conclude with satisfaction: 'C'est cette photographie qui est au plus près de celle qui n'a pas été faite de la jeune fille du bac' (21).[40]

Masculinity, a gender category just as problematic as that of femininity, is also shown in the text to be tied to aspects of performance. The lover inhabits a 'garconnière' (batchelor flat), a space more or less exclusively intended for his amorous activities, but, as noted earlier, when the girl asks him to enact the performance, throw her on the bed and rip off her clothes, he breaks down half-way through, dissolves into tears, and has to be himself tenderly undressed by the inexperienced girl. If in some respects he plays the role of perfect lover, he does not do so entirely in accordance with Hollywood film tradition since the narrator describes his body in terms of a series of lacks of conventional Western masculinity: 'La peau est d'une somptueuse douceur. Le corps. Le corps est maigre, sans force, sans muscles, il pourrait avoir été malade, être en convalescence, il est imberbe, sans virilité autre que celle du sexe, il est très faible, il paraît être à la merci d'une insulte, souffrant' (49).[41] This description makes clear how categories of race and gender identity are imbricated in the text, and further links the lover both to the little brother, also described in a blurring of gender and race as a little coolie, and to the girl herself, with her barely formed body 'encore sans formes arrêtées, à tout instant en train de se faire' (121). The lover's room is similarly described as a 'passage', and it becomes a borderland—a place built for the poor Chinese, furnished impersonally in modern Western style, open to the sounds and smells of the crowd in the street, a place which suits the girl perfectly because it is a displacement: 'Elle est là où il faut qu'elle soit, déplacée là' (47).[42]

---

[40] 'He's in California with his friends Erika and Elisabeth Lennard. He looks thin, so thin that you would think he was a white Ugandan as well'; 'He wants to take on a twisted image of a young layabout'; 'This is the photograph that comes closest to the one which was never taken of the young girl on the ferry.'

[41] 'His skin is sumptuously soft. His body. His body is thin, with no strength, no muscles, as if he has been ill, as if he was convalescing, he has no beard, no sign of virility other than his penis, he is very weak, he seems to be open to insult, distressed.'

[42] 'It is still without finished form, at every moment still in the making'; 'She is where she should be, displaced.'

For Gloria Anzaldua, the consciousness of the borderlands is the consciousness of the future, because the future 'depends on the breaking down of paradigms, it depends on the straddling of two or more cultures' and on an abandonment of dualistic thinking.[43] In this sense *L'Amant* may be a text which takes events of the past as its focus but it is inhabited by a very contemporary sensibility.

Conclusions

L'Amant is a love story, a post-colonial narrative, a confessional text. It evokes, directly and indirectly, many other texts in its pages. The seasoned Duras reader is directly addressed by the narrator-as-author and reminded of the more low-key version of events given more than thirty years earlier in *Un Barrage contre le Pacifique* (1950). This reader will also recognize the beggar woman, and the distraught colonial wife whose young lover commits suicide, and find echoes of other figures from Duras's fictional and film narratives. This form of intertextuality, in which a single work by an author explicitly takes its place within an already existing *œuvre*, reworking familiar themes and characters, echoes the practice of other contemporary authors such as Michel Tournier and, to a lesser degree, Annie Ernaux. One of its main effects is to displace the centre of interest from the primary material with which the text deals to the ways in which the material is handled, to the writing or filmic process itself.

Less intentional and explicit echoes may also sound for some readers of an author of an earlier generation writing about rather different experiences of the French colonies of 1920s Indo-China. André Malraux's expedition into the Cambodian jungle, his subsequent trial and conflict with the colonial regime took place at much the same time as the events recounted in *L'Amant*, and are fictionalized in *La Voie royale* (1933). Malraux's focus on man's metaphysical struggle with destiny, symbolized in the threatening and alienating force of the Cambodian jungle and its native inhabitants, differs sharply from Duras's text, yet his protagonists too are uncertain of their identity, occupy borderlands, and are fixated by gender and sexual performance, threatened by impotency. Further back still, *L'Amant* has many resonances with the tradition of the French confessional text, in which a male, often curiously feminized first-person narrator confesses his own part in a love affair which has destroyed the other partner.[44] Here the tale is turned on its head since the woman both

---

[43] Anzaldua, *Borderlands*, 79–80.

[44] Chateaubriand's *René* (1802), Musset's *Confession d'un enfant du siècle* (1836), and Constant's *Adolphe* (1816) are famous examples.

survives and narrates, but her narrative does resemble in some ways the confessional tale of Chateaubriand's René, driven overseas to live with the Natchez Indian tribe in the French American colonies in an unsuccessful attempt to bury a history of incestuous desire. In its runaway popular success, can *L'Amant* be said to have anything in common with less high culture? Its confessional tone certainly has links with popular romance, and its focus on the female narrator and her experiences is one shared by many best-sellers. The strong emphasis on the visual connects it to the influential film culture of contemporary France, a connection made evident by the film version of the text made by Jean-Jacques Annaud released in 1992. Although the film gained international success, its reception was dominated by the weight of its erotic material—it is perhaps inevitable that the cinematic exploration of sexuality carries an impact of such potency that it shifts the balance of the written text.

Novels highly acclaimed in their time by no means always retain their status for later generations. *L'Amant* was undoubtedly *the* text of the 1980s and, if it has a single characteristic which may guarantee its future, it may be its open, exploratory nature. Open to other tellings, open to other texts, and open, most importantly, to other readers.

2 Detective fictions: Daniel Pennac's *Au bonheur des ogres* (1985)

Setting the (Malaus)sène

A bomb explodes in a Parisian department store. An elderly man is killed; Benjamin Malaussène, an employee of the store, witnesses the explosion but is unharmed. Police investigations prove fruitless. A second bomb explodes in the store, this time killing an elderly brother and sister; Malaussène witnesses the explosion but is unharmed. A third explosion kills an elderly man; Malaussène witnesses the explosion but is unharmed. For the fourth explosion, which perhaps unsurprisingly kills an elderly man, Malaussène is not present, but one of his sisters is near the scene. Malaussène is the principal suspect of the police and his fellow employees; interrogated by the former, he is also subjected to a vicious beating by a group of the latter. Only his dysfunctional family and a certain police Commissioner Coudrier, who shares his passion for good coffee, seem to accept his protestations of innocence. Eventually, however, the truth emerges. By the time the fifth bomb explodes, killing an elderly man whilst Malaussène looks on unharmed, it has become clear that Malaussène is not the perpetrator but the victim of the crimes: an innocent bystander, a saint even, whom a group of cannibalistic devil-worshippers with astrological leanings has decided to discredit by making him seem responsible for what are in fact their suicides. His innocence established, Malaussène can go home to his family of half-brothers and half-sisters. Finally, their mother returns, pregnant once again, and unaccompanied by her next child's father.

This, in brief, is the plot of *Au bonheur des ogres*, the first of what is now a six-volume series of novels in which Malaussène plays the role of eternal victim and perpetual suspect.[1] In subsequent volumes, Malaussène is incriminated in a series of murders including that of a policeman (*La Fée carabine*, 1987), he is shot through the head by a psychopathic serial killer and only recovers by means of a transplant of multiple organs taken from

---

[1] References to the six volumes of the Malaussène series, *Au bonheur des ogres, La Fée carabine, La Petite Marchande de prose, Monsieur Malaussène, Des chrétiens et des maures*, and *Aux fruits de la passion* (Paris: Gallimard, 1985, 1987, 1989, 1995, 1996, and 1999 respectively; all Folio edns. except the latter) are given in the text. Pennac has also published a one-man play, *Monsieur Malaussène au théâtre* (Paris: Gallimard, 1996), which draws on material from *Monsieur Malaussène* and previous novels in the series.

his attacker (*La Petite Marchande de prose*, 1989), and he is imprisoned for twenty-one murders, including all those committed in the first three volumes of the cycle (*Monsieur Malaussène*, 1995); in a variant on the pattern, in the most recent novel of the series (to date) Malaussène expects to be imprisoned but it is actually his sister Thérèse who is arrested for her husband's murder (*Aux fruits de la passion*, 1999). Each of the novels is punctuated by violent crimes, but also by the births of further additions to the Malaussène family, and eventually in *Monsieur Malaussène* by that of his own child, born from the womb of a virgin nun. Pennac's work contains numerous elements typical of detective fiction: mysterious crimes investigated by dogged police officers, red herrings and unexpected twists of the plot, suspicion and guilt, innocence and evil. Indeed, the first two volumes in the Malaussène series, *Au bonheur des ogres* and *La Fée carabine*, were initially published in Gallimard's *série noire*, a series specifically targeted at devotees of detective fiction. However, Pennac's appeal has extended beyond that specialist audience; whilst the detective format remains central to the construction of the Malaussène novels, they are also driven, as the above summaries perhaps indicate, by a playful exorbitance in the narrative and an impressive linguistic creativeness. They combine an adherence to the detective format with a highly self-conscious literariness. The title of *Au bonheur des ogres* alludes to Emile Zola's *Au bonheur des dames*, the eleventh of his twenty-volume Rougon-Macquart series, published almost exactly a century before Pennac's novel in 1883. Zola's title refers to the name of a large shop specializing in women's clothes, a place intended to bring happiness to women; the title of Pennac's novel (which also, in its way, is part of a series depicting the fortunes of a family dynasty) indicates that the department store where Malaussène works is more likely to bring happiness to ogres than to women. Pennac thus gives a mythical spin to Zola's Naturalism, and it was immediately clear to his earliest readers that his novels could not be classified simply under the rubric of detective fiction.[2] This was recognized by Gallimard when they published the third volume of the series, *La Petite Marchande de prose* in their *série blanche*, a series aimed at a more general, less specialized market than the *série noire*; and all of the novels are now available in the Folio paperback series.

One critic has described Pennac's work, along with that of Jean Echenoz and others, as 'post-literary', explaining that this term 'designates not the

---

[2] The ogrish nature of the department store is anticipated in Zola's *Au bonheur des dames*, from which Pennac's novel derives its title; for discussion, see Sophie Guermès's 'Préface' to Emile Zola, *Au bonheur des dames* (Paris: Fasquelle, 1998; Livre de Poche edn.), 7. On mythical elements in titles of Pennac's other Malaussène novels, see Colin Nettelbeck, 'The "Post-Literary" Novel: Echenoz, Pennac and Company', in *French Cultural Studies*, 5/2 (1994), 113–38, especially 132.

demise of the literary, but the displacement of a cultural dominant, and the relativization of what had been a quasi-absolute social value';[3] literature no longer has the cultural prestige it once had, and the most important influences on 'post-literary' writers are not the canonical authors of the literary tradition so much as popular and mass culture, including detective fiction, science fiction, the cinema and television, comic strips and popular music.[4] But this does not mean that literary authors such as Pennac and Echenoz have simply abandoned the high ambitions of their art. Pennac's fiction, like much of the most successful work written during the period covered in this book, is at the meeting-point of high art and popular culture; rather than tending to abolish the distinction, it exploits the possibility that different readers may take different forms of pleasure in the same works, or even that the same reader's pleasure may be subtly differentiated, so that the desire to discover 'whodunit' does not in any way exclude enjoyment of aspects of the text which have little to do with plot development. This is indicated in *Au bonheur des ogres* by Malaussène's own activities as a nightly purveyor of stories to his very different siblings. In the same narrative he succeeds in giving to each of his listeners what he or she wants, combining a story of ogres with a war story, providing an element of humour as well as good practice for one of his sisters who, as a trainee secretary, types up his stories as he tells them (28–9). Everyone hears the same story, but everyone gets something different out of it.

Much of the success of the Malaussène novels depends on the character of Malaussène himself. The founding conceit of the series is that his status as perpetual suspect is not simply a matter of bad luck, being in the wrong place at the wrong time, but an essential aspect of his nature. Malaussène arouses the hostility of the mob, or the police, because he is in fact a paragon of innocence, too pure to survive unscathed in a wicked world. He is the person who attracts to himself all the guilt for the crimes of others. This is illustrated by his job at the department store. In principle Malaussène is responsible for technical control on goods sold in the store, but he explains the real nature of his job to Commissioner Coudrier:

> Je lui explique alors que la fonction dite de Contrôle technique est absolument fictive. Je ne contrôle rien du tout, car rien n'est contrôlable dans la profusion des marchands du temple. A moins de multiplier par dix les effectifs des contrôleurs. Or donc, lorsqu'un client se pointe avec une plainte, je suis appelé au bureau des Réclamations où je reçois une engueulade absolument terrifiante. Mon boulot consiste à subir cette tornade d'humiliations, avec un air si contrit, si paumé, si profondément désespéré, qu'en règle générale le client retire sa

> plainte pour ne pas avoir mon suicide sur la conscience, et que tout se termine à l'aimable, avec le minimum de casse pour le Magasin: Voilà. Je suis payé pour ça. Assez bien, d'ailleurs. (80)[5]

In later volumes in the series, Malaussène will exercise a similar function in a publishing company. His role is essentially to take the blame for the faults of others, or to disarm anger addressed to others by directing it towards himself. There is a serious point behind this role: it represents a comment on the nature of modern capitalism which sacrifices quality on the altar of increased profit margins. As Sainclair, the store manager, explains to Malaussène, 'Vu le nombre d'articles qui sortent d'un grand magasin en une journée, comment voulez-vous que le contrôle technique puisse contrôler quoi que ce soit?' (101).[6] By playing his role to perfection, Malaussène becomes a sort of Christ-figure, taking on himself the sins of others. There is, therefore, a direct connection between his professional employment and the criminal intrigue into which he gets drawn, since in both he displays his peculiar ability to attract blame for crimes or misdemeanours that he has not committed. Malaussène acquires a sort of mythical status: he is not simply a man unjustly accused, but the embodiment of Wronged Innocence, or, in the terms used throughout the series of novels, *le Bouc émissaire* (Scapegoat). The designation of Malaussène as *bouc* (goat) is subject to a certain amount of play through the novels, suggesting both his malodorousness (*puer le bouc*, to stink like a goat) and his active libido (*un bouc*, a lubricious man). But its most important association, the one on which the central dynamics of innocence and victimization depend, is with the scapegoat, in particular as it is theorized in the work of René Girard.

Rounding up the suspects

Girard is an eclectic thinker and literary critic who has spent most of his career teaching in the United States. The importance of his thought to *Au*

---

[5] 'So I explain to him that the function of so-called Technical Inspection is absolutely fictitious. I don't inspect anything at all, since nothing can be inspected in the profusion of merchants in the temple. Unless they were to multiply by ten the numbers of inspectors. So when a client turns up with a complaint, I'm called in to the Complaints Office where I get an absolutely terrifying bawling out. My job consists in undergoing this tornado of humiliation, looking so contrite, so lost, so deeply in despair, that as a general rule the customer withdraws his complaint so as not to have my suicide on his conscience, and everything ends amicably, with the minimum loss to the Shop. That's it. I am paid for that. Fairly well, in fact.'

[6] 'Given the number of articles leaving a department store in a day, how do you expect that technical inspection can inspect anything at all?'

bonheur des ogres is signalled by the epigraphs to the novel; two out of the three epigraphs are taken from Girard's *Le Bouc émissaire* which Pennac has acknowledged reading shortly after its publication in 1982 (the third epigraph to the novel is an unreferenced quotation attributed to Woody Allen).[7] *Le Bouc émissaire* represents the latest stage in the development of Girard's thought which begins with his first book, *Mensonge romantique et vérité romanesque* (1961) and which is taken further in his subsequent work, notably *La Violence et le sacré* (1972) and *Des choses cachées depuis la fondation du monde* (1978). His central interest has always been in the role of violence in the formation and maintenance of human communities. In *Mensonge romantique et vérité romanesque*, which is largely a work of literary criticism, Girard lays the foundation for his later studies of history and myth with his account of what he calls *le désir triangulaire* or *le désir mimétique*.[8] The human subject, according to Girard, is constituted by desire; but desire is not, as the Romantics wanted, the spontaneous expression of a unique being. It is aroused only through a process of what Girard calls mimeticism; in effect, we desire an object because, and only because, we see that others desire it, we *copy* the desire of others, and without that copying we would be incapable of desiring anything at all. Desire is triangular in that it requires three positions to be occupied: the desiring subject, the desired object, and—crucially—a mediator who provokes the subject's desire by establishing the object as desirable. I want what the mediator wants, and I want it only *because* the mediator wants it. Thus, rivalry for the object of desire is not a matter of bad luck; it is the very condition of desire.

The theory of mimetic desire explains both the formation of communities and the persistence of conflict within those communities. I am bound to my fellow beings because I want the same things as them, but I am in rivalry with them because each of us prevents the others from fully possessing what we think we want. *Mensonge romantique et vérité romanesque* describes humans as members of antagonistic communities which are constantly in danger of falling apart through the pressure of precisely what holds them together, the imbrication of an individual's desire with that of others. In *La Violence et le sacré* Girard extends his theory through the use of ethnographic and psychoanalytic material, as he considers what happens within communities when their inherent tensions reach breaking-point. At times, conflict inevitably develops into crisis; if the community is to survive, it requires some means of turning

---

[7] Pennac acknowledges his debt to Girard, for example in interview with Aliette Armel, 'Daniel Pennac: Au bonheur des enfants', in *Magazine littéraire*, 357 (Sept. 1997), 98.

[8] 'triangular desire'; 'mimetic desire'.

that crisis to its own advantage. Girard argues that ritual sacrifice establishes a mechanism which preserves the cohesion of the community by channelling its internal conflicts towards a single victim. The community comes together to expel or destroy that victim, giving expression to its inherent antagonisms but bringing its members closer together in the act of communal persecution. Sacrifice strengthens the community, if only for a while, by ridding it of what it holds to be responsible for its collective ills: 'C'est la communauté entière que le sacrifice protège de *sa* propre violence, c'est la communauté entière qu'il détourne vers des victimes qui lui sont extérieures. Le sacrifice polarise sur la victime des germes de dissension partout répandus et il les dissipe en leur proposant un assouvissement partiel.'[9]

It is a crucial aspect of Girard's analysis that the community misunderstands the workings of sacrificial violence; it genuinely believes that the *victime émissaire* is responsible for the crisis that besets it, whereas Girard insists that the identity or real guilt of the victim are largely irrelevant to its sacrificial function. Sacrificial violence is an expression and temporary assuagement of conflicts inherent in communities. So the victim is an innocent scapegoat made to pay the price for crimes s/he has not committed. In *Le Bouc émissaire* Girard outlines four 'stereotypes of persecution', which are elements typically found in texts where the mechanism of scapegoating can be observed, whether the texts are historical, literary, or mythological:[10]

1. The first is the stereotype of crisis. The search for a scapegoat begins when the cohesion of a community is under threat. Rather than blaming themselves for the crisis, members of the community blame either society as a whole, or certain individuals thought to be particularly harmful.

2. This leads to one or more of a number of stereotypical accusations against the scapegoat. They generally involve crimes that attack the security or fundamental principles of a society: crimes of violence, particularly those directed against members of society held to be most important (the king, the father) or the most weak, such as children; sexual crimes, such as rape, incest, homosexuality, or bestiality; or religious crimes, such as the profanation of the host.

3. The third kind of stereotype concerns the identity of the scapegoat. The victims typically belong to one or more groups which are particularly

---

[9] 'It's the entire community that sacrifice protects from *its* own violence, it's the entire community that it turns aside towards victims who do not belong to it. Sacrifice polarizes on to the victim seeds of dissension which are everywhere and it dissipates them by offering them a partial satisfaction.' René Girard, *La Violence et le sacré* (Paris: Grasset, 1972), 22.

[10] See in particular René Girard, 'Les Stéréotypes de la persécution', ch. 2 of *Le Bouc émissaire* (Paris: Grasset, 1982), 23–36.

exposed to persecution. They may come from ethnic or religious minorities, have some physical deformity such as a limp or a hunchback, or simply be different from the mainstream in some way: foreign, provincial, orphaned, unemployed, poor, or even very rich or exceptionally beautiful. When scapegoats are required, deviation from the norm becomes a crime in itself: 'Plus on s'éloigne du statut social le plus commun, dans un sens ou dans l'autre, plus les risques de persécution grandissent.'[11]

4. The fourth stereotype is that of violence. Once the necessary critical conditions are in place and the accusations are made, the victim is identified, drawn into the circle of the victimizers, and violently punished for the crimes for which he or she is deemed responsible. The group regains its cohesion though collective violence against the chosen scapegoat.

Malaussène refers to himself as a scapegoat, and other characters make explicit that this is not just a job, but a mythical function. Julia, the journalist who becomes Malaussène's lover, describes the scapegoat as 'Le mythe fondateur de toute civilization!' (118),[12] referring to its role in Judaism and Christianity, as well as its manifestations in modern secular societies, such as the show trials of the Stalinist Soviet Union. If the scapegoat didn't exist, we would have to invent it: 'Et nous, qui croyons qu'il ne faut croire en rien, comment penses-tu que nous réussissons à ne pas nous prendre pour des merdes? En reniflant le parfum de bouc du voisin [. . .] et s'il n'y avait pas de voisin on se couperait en deux pour se faire un bouc à nous, portatif, qui puerait à notre place!' (119).[13] Commissioner Coudrier also expands on the notion of the scapegoat, insisting that it serves to explain what could not otherwise be explained:

> **Voyez-vous, le Bouc Emissaire n'est pas seulement celui qui, le cas échéant, paye pour les autres. Il est surtout, et avant tout, *un principe d'explication*, Monsieur Malaussène. [. . .] Il est la cause mystérieuse mais *patente* de tout événement inexplicable. [. . .] D'où l'explication des massacres de juifs durant les grandes pestes du Moyen Age. [. . .] Pour certains de vos collègues, en tant que Bouc Emissaire, vous êtes le poseur de bombes, pour la seule raison qu'ils ont *besoin* d'une cause, que cela les rassure. [. . .] Ils n'ont aucun besoin de preuves. Leur conviction leur suffit. Et ils recommenceront si je n'y mets pas bon ordre. (149)[14]**

---

[11] 'The more distant someone is from the most common social status, in one or another direction, the greater are the risks of persecution.' Girard, *Le Bouc émissaire*, 31.

[12] 'The founding myth of all civilization!'

[13] 'And we, who believe that you shouldn't believe in anything, how do you think we succeed in not taking ourselves for dirt? By sniffing the goat's scent of our neighbour [. . .] and if we didn't have a neighbour we would cut ourselves in two in order to make our own goat, a portable one, who would stink in our place!'

[14] 'You see, the Scapegoat is not only someone who, if necessary, pays for others. He is especially and above all *a principle of explanation*, Mr Malaussène. [. . .] He is the mysterious but *obvious* cause of

If the epigraphs to *Au bonheur des ogres* indicate that Pennac has read Girard's *Le Bouc émissaire*, such comments from Julia and Coudrier suggest that Pennac's characters have been reading the book as well.[15] Girard's thought is an essential influence on *Au bonheur des ogres*, since Malaussène is conceived as a character who occupies the role of scapegoat by profession and by nature. The four stereotypes of persecution outlined by Girard can be seen to operate in the events which lead to the victimization of Pennac's protagonist in *Au bonheur des ogres*:

1. The crisis which afflicts the society in which the novel is based is not so much an event or series of events which threaten the community as a permanent state of late capitalism, as represented by the department store. This is a society in which profit has outstripped the ability to monitor the quality of the goods on sale, so that the technical inspection that Malaussène is deemed to exercise is a purely fictional function. There is a permanent need for scapegoats, as the minor crises which betray a deeper societal dysfunction (not a plague or a war, but a fridge that doesn't work or a bed that collapses) become an everyday occurrence. The series of explosions which afflict the store, and the various crimes and murders in the later Malaussène novels, thus appear to be symptoms rather than causes of the crisis in society.

2. As Girard points out, the scapegoat is accused of heinous crimes which strike at the very heart of society. In the Middle Ages, Jews were accused of poisoning the water supply in order to cause random, widespread suffering. A series of explosions without apparent pattern or motive (which may remind the reader of the bombs set off in Paris the year after the publication of *Au bonheur des ogres*) serves as a suitable modern version of such an accusation. One of the defining fantasies and fears of modern popular culture is the terrorist or the random serial killer who, because he or she has no *particular* target, puts all of us at risk.

3. Even without the circumstantial evidence which implicates him in the crimes, Malaussène is in a near-ideal position to be designated as scapegoat. Although not himself homosexual or foreign, or from a religious or ethnic minority, his friends are almost all in some way marginal to the white heterosexual French mainstream. He lives in, and loves, Belleville, a working-class and immigrant district rife with crime.

every inexplicable event. […] Which explains the massacre of Jews during the great plagues of the Middle Ages. […] For some of your colleagues, in as far as you are the Scapegoat, you are the person planting the bombs, for the sole reason that they *need* a cause, and that reassures them. […] They don't need proof. Their conviction is quite enough. And they will do it all again if I don't sort things out'.

[15] Coudrier's reference to the Middle Ages here may be a direct reference to the first chapter of Girard's *Le Bouc émissaire*, which discusses a 14th-cent. text by Guillaume de Machaut.

And his family situation is to say the least unusual, as he finds himself effectively the head of a bizarre family of illegitimate half-brothers and half-sisters who seem not to know their fathers and to have been deserted by their mother.

4. The stereotypes of persecution inevitably lead to violence. Malaussène is viciously beaten up by a group of fellow employees at the department store, thus bringing to its culmination the persecutory mechanism in which he is caught (see 143–4).

Girard coins the term *textes de persécution* (persecutory texts) to refer to texts which are unconsciously structured by the sacrificial logic that he has uncovered.[16] However, after *La Violence et le sacré*, in *Des choses cachées depuis la fondation du monde* Girard introduces a development in his thought which he will explore further in *Le Bouc émissaire*. What he calls *textes de persécution* are texts, be they historical or mythical, which are complicit with the designation and persecution of scapegoats; for example, anti-Semitic texts are written as if their authors really believed in the guilt of the Jews, so such texts actively encourage and participate in the violence of the persecutory mechanism. But there is also a unique body of texts which reveal and denounce this sacrificial process, namely the Gospels. What is unprecedented about the Gospels, according to Girard, is their insistence on the innocence of the sacrificial victim. So, although it is true that the crucifixion of Christ follows the same pattern of scapegoating that can be found in other religions, it is different in as far as the Gospels are written unambiguously from the standpoint of the victim; Christ's innocence is stressed as it is in no other version of the same story, and the extent to which the persecutors are obeying a logic of which they have no understanding is unambiguously brought to light. Christ's words, 'Forgive them father for they know not what they do', are to be taken absolutely literally, since it is only in the Gospels, and subsequently in Girard's own work, that the stereotypes of persecution are made explicit.

This is another important lesson that Pennac learns from Girard in the composition of *Au bonheur des ogres*. The text is narrated throughout by Malaussène; the novel is thus written from the perspective of the innocent victim of persecution, and clearly illuminates the prejudice and injustice to which he is subjected by those around him. According to Girard, what separates the Gospels from the *textes de persécution* is that in the latter the stereotypes of persecution inform the underlying structure of the text, whereas the Gospels explicitly thematize those stereotypes. For the *textes de persécution* the scapegoat is 'le bouc émissaire *du* texte', with whose

---

[16] See Girard, *Des choses cachées depuis la fondation du monde* (Paris: Grasset, 1978; Livre de Poche edn.), 176–211.

persecution the text is complicit, whereas in the Gospels Christ is 'bouc émissaire *dans* le texte et *pour* le texte',[17] clearly depicted as the innocent victim of the mechanism of persecution.[18] *Au bonheur des ogres*, then, aligns itself with the Gospels, with Malaussène as an improbable Christ-figure, by insisting on the innocence of the scapegoat. If this reference to the Gospels seems to aggrandize *Au bonheur des ogres*, and in particular Malaussène's role in it, the comparison is justified at least to some extent in the novel itself. Malaussène tells Julia about how he makes a living 'en endossant la faute originelle de la société marchande' (121), and Julia concurs that he is 'une sorte de saint' (127).[19] Later Malaussène puts himself directly into the role of Christ by quoting his words on the cross: 'Père, pourquoi m'as-tu abandonné?' (244).[20] The last of the suicidal bombers reiterates the identification of Malaussène with Christ: '—En vous chargeant des fautes de tous, en prenant sur vos épaules tous les péchés du Commerce, c'est en saint que vous vous comportez, voire en Christ! . . .' (252).[21] There is doubtless much irony in this identification of Malaussène with Christ; at the same time, the plots of each of the Malaussène novels are driven by his status as innocent victim. *Au bonheur des ogres* and its sequels take Girard's ideas from *Le Bouc émissaire* and show the persistence into the modern world of the processes of scape-goating; they denounce the manner in which society seeks to restore its endangered cohesion through the violent expulsion of innocent scape-goats deemed responsible for otherwise inexplicable woes.

Telling the story

It is the singular achievement of *Au bonheur des ogres* that it combines ideas derived from Girard with what remains a highly entertaining, plot-driven detective story. In fact, this convergence of popular fiction and intellectual seriousness has important precedents in post-war France. The end of the Second World War brought new possibilities for the dissemination of American popular culture to a wide French audi-ence. The Blum–Byrnes agreement of 1946 offered France economic aid from the United States in exchange for, amongst other things, increased access of American films to French cinemas.[22] The newly-discovered

---

[17] 'the scapegoat *of* the text'; 'scapegoat *in* and *for* the text'.   [18] Girard, *Le Bouc émissaire*, 170.

[19] 'by taking on the original sin of consumer society', 'a sort of saint'.

[20] 'Father, why have you forsaken me?'

[21] '—By taking onto yourself the faults of all, by taking on your shoulders all the sins of Commerce, you are behaving like a saint, indeed like Christ! ...'

[22] See Jill Forbes and Michael Kelly (eds.), *French Cultural Studies* (Oxford: OUP, 1995), 140–1.

films of directors such as John Ford and Howard Hawks appealed to intellectuals as much as to a wide popular audience; they were examined and praised by the critics of the influential *Cahiers du cinéma*, many of whom went on to become leading directors of the so-called *nouvelle vague* (new wave) of French cinema in the late 1950s and 1960s: Jean-Luc Godard, François Truffaut, Claude Chabrol, Jacques Rivette, Eric Rohmer.[23] These directors developed their own ideas about cinema in part through watching American popular film. Godard's first feature film, *A bout de souffle* (1959), is dedicated to Monogram Pictures, makers of Hollywood B movies, and its central character, played by Jean-Paul Belmondo, is a dangerous petty criminal who models himself on the screen persona of Humphrey Bogart. The film develops its own aesthetic by self-consciously incorporating elements of Hollywood cinema; popular culture is thus not a straight alternative to experimental cinema so much as an element in its creation.

The dissemination of American cinema in France was matched by the new availability of American popular fiction. Gallimard's *série noire* was established in 1945, initially publishing translations of English and especially American detective fiction by authors such as Dashiell Hammett and Raymond Chandler. Even the earliest French-authored novels to be published in the series were written under American-sounding pseudonyms. Just as Godard and others were drawn to Hollywood cinema, many serious experimental writers were drawn to the detective genre as popularized by the *série noire*. In particular, the plot of the detective story, entailing an ultimately successful search for an initially hidden truth, seemed a perfect instance of the presumptions of sense and coherence which avant-garde writers wished to undermine. Practitioners of the *nouveau roman* such as Michel Butor in *L'Emploi du temps* (1953) and Alain Robbe-Grillet in *Les Gommes* (1957) played on and transgressed the detective format. *Les Gommes*, for example, ends with a detective killing the person whose murder he had been sent to investigate. New narrative possibilities, and more elusive, playful relations between text and reader, emerge through the deliberate flouting of generic conventions. Since the heyday of the *nouvelle vague* and the *nouveau roman* the detective format has remained a constant element in some of the most interesting French artistic works which occupy the boundary between popular and high culture. This can be seen in novels such as Patrick Modiano's Goncourt prize-winning *La Rue des boutiques obscures* (1978) (in which a private detective suffering from amnesia sets out to discover his own true identity), Jean Echenoz's *Cherokee* (1987) or Michel del Castillo's *Mort d'un*

[23] Forbes and Kelly, *French Cultural Studies*, 173–6.

poète (1989), and in such films as Alain Corneau's *Série noire* (1979) (with dialogue by the writer Georges Perec), Jean-Jacques Beineix's *Diva* (1981) (itself based on a novel published in the *série noire*), Michel Deville's *Péril en la demeure* (1985), Luc Besson's *Nikita* (1990), or Patrice Leconte's *Monsieur Hire* (1989) (based on a novel by Simenon).[24]

Meanwhile, the *série noire*, as one of the principal outlets of the *roman policier* or the *polar* as it has become known, was also broadening its scope to include more works by French authors (writing now under French names), often dealing directly with the sort of social and political issues which are usually at most only implicit in detective fiction. In particular, the phenomenon of the so-called *néo-polar* arose at the beginning of the 1970s as the 'hard-boiled' heritage of Chandler and Hammet was combined with the political concerns of the post-68 generation.[25] The *néo-polar* of writers such as Jean-Patrick Manchette, Pierre Siniac, and Jean Vautrin was overtly politicized, belonging either to the extreme left or the extreme right, setting crime against the corrupt triumvirate of the police, political power, and the capitalist state. By the late 1970s, however, the influence of extreme politics in France had eased off somewhat (only later to be revived to some extent by the rise in popularity of the *Front National* in the late 1980s and 1990s and the concomitant increased appeal of the French Communist Party). In his essay on the *néo-polar* François Cote observes that by the early 1980s popular detective fiction was typically less unambiguously political, and less virulent in its attack on the police.[26] This is certainly reflected in Pennac's Malaussène novels. They contain their fair share of corrupt policemen and politicians (in particular in *La Fée carabine*); but on the other hand the detectives Coudrier and Caregga (in all the novels), Pastor (in *La Fée carabine*), Van Thian (in *La Fée carabine* and *La Petite Marchande de prose*) and Van Thian's adoptive daughter, the nun-detective Gervaise (in *Monsieur Malaussène*), are all portrayed in a fairly unambiguously positive light. And Malaussène himself refuses any engagement in politics; echoing the widespread disaffection of the mid-1980s, he doesn't take part in a union demonstration at the store, and when interviewed by Coudrier he gives a rare piece of information about his life before the events described in the novels:

---

[24] On modern French film makers' use of the thriller format, and in particular the development of the 'postmodern thriller', see Jill Forbes, *The Cinema in France. After the New Wave* (London: Macmillan, 1992), 47–75, and Emma Wilson, *French Cinema Since 1950. Personal Histories* (London: Duckworth, 1999), 68–82.

[25] For an account of the history of the *néo-polar*, see François Cote, 'Le Néo-polar français et les policiers', in *Esprit*, 135 (1988), 46–50.

[26] See ibid. 49.

-Avez-vous jamais milité dans une organisation quelconque?
Ni dans une quelconque ni dans une distinguée. Du temps où j'avais des amis, ils le faisaient à ma place, troquant l'amitié pour la solidarité, le flipper pour la ronéo, le clair de lune pour l'éclat du pavé, Gadda pour Gramsci. Savoir qui d'eux ou de moi avait raison est une question qui dépasse tous ceux qui lui donnent une réponse. (150)[27]

Against this background, the appearance of Pennac's *Au bonheur des ogres* and *La Fée carabine* in the *série noire* by no means prejudges their aesthetic, intellectual, or sociological ambition. The modern *polar* is highly self-conscious about its governing conventions and its relationship with its readers. In Pennac's writing this reaches its most extreme point in *Monsieur Malaussène*. After Malaussène has been imprisoned as a serial killer, chapters 47 to 54 of the novel describe his experiences in gaol, the visits he receives, interviews with lawyers and the *juge d'instruction*, all of which lead inexorably to his trial and the inevitable guilty verdict. The whole passage may remind the reader of the imprisonment and trial of Meursault in Albert Camus's *L'Etranger*. However, in chapter 55 it is abruptly revealed that the preceding eight chapters are in fact all a story written by Malaussène's brother Jérémy, who has embarked on a fictionalized four-volume account of Malaussène's life not unlike the first four volumes written by Pennac. Malaussène is aware that his reader will feel deceived by the lengthy account of events that turn out not to have taken place:

Je sais, je sais, on peut tout dire, mais on n'a pas le droit de trimballer le lecteur sur une profondeur de huit chapitres en lui annonçant à l'orée du huitième que toute cette tension tragique, ce sentiment d'injustice qui croissait à chaque mot, cet effroyable verdict enfin, que tout cela était une blague, et que les choses se sont passées différemment. Ça relève de l'abus de confiance, ce genre de procédé, ça devrait être puni! Défenestration du bouquin, pour le moins! (*Monsieur Malaussène*, 522)[28]

But then Malaussène turns on his reader: why do we feel so deceived? Because it would have been more coherent, more in line with the rest of the narrative, if the trial had gone on as described? But in that case, our

[27] '—Have you ever been a militant in any sort of organization?; Neither in any sort of one, nor in a distinguished sort of one. In the days when I had friends, they did it in my place, swapping friendship for solidarity, pinball for a Roneo, moonlight for the glare of the street, Gadda for Gramsci. To know who was right, them or me, is a question that is too hard for anyone who tries to answer it.'

[28] 'I know, I know, you can say anything, but you don't have the right to drag along the reader through eight chapters and announce to him at the edge of the eighth that all that tragic tension, that sense of injustice that was growing with each word, finally that terrible verdict, all that was a joke, and that things happened differently. That's an abuse of confidence, that sort of practice, that should be punished! Defenestration of the book, at the very least!'

desire for coherence from the detective novel is no better than, indeed directly complicit with, the desire of judges and police for an explanation of events which makes sense *even if it is wrong*: 'Besoin de cohérence, hein! Comme les juges! Vous sacrifieriez un innocent à votre besoin de cohérence ... Plutôt une bonne erreur judiciaire qu'un mauvais procédé littéraire, c'est ça?' (*Monsieur Malaussène*, 523).[29]

Pennac frequently uses this device of deceiving the reader as he sets up expectations in order to frustrate them. In *Au bonheur des ogres* Malaussène describes what appears to be a vicious beating, only to reveal that he is in fact describing an attacking manœuvre in chess (88); later he quotes part of the previous passage word for word, but concludes it with the information that 'ce n'est pas une partie d'échecs' (143).[30] This time he really is being beaten up. A similar temporary deceit of the reader is practised in chapter 26, which narrates what appear to be the preparations for the final arrest of the murderer who has been planting bombs in the store; it turns out, however, that this is Malaussène's fictionalized resolution of events, recounted as the bedtime story for the rest of his family. *Au bonheur des ogres* and the rest of the Malaussène series are in fact centrally concerned with the question of storytelling. Important passages of the first novel describe Malaussène telling stories to his family; and in the later novels Malaussène is replaced as the principal family storyteller in turn by Risson (a drug-addicted former bookseller adopted by the family), the detective Van Thian and Malaussène's brother Jérémy. One of the main threads of the plot of *La Fée carabine*, the murder of old women in Belleville, is finally explained as a crime committed on behalf of literature: Risson turns out to have been killing the women in order to buy drugs which make it possible for him to bring back to memory the stories that he tells the Malaussène family at night. In Risson's account, he has committed the murders quite simply 'Pour sauver la littérature' (*La Fée carabine*, 249).[31] The murders in *La Petite Marchande de prose* also turn out to have been committed for literary motives, as a dispossessed author takes revenge on those who have stolen and published his writings; and in *Des chrétiens et des maures* the father of le Petit, one of Malaussène's half-brothers, is revealed to be the hero of a series of detective novels, so that the child is doubly fictional: a character in a novel engendered by a character from other novels.

Literature and storytelling in general are thus central themes in the Malaussène novels. Malaussène is highly aware of his role as storyteller,

---

[29] 'Need for coherence, eh! Like judges! You would sacrifice an innocent man to your need for coherence ... Better a good judicial error than a bad literary practice, is that it?'
[30] 'it isn't a game of chess'.   [31] 'To save literature'.

and he 'corrects' his lived experience to enhance its literary merit. He realizes that his initial meeting with Inspector Caregga lacks narrative dynamism:

> Mais je tiens déjà le récit que je servirai ce soir aux enfants. Ce sera le même, à ceci près que les répliques fuseront, marquées au sceau d'un humour définitif, qu'on se séparera dans un mélange explosif de haine, de méfiance et d'admiration, et que les flics seront deux, deux affreux de mon invention que les enfants connaissent bien: un petit, hirsute, avec une laideur tourmentée de hyène, et un énorme chauve—à l'exception des deux pattes 'qui abattent leurs points d'exclamation sur ses maxillaires puissants'. (33–4)[32]

This process of turning life into something more dramatic, more narratively satisfying, is not restricted to literary production. Malaussène observes that the newspaper which reports the first of the explosions in the store seems disappointed that there was only one victim, so it describes what *might* have happened: 'Comme un seul mort ne suffit pas, l'auteur de l'article décrit le spectacle auquel on *aurait pu* assister s'il y en avait eu une dizaine! (Si vous voulez vraiment rêver, réveillez-vous ...)' (36).[33] Fictionalizing occurs both inside and outside the confines of literature. It crosses over into reality, and impinges on the plot: the typed-up version of the story Malaussène has been telling his family, based on the explosions in the store, is obtained by the police, and provides further incriminating evidence of his involvement in the affair (238). The novel that Malaussène is making out of the novel that we are reading threatens to affect the outcome of events as they unfold. In *Monsieur Malaussène*, the fourth volume in the series, Jérémy is explicit that he intends to write *four* novels about his brother's life, the final one being 'pour ce qui t'arrive maintenant' (*Monsieur Malaussène*, 478).[34] The novel is being written *as events occur*. The process of making fiction, and making sense, is part of the reality to be fictionalized and explained.

The importance of this thematization of storytelling in the specific context of detective fiction lies in its close connection to the activities of both detectives and readers. Detection, like reading, is an exercise in coherence-building. The detective gathers clues, attempts to distinguish

---

[32] 'But I already have the story that I will serve to the children this evening. It will be just the same, except that the dialogue will sparkle, marked with the seal of definitive humour, that we will separate in an explosive mixture of hatred, distrust, and admiration, and that there will be two coppers, two terrible types of my own invention that the children know well; one is small, hairy, with the tormented ugliness of a hyena, and one is huge and bald except for his sideboards "which bring down their exclamation marks on his powerful jaws".'

[33] 'As if just one dead person isn't enough, the author of the article describes the spectacle which one *might have* seen if there had been around ten! (If you really want to dream, wake up ...).'

[34] 'for what is happening to you now'.

between the significant and the insignificant, and to build a coherent story out of initially bewildering material. Readers are in the same position as they begin a new text; we are confronted with unknown characters and thrown into a situation about which we know nothing. Both detectives and readers are thus engaged in a process of making coherent sense out of incomplete evidence. The Malaussène novels, written from the standpoint of the innocent suspect rather than the enquiring detective, repeatedly make the point that the search for coherence is essentially a fictionalizing activity. As *Monsieur Malaussène* makes explicit, apparent coherence is no guarantee of the truth:

> Cette implacable logique que les honnêtes gens prêtent aux criminels.
> Comme ils vous emboîtent la petite enfance, le caractère, les mobiles, la préméditation, les moyens mis en œuvre, l'assassinat proprement dit et le service après crime ... Tout se tient! Tenons et mortaises! Tout 'fait sens' ... paroles et silences ...
> Ce qu'ils veulent, ce n'est pas la vérité, voyez-vous, c'est la cohérence.
> Une erreur judiciaire est toujours un chef-d'œuvre de cohérence. (501–2)[35]

In his essay on reading entitled *Comme un roman* (1992) Pennac refers to 'la vertu paradoxale de la lecture qui est de nous abstraire du monde pour lui trouver un sens'.[36] Reading helps us stand back from the world in order to find in it a meaning which might not be otherwise apparent. If this is true of reading in general, it is especially the case in detective fiction, where readers join the protagonists in trying to make sense of unintelligible data. But as the above passage from *Monsieur Malaussène* indicates, coherent explanations are not necessarily correct. Apparent sense may be disastrous error. *Au bonheur des ogres* illustrates this by offering competing explanations for the series of bombs that explode in the department store. In Malaussène's fictionalized account, the murderer is taking revenge for his father whom he believes has been cheated out of the credit for his inventions; Thérèse explains the deaths in terms of astrology, as each of the victims was fated by the stars to die violently; the police, with the exception of Coudrier, blame Malaussène because of the weight of incriminating evidence which points towards him. In the end it turns out that Thérèse was in a sense right, even if the deaths might be explained by

---

[35] 'That implacable logic that honest people ascribe to criminals. | How they fit together for you early childhood, character, motives, premeditation, the means used, the murder itself and what happens after the crime ... Everything hangs together! Lock, stock and barrel. Everything "makes sense" ... speech and silence ... | What they want is not the truth, you see, it's coherence | A judicial error is always a masterpiece of coherence.'

[36] 'the paradoxical virtue of reading which is to take us away from the world in order to find a meaning for it'. Pennac, *Comme un roman* (Paris: Gallimard, 1972; Folio edn.), 19.

the *belief* in astrology rather than by the actual workings of destiny.[37] The victims are in fact former members of a cannibalistic cult which met in the store whilst it was closed for six months during the Second World War in 1942. Because the cult members share Thérèse's belief in astrology, they can also foresee the time of their own violent deaths; in order to retain some measure of freedom they make themselves the agents of their own demise on the date prescribed by the stars, on the site of their own former crimes. So, of the various explanations we are given for the explosions, the least likely—the one offered by Thérèse—turns out to be closest to the truth. Moreover, the presence of Malaussène at all but one of the explosions, which throughout the novel had appeared to be merely bad luck, is finally revealed after all to be motivated; the cult members had observed Malaussène's saint-like innocence and purity and had wanted to incriminate him in their crimes as their final act of wickedness. Coudrier explains their motives: 'Compromettre un saint authentique, le convaincre d'assassinat, le désigner comme coupable à la vindicte publique, c'était une jolie tentation pour ces vieux diablotins, non?' (283).[38] By the end of *Au bonheur des ogres*, as in all of the Malaussène novels, the various strands of the plot have come together, the loose ends have been tied up, the crimes explained, and the guilty punished. All this is in the best tradition of the detective novel. However, the reader may find these final explanations much less plausible than some of the rather more sober versions of events previously suggested; in particular, the hypothesis that Malaussène is the guilty party provides a simple, credible solution which does not rely on recourse to bizarre cannibalistic cults. The point that the novel makes is precisely that simple, coherent solutions are to be distrusted; they may be in line with the principles of realistic storytelling, but they do violence to innocent parties. Making sense also entails making mistakes, and the process of weaving stories out of disparate evidence does not by any means lead inevitably to truth.

By convention, the detective novel tells two stories: the story of the crime and the story of the enquiry into the crime.[39] *Au bonheur des ogres* goes further in as far as storytelling, and the distortions and errors that go along with it, is one of its central themes. Storytelling, as the building of

---

[37] In *Au bonheur des ogres* it is not certain that Thérèse has been able to predict the bombings because of supernatural powers; it may simply be coincidence that she shares the same astrological beliefs as the bombers, and so makes the same calculations as them. In later novels of the Malaussène series, such a rational explanation of her powers is less easy to maintain, as when she predicts Gervaise's pregnancy in *Monsieur Malaussène*.

[38] 'To compromise an authentic saint, to get him convicted of murder, to expose him as the guilty party for public condemnation, that was a fine temptation for those old devils, wasn't it?'

[39] See Tzvetan Todorov, 'Typologie du roman policier', in *Poétique de la prose, suivi de Nouvelles recherches sur le récit* (Paris: Seuil, 1971, 1978; Points edn.), 11.

coherent narratives, turns out to be a dangerous business, in that it can incriminate you in murder or lead to utterly false conclusions about guilt and innocence. But it also has a more positive side, as Pennac emphasizes in *Comme un roman*. Pennac bemoans the transformation of literature into a quasi-sacred object to be respected more than enjoyed; he criticizes families and the education system which make reading into work rather than pleasure. Books and stories should be something we share with those we love, a means of consolidating the bond between us. This is the role it plays within the Malaussène family. The storytelling ritual is a nightly communal event which binds together a disparate set of individuals with little in common despite the fact that they have the same mother. For all its dangers and distortions, storytelling is thus also a source of pleasure and a force of cohesion. It is a fundamental mode of survival for both the individual and the community. In Sartre's *La Nausée*, the protagonist Roquentin insists that living and storytelling are incompatible since storytelling alienates the storyteller from the immediacy of experience: 'Mais il faut choisir: vivre ou raconter'.[40] Whilst not necessarily disagreeing with this, Pennac's writing suggests a very different evaluation of the role of storytelling. In *La Fée carabine* Thérèse helps Van Thian, who has been shot, to survive by encouraging him to replace Risson (who has replaced Malaussène) as the family storyteller; she alludes to but crucially alters the antithesis offered by Sartre's Roquentin: 'A vous de choisir, donc: mourir ou raconter' (*La Fée carabine*, 306).[41] By surviving to tell stories, Van Thian reconquers his place within the community.

Storytelling in Pennac's fiction is therefore an all-pervasive activity, one which is consistently celebrated despite the dangers that attend it. This marks an important point of difference from Girard's view of myth as elaborated in *Le Bouc émissaire*. According to Girard, myths are typically stories that communities tell themselves to justify the violence they have exercised over their chosen scapegoats. They conceal the original crime of the community by transforming the persecution of innocence into the story of guilt justly punished. Thus, behind the story of Oedipus (a man who has committed terrible crimes and is sent away from the community) it is possible to see all the stereotypes of persecution which suggest that Oedipus is in fact a scapegoat: the city is beset by plague, so a man who limps (and who therefore has a distinguishing feature which marks him out to be chosen as a victim of persecution) is accused of parricide and

---

[40] 'But you have to choose: to live or to tell stories'. Sartre, *La Nausée* (Paris: Gallimard, 1938; Folio edn.), 62.

[41] 'It's for you to choose, then: to die or to tell stories.'

incest, and expelled from the city. The story as it survives masks the persecution of the innocent which is at its origin; it binds the community together by hiding the violence which it has communally committed. Pennac's fiction, on the other hand, is written from the standpoint of the victims not the victimizers; unlike Girard's myth, Pennac's storytellers keep the family together by celebrating its innocence, with the thread of stories tying together narrator and listener in a bond of pleasure. Whereas Girard sees guilt behind the myth, Pennac sees innocence within the story.

Ultimately, then, the community in Pennac's writing is strengthened though the trials it endures and the stories it tells. But Pennac's use of Girard's analysis of the *bouc émissaire* may provoke distrust towards this refound cohesion: perhaps it is also based on exclusions, on the displacing rather than the abolition of the logic of scapegoating?

Happy endings

At the end of Pennac's novels, the guilty have been punished and the innocent, if not positively rewarded, have at least been recognized. Although the novels contain numerous deaths, they are also punctuated by births, looking forward—perhaps—to a better future. *Au bonheur des ogres* ends with the return of Malaussène's mother to her family, pregnant once again; at the end of *La Fée carabine* Van Thian joins the Malaussène clan as chief storyteller and the only person capable of placating the infant Verdun; in *La Petite Marchande de prose* Malaussène finally recovers from the near-fatal bullet through the brain, and the family is extended through the birth of his sister Clara's child, given the name C'Est Un Ange; *Monsieur Malaussène* ends with the departure of Malaussène's mother, who is in love again, and the birth of Malaussène's own child; and at the end of *Aux fruits de la passion* his sister Thérèse gives birth to a daughter who extends the family still further. Despite the proximity of death, the novels celebrate life and love in a manner which at times can be surprisingly sentimental.[42] Nettelbeck describes this as 'Pennac's faith that *eros* is stronger than *thanatos*'.[43] In fact, the endings of Pennac's novels are reminiscent of the final pages of the Astérix cartoons, which invariably depict a banquet held to celebrate the return of the heroes to their village after their adventures in the wide world. The community is strengthened, extended, and reconciled with itself by the trials which it has undergone.

---

[42] This is made explicit in *Monsieur Malaussène*, when Julie attacks what she calls Malaussène's 'religion de l'amour' (religion of love); see 328–30.

[43] Nettelbeck, 'The "Post-Literary" Novel', 136.

The family, and more broadly the community, plays a central role in Pennac's fiction. His novels certainly do endorse family values, though one of their most moving aspects derives from their redefinition of what family values might mean. The Malaussène family is a collection of half-siblings and their usually absent mother. Crucially, this is a family without fathers. As Malaussène suggests in *Monsieur Malaussène*, 'On peut très bien s'en passer, du père! C'est une invention moderne! Une hypothèse du travail! [. . .] Ce n'est pas le père, qui compte, c'est la suite!' (*Monsieur Malaussène*, 160);[44] and Malaussène's brother Jérémy echoes this view in *Des chrétiens et des maures* when he insists that 'le père est une hypothèse dont on peut fort bien se passer' (14).[45] Each of the children of the Malaussène family has a different father; and with the exception of *Des chrétiens et des maures*, which explains how Malaussène's brother le Petit resulted from the affair of his mother with a fictional character, none of the fathers appears in any of the novels. Malaussène has never met his father, as he tells Coudrier: 'Un des mecs de ma mère. Le premier. Elle avait quatorze ans. Jamais vu: pleurez, commissaire' (150).[46] The family here is not a tightly-knit, coherent unit held together by a dominant father; it is a chaotic assembly of the most diverse individuals. The diversity, rather than the unity, of the family is what keeps it together. Moreover, the family is extended to include numerous others who are not tied by blood to Malaussène and his half-siblings: the homosexual dandy Théo and the chess-playing Serbian night porter Stojilkovitch count as uncles; Yasmina, the wife of a local Arab restaurateur, takes the maternal role in the absence of the real mother (53), and her son Hadouch thus has the position of brother. In later novels the Malaussène family will be designated rather as a tribe, and extended by many other honorary uncles, aunts, and grandfathers.

In Pennac's writing the family is at the centre of a different sort of social organization from that sustained by the conventional nuclear unit comprising father, mother, and children. Rather than a source of social stability rooted in paternal authority, it is open-ended and permissive, founded on affection as much as on consanguinity. And Belleville, the area of Paris in which the Malaussène novels are set, plays an important role in this vision of an alternative social construction. Belleville has traditionally had a high proportion of immigrant and working-class inhabitants. In the Malaussène novels it appears as a sort of utopian space, despite the problems of drugs, crime, and poverty which afflict it,

---

[44] 'You can very well do without the father! He's a modern invention! A working hypothesis! [...]
It's not the father who matters, it's what comes after!'

[45] 'The father is a hypothesis that you can very well do without.'

[46] 'One of my mother's blokes. The first. She was fourteen. Never seen him: weep, commissioner.'

because it provides an image of an extended multi-ethnic, multi-cultural family in which differences of race, colour, religion, and sexual preference give rise to tolerant, loving respect rather than open conflict. This utopian space is, however, under threat; throughout the Mitterrand years, much of Belleville was pulled down and replaced by modern buildings. In the Malaussène novels, the modernization and gentrification of Belleville is depicted with dismay; it is an act of destruction no less criminal than the bombs which explode in the department store: 'Il n'y a pas que le Magasin qui saute. Belleville aussi. Avec toutes ces façades manquantes le long de ses trottoirs, le Boulevard ressemble à une mâchoire édentée' (51).[47] It is no coincidence that one of the villains behind the crimes in *La Fée carabine* turns out to be an architect who has been raising new buildings in Belleville; and *Monsieur Malaussène* revolves in part around the disappearance of the last cinema in Belleville. That novel is dedicated, rather wistfully, 'A Belleville (à ce qu'il en reste)'.[48] The disappearance of Belleville puts at risk what the novels present as the radical possibility of an alternative social organization which is more tolerant, more inclusive than one built around the dominant popular image of the white middle-class nuclear family.

So, one of the fundamental themes of Pennac's detective stories is the community or family put at risk, eventually regaining its cohesion by the discovery and punishment of the guilty party or parties. But in the context of Pennac's use of Girard's work on the scapegoat, this description may arouse a suspicion. In Girard's analysis, the process of scapegoating is set in motion, and persecutory texts come into their own, precisely at the moment when the community finds itself in crisis. *Au bonheur des ogres* looks as if it has learned one of Girard's fundamental lessons in its insistence on the innocence of Malaussène, the scapegoat. At the end of the novel, as at the end of all the Malaussène novels, Malaussène's innocence is acknowledged by all; he is recognized as the victim of persecution rather than the perpetrator of crime. However, despite its insistence on the innocence of one particular scapegoat, the novel remains complicit with the process of scapegoating. According to Girard, a community seeks scapegoats as a principle of explanation to account for ills which cannot otherwise be understood. Bewilderment in face of the modern world is Malaussène's characteristic attitude, and the Malaussène novels replicate Girard's 'stereotypes of persecution' in order to circumscribe the danger of an unintelligible reality. They are set in a society in permanent

---

[47] 'It's not just the Shop that's being blown up. Belleville as well. With all those missing façades along its pavements the Boulevard looks like a toothless jaw.'
[48] 'To Belleville (to what is left of it)'.

crisis; threatened by crime, drugs, and the destruction of beloved Belleville, dominated by a materialist capitalism which has abandoned all quality control, the community needs someone to blame. In modern culture, and in the modern detective novel in particular, the witches and water-poisoners of earlier times have been replaced by satanic cults, psychopathic serial killers, drug barons, corrupt policemen, and dishonest politicians. These turn out to be precisely the culprits of the Malaussène novels; and seen in this light, their break from the stereotypes of persecution is less radical than might have appeared. Indeed, the *polar* may be one of purest examples of the persecutory text, as it identifies a restricted number of individuals as the immediate cause of social crisis and then brings about their expulsion as the price of society's reconquered cohesion.

The extent to which scapegoating is still operative in Pennac's fiction is most evident in the return of characters from *Au bonheur des ogres* in the fourth of the Malaussène novels, *Monsieur Malaussène*. In the first novel of the series, Malaussène was initially given his job as scapegoat by the store manager, Sainclair; the Complaints Office in the store is presided over by Lehmann; and the fellow employees who beat him up, thinking he is responsible for the bombs, include the store detective Cazeneuve. These, then, constitute a band of representative persecutors. In *Monsieur Malaussène* Sainclair reappears, now the director of a medical journal. Malaussène meets him when he has just been told that Julie's pregnancy will have to be terminated, and he takes out his frustration on the loathed Sainclair. At this moment, Malaussène realizes that he has been acting out the same persecutory tendencies that make of him the scapegoat for others: 'besoin de me payer mon bouc, moi aussi' (*Monsieur Malaussène*, 169).[49] This is a moment of extraordinary insight, as the text makes explicit that the scapegoat also needs his own scapegoats, even though they may have no relation to the actual crimes or misfortunes for which they are punished. However, following the mechanism of the persecutory text, subsequent events in the novel show that Sainclair, along with Lehmann and Cazeneuve, is after all responsible both for the murders which constitute the mainspring of the plot and for the forged letter which tells Julie that her pregnancy must be terminated. The scapegoat turns out to be guilty after all, and Malaussène's violence against him is less unmotivated than he or we knew at the time. The persecutors from *Au bonheur des ogres* reappear as the perpetrators of crime in *Monsieur Malaussène* and can thus be subjected to the same opprobrium with which they had treated Malaussène.

---

[49] 'need to treat myself to a scapegoat, me too'.

This reversal of perspective, whereby the persecutors of the scapegoat turn out to be the guilty parties, does not entail the abandonment of the persecutory mechanism analysed by Girard and adopted by Pennac in the composition of the Malaussène novels. The targets may be different, but the process is still in operation, as the cycle of novels depicts a potentially harmonious society threatened by Satanists, psychopaths, and politicians. Whilst the happy endings of Pennac's novels support the argument that he depicts *eros* as stronger than *thanatos*, this optimism is mitigated by the fragile, temporary nature of the happiness his characters achieve. Death is offset by birth, but each birth may soon be followed by more killing. In the world depicted in the Malaussène novels, even the most compelling evidence may not lead to truth; the innocent may look guilty, violence may break out at any moment and the instinct for persecution may take over. Faced with events that do not seem to make sense, in the midst of a crisis that threatens to be without end, the community can only survive by designating its scapegoats and expelling them. If Malaussène is ultimately saved, the novels in which he appears nevertheless continue to participate in the frenzy of persecution by pointing the finger at the usual suspects.

Moreover, it is important that the satanic cult responsible for the bombs in *Au bonheur des ogres* initially flourished during the moral vacuum of the Second World War. In the 1970s and 1980s Pennac, along with many others of his generation who never lived through the war, found himself still suffering from the aftershock of events which took place over forty years previously. In *Au bonheur des ogres* the war is spectrally present as an unliquidated trauma, one which has been largely forgotten, but which erupts unexpectedly and violently into the lives of people who did not realize they were influenced by it. The war continues to impinge on the present, and the renewed urgency of coming to terms with it is the central theme of the next chapter, on Semprun's *La Montagne blanche.*

3 Recalling the past: Jorge Semprun's *La Montagne blanche* (1986)

The return to history

As we saw in the previous chapter, the buried trauma around which the events of Pennac's *Au bonheur des ogres* turn out to revolve originates in the Occupation. Pennac's novel is thus picking up on one of the major problems of writing and film-making in the 1970s and 1980s: the painful recovery of a forgotten past, in particular the semi-occluded memory of the Second World War. Jorge Semprun's *La Montagne blanche* takes this problem as its central, obsessive theme, describing the effects of recovered memory on a survivor of Buchenwald. Forty years after his deportation, the protagonist of the novel finds that his repressed past erupts into the present and leads to his suicide.

Although this chapter will not dwell on the biographical aspects of the novel, it is clear that in some respects *La Montagne blanche* reflects Semprun's own life.[1] Semprun was born in 1923 in Madrid; his family went into exile during the Spanish Civil War, living first in the Netherlands and then in France. Whilst in France, Semprun joined the Communist Party, and was arrested in 1943 as a member of the Resistance, tortured, and sent to Buchenwald. After his return to France he became a leading member of the Spanish Communist Party and was engaged in clandestine missions in Fascist Spain until his expulsion from the party for ideological reasons in 1964. By that time he had already begun to write, his first novel *Le Grand voyage* (1963) being rapidly acknowledged as one of the first works in French to deal with the Holocaust in a sophisticated literary form. Having spent most of his life in France, he continues to write principally in French; and since his break with the Communist Party he has produced an impressive series of novels,[2] filmscripts,[3] and memoirs.[4]

---

[1] See Jorge Semprun, *L'Écriture ou la vie* (Paris: Gallimard, 1994), 252–5. References to *La Montagne blanche* (Paris: Gallimard, 1986; Folio edn.) are given in the main text.

[2] *L'Évanouissement* (1967), *La Deuxième Mort de Ramón Mercader* (1969), *L'Algarabie* (1981), *La Montagne blanche* (1986), *Netchaïev est de retour* (1987).

[3] *La Guerre est finie* (1966) and *Stavisky* (1974), directed by Alain Resnais; *Z* (1966), *L'Aveu* (1970), and *Section spéciale* (1975), directed by Constantin Costa Gavras.

[4] *Autobiografía de Frederico Sánchez* (1977, originally written in Spanish), *Quel beau dimanche!* (1980), *L'Écriture ou la vie* (1994), and *Frederico Sanchez vous salue bien* (1993).

In 1988, after the death of Franco and the end of the Fascist regime, he returned to Spain as Minister of Culture in the Socialist government, a post which he held until 1991.

The protagonist of *La Montagne blanche*, Juan Larrea, is, like Semprun, a successful writer (albeit a playwright) of Spanish origin, haunted by his experiences in Buchenwald. The plot of the novel is relatively simple, even if the narration is made more complex and confusing by the constant oscillations between characters and different moments in time. The novel is set over two days, 24 and 25 April 1982. Juan goes to the house of his friend Antoine de Stermaria, a painter, and Antoine's wife Franca Castellani, for a double celebration: it is the fortieth anniversary of the first meeting of Juan and Antoine, and also Franca's fortieth birthday. Franca is the wife of Antoine, but the coincidence of her age and Juan and Antoine's meeting leads the two men to consider her to be the mythical offspring of their long-standing friendship; moreover she is, it transpires, having an affair with Juan. This *ménage à trois* risks expanding into a *ménage à quatre* because Juan is accompanied by his lover Nadine Feierabend (whom Antoine asks Juan to give to him in return for a lover shared when they first met), and then into a *ménage à cinq* by the arrival of Juan's friend Karel Kepela, an exiled Czech director of plays and films who is attracted to both Nadine and Franca. The stakes of this rather convoluted domestic drama of sexual mores amongst artists are raised by the broader historical, political, and cultural issues which are never far from the foreground of the novel. By the morning of 25 April, the marital difficulties of Antoine and Franca appear to have been resolved. Juan has recounted his experiences in Buchenwald for only the fourth time since his return in 1945, and the novel ends as he kills himself by drowning.

The central tension of *La Montagne blanche* is between memory and forgetting, between the need for a lucid confrontation with the past and the equally urgent necessity of blocking out a past which is too traumatic to bring back to memory. In *L'Ecriture ou la vie* Semprun recounts his own struggle to survive by suppressing his memories of Buchenwald; and in *La Montagne blanche* each of the male characters is torn apart by the need to keep at bay memories of a traumatic past. Antoine is troubled by the memory of the incestuous inauguration of his sexuality and the excitement he felt when watching his aunt and his female art teacher engaged in sexual activities, a memory revived in the year preceding the events of his novel by his wife's lesbian display in a Dutch nightclub; Kepela is disturbed by the memory of his betrayal by his first wife to the Czech Communist authorities and by his recent discovery that his lover Ottla has repeated this betrayal by recording their conversations for the secret police; and most importantly, Juan is traumatized by his experiences in

Buchenwald, in particular the memory of the stench from the cremat-
orium of the smoke from burning human bodies. Memory, here, is not
a splendid Proustian epiphany through which lost time is magically
recovered; rather it is the revival of a pain too awful to confront. The
difference from Proust is suggested by an explicit allusion. Passing the
power station at Porcheville on the way to the house of Antoine and
Franca, Juan initially misreads the name as Forcheville, which reminds
him of Proust's Gilberte Swann (32);[5] shortly afterwards, smoke from one
of the power station chimney's gives him an experience of quasi-
Proustian involuntary memory, but without the ecstatic sense of continuity with the past:[6]

> **Dans la quiétude de l'après-midi d'avril, un panache de fumée couronne l'une
> des cheminées de la centrale électrique de Porcheville. Une fumée floconneuse,
> presque immobile, couleur de cendre grise, sur la boucle de la Seine.**
> **Comme la fumée du crématoire, autrefois.**
> **La fumée sur la colline de l'Ettersberg, autrefois, dans une mort antérieure.**
> **Il essaye de résister au flot d'angoisse qui monte en lui. (39)[7]**

When memory is experienced as appalling trauma, forgetting becomes
a strategy of survival: 'Il avait décidé de ne rien dire, du moins. Garder
pour soi l'angoisse nauséeuse: fumée de Porcheville sur la vallée de la
Seine, comme celle jadis du crématoire sur l'Ettersberg. Garder, enfouir,
refouler, oublier' (109).[8]

The tension between memory and forgetting which becomes the
central drama of *La Montagne blanche* was one which was being enacted
on a much broader scale through the 1970s and 1980s in French attempts
belatedly to come to terms with some aspects of the Second World War.
Marcel Ophüls's documentary on Collaboration, *Le Chagrin et la pitié*,
was banned from French television when it was released in 1971, and
could only be shown in private cinemas. Louis Malle's film *Lacombe
Lucien* (1974) caused outrage in some quarters by depicting Collaboration

---

[5] In Marcel Proust's *A la recherche du temps perdu* the Comte de Forcheville is a member of the
Verdurin circle who marries Odette Swann after the death of her husband and adopts her daughter
Gilberte, the object of the narrator's childhood love.

[6] The allusion to Proustian involuntary memory, and its potential link with anguish rather than joy,
is anticipated in Semprun's *Le Grand Voyage* (Paris: Gallimard, 1963; Folio edn.), 149–50, where the
narrator describes how the taste of bread transports him back to his time in Buchenwald.

[7] 'In the calm of the April afternoon, a trail of smoke crowns one of the chimneys of the power station
of Porcheville. A fluffy smoke, almost motionless, the colour of grey ash, over the bend in the Seine.
| Like the smoke from the crematorium, in the past. | The smoke over the Ettersberg hill, in the past,
in a previous death. | He attempts to fight against the wave of anguish which rises in him.'

[8] 'He had decided to say nothing, at least. To keep for himself the nauseous anguish: smoke of
Porcheville over the Seine valley, like that in former times over Ettersberg. To keep, to bury, to
repress, to forget.'

without overt condemnation, and failing to draw a simple contrast between evil collaborators and heroic resisters. Numerous writers began to look back at the war and present it in a more ambiguous light; in particular the still-powerful myth of the Resistance was put into question, the story of France during the war being recounted as much as a story of Collaboration as of heroism. This re-evaluation was fiercely resisted in many quarters, and it was not until 1983 that collaboration was actually acknowledged in French school textbooks. Even more recently, films such as Malle's *Au revoir les enfants* (a much more sentimental film about the war than the same director's glacially problematic *Lacombe Lucien*) or Claude Berri's *Ils partiront dans l'ivresse*, based on the wartime experiences of the resistance hero Lucie Aubrac, have been popular in part because they promote a more reassuring and predominantly heroic image of the French in the war.

There are now, however, a large number of competing representations; and one of the insights that emerge very clearly from the re-evaluation of the war in France is that there is no single narrative or version of events, be it of Resistance or Collaboration, which can be claimed to be the one true story of France during the war. Instead, there has been an explosion of films and novels which give different accounts of a more complex reality. The literary experimentations of the post-war avant-garde associated with the *nouveau roman*, the *nouveau nouveau roman*, Oulipo, the *Tel Quel* group, or the practitioners of *écriture féminine*, were sometimes accused (often unfairly) of entailing a rejection of historical reference or lived experience as the subject-matter of literature. But the 'return to history' that can be observed in the 1970s and 1980s has significantly involved, not a rejection of modernist narrative experimentation, but an acceptance of its relevance for a view of history as untotalized, containing numerous alternative or competing narratives that cannot easily be resolved. Thus Semprun, who has sometimes been associated with the *nouveaux romanciers*, typically adopts kaleidoscopic narratives with unstable points of view and chronology; his texts are ambiguous and fragmented, never giving their readers the complete story, ending with as many questions unresolved as resolved. They are every bit as self-regarding as the most narcissistic works of fiction; when Juan in *La Montagne blanche* first meets Antoine, the future writer is reading a copy of Gide's *Paludes*, a novel about a man writing a novel entitled *Paludes*; this example of *mise-en-abyme* is itself reflected in Semprun's novel, in which Juan is working on a project under the title *La Montagne blanche*. But in the work of Semprun, this knowing (and sometimes irksome) self-referentiality, as well as the highly complex, disorientating construction of his narrative, is not an alternative to historical, experiential subject-matter; it is, on the contrary, its most suitable format, when history itself is conceived as a broken, incoherent story, and the meaning of experience appears as elusive, always beyond full comprehension.

Semprun's novel can be seen, then, as part of a broader endeavour to come to terms with the past, and as an attempt to find sophisticated narrative forms to account for the complex interrelations between past and present, memory and repression. The specific question of Holocaust testimony, its possibility and credibility, was an issue of particular urgency in the early 1980s. It had come to the centre of French debate through the Faurisson affair, to which *La Montagne blanche* clearly alludes, and which requires some explanation.

The theft of memory

Nadine, Juan's lover, is working on an academic thesis: 'Nadine préparait, cet hiver-là, une thèse universitaire sur l'extermination des Juifs européens, en réponse, d'une certaine façon, aux idéologues niant l'existence des chambres à gaz. [. . .] Les conclusions de ce travail avaient paru, au début du printemps dans la revue *Esprit*, aux côtés d'un essai sur le même thème de Pierre Vidal-Naquet' (113).[9] *La Montagne blanche* constantly merges the fictional with the real; the occasion on which Juan and Kepela first meet, for example, is also attended by the film directors Alain Resnais and Milos Forman; and Franca Castellani is both the central female character of the novel and one of its dedicatees (the other being Semprun's wife). The novel thus suggests that fiction and reality cross over into one another. And in this instance, if Nadine Feierabend is fictional, then Pierre Vidal-Naquet, the journal *Esprit* and the controversy over the denial of the gas chambers are not. Vidal-Naquet is a prominent Jewish historian whose work deals principally with classical antiquity, but who has also written extensively on matters of Jewish history. Although the chronology is not precisely correct (Semprun's text suggests that the article should have appeared in spring 1982), it is likely that the allusion here is to Vidal-Naquet's essay 'Un Eichmann de papier', which was published in *Esprit* in September 1980 (reprinted in 1987 in Vidal-Naquet's *Les Assassins de la mémoire*) and which was a direct response to the so-called revisionist controversy fuelled by the work of Robert Faurisson.[10]

---

[9] 'Nadine was preparing, that winter, a university thesis on the extermination of the European Jews, to a certain extent in response to the ideologues who were denying the existence of the gas chambers. [...] The conclusions of her work had appeared at the beginning of spring in the review *Esprit*, alongside an essay on the same topic by Pierre Vidal-Naquet.'

[10] See Pierre Vidal-Naquet, 'A Paper Eichmann', *The Assassins of Memory. Essays on the Denial of the Holocaust*, trans. Jeffrey Mehlman (New York: Columbia University Press, 1992), 1–64.

Ever since the end of the Second World War there have been people who deny that the systematic murder of Jews and gypsies had really taken place, but the work of Faurisson and others gave their beliefs a semblance of academic respectability.[11] In December 1978, yielding to legal pressure, the newspaper *Le Monde* published an article by Faurisson, a professor of literature at Lyon University, entitled 'The Problem of the Gas Chambers or the Rumour of Auschwitz'. Faurisson's article is summarized by Jeffrey Mehlman:

> **Faurisson's argument lay in positing that the technological requirements for mass gassings were totally incompatible with the installations described by numerous witnesses, and would have resulted in a 'catastrophe' for those administering the gas chambers themselves. Moreover, since numerous eyewitness reports had already been discredited, on what basis could one accept *any* such testimony? The hell of Auschwitz, for Faurisson, was that of a protracted typhus epidemic: whatever gassing (of lice)—or cremation (of infected corpses)—may have been going on at Auschwitz was part of an effort to control that epidemic.[12]**

Part of the seduction of Faurisson's argument, since developed in further publications and interviews by him and others, lay in its claim to have no political or historical axe to grind beyond a commitment to the truth. He made it possible for some to regard 'revisionism' as a rigorous school of historical thought, opposed to the 'exterminationists' (those who maintain that the Nazis did follow a policy of systematic extermination) but holding equally tenable views. Holocaust denial had made the great achievement of getting itself taken seriously, since it could no longer simply be dismissed as the aberration of a small number of extremist cranks. The revisionists are adept at using even the most unambiguous documentation to support their views; and they suggest that the testimony of witnesses cannot be trusted, since their very survival undermines their assertions that Jews and others were systematically murdered. So the argument of the 'exterminationists' begins to look decidedly weak if two of its cornerstones, historical documents and eyewitness testimony, are rejected on the grounds that they are not reliable evidence for their case.

Many French intellectuals were unwilling to argue with the revisionists on their own terms, since this would effectively be to concede the intellectual legitimacy of their argument; on the other hand, to let their views go unopposed risked giving the impression that their conclusions were historically incontrovertible. 'Un Eichmann de papier' represents

[11] For a detailed account of the extent of Holocaust denial, see Deborah Lipstadt, *Denying the Holocaust. The Growing Assault on Truth and Memory* (London: Penguin, 1994).

[12] Jeffrey Mehlman, in Foreword to Pierre Vidal-Naquet, *The Assassins of Memory*, p. xii.

Vidal-Naquet's reluctant participation in the debate; he analyses the background and procedures of the revisionist argument, and outlines a number of common principles: the testimony of Jews is treated as a lie or a fantasy; documents preceding the liberation of the camps are regarded as forgeries; Nazi testimony given after the war is considered as having been obtained through torture or intimidation; technical arguments are adduced to demonstrate the material impossibility of mass gassings; and any compelling evidence of the Holocaust is either unacknowledged or falsified.[13] Vidal-Naquet presents Faurisson as 'a paper Eichmann' because he pursues on paper the work of extermination that Eichmann undertook in reality. Semprun's reference to Vidal-Naquet in *La Montagne blanche* is parallelled towards the end of 'Un Eichmann de papier' by a reference to Semprun and Resnais's film *La Guerre est finie*, followed by an assertion of the necessity of memory: 'My generation, now fifty years old, is more or less the last for whom Hitler's crime still remains a memory. That one must fight against the disappearance—or, worse yet, the debasement—of memory seems to me obvious.'[14]

This sentiment is echoed in *La Montagne blanche* when Juan contemplates the possibility that future generations might cease to believe in the Holocaust when there are no remaining survivors with direct memories of it: 'Quand nous serons tous morts, pensa-t-il, y croira-t-on encore?' (42).[15] Part of the duty of the survivor is to protect memories of catastrophe from forgetfulness or wilful suppression. In 1995, to commemorate the fiftieth anniversary of the liberation of the camps, Semprun took part in a dialogue with the Nobel prize-winning writer and Holocaust survivor Elie Wiesel published under the title *Se taire est impossible*.[16] As this title suggests, testimony is a moral imperative for the survivors of atrocity. But bearing witness is no easy matter. Holocaust narrative is characteristically haunted by the knowledge that what it has to tell is both unspeakable and unbelievable. Robert Antelme, one-time husband of Marguerite Duras and fellow internee with Semprun at Buchenwald, begins his account of deportation with an acknowledgement that his story cannot easily be told.[17]

---

[13] Ibid. 21–4.   [14] Ibid. 57.

[15] 'When we are all dead, he thought, will people still believe it happened?'

[16] 'To be silent is impossible'. Jorge Semprun and Elie Wiesel, *Se taire est impossible* (Paris: Editions Mille et une nuits/Arte Editions, 1995).

[17] See Robert Antelme, *L'Espèce humaine* (Paris: Gallimard, 1957; Tel edn.), 9: 'Comment nous résigner à ne pas tenter d'expliquer comment nous en étions venus là? Nous y étions encore. Et cependant c'était impossible. A peine commencions-nous à raconter, que nous suffoquions. A nous-mêmes, ce que nous avions à dire commençait alors à nous paraître *inimaginable*' ('How could we resign ourselves not to attempt to explain how we had come to that point? We were still there. And yet it was impossible. Hardly did we begin to recount that we suffocated. Even to ourselves, what we had to say began then to seem *unimaginable*').

David Rousset, also interned in Buchenwald, describes the experience of survivors as 'impossible à transmettre'.[18] Wiesel summarizes the survivors' dilemma as a choice between impotent silence and inadequate speech: 'comment en parler et comment ne pas en parler?'[19] The need to bear witness is made more acute by the awareness of the inadequacy of language and the disbelief of those who hear; the response of the revisionists is one with which survivors are all too familiar. Testimony thus emerges as both urgent and impossible, as a risk which must be taken and cannot succeed.

The crisis of testimony is complicated in Semprun's writing by a deliberate, strategic suppression of memories of the war. Semprun has written extensively about this at an autobiographical level in *L'Ecriture ou la vie*, which describes his attempts over fifty years firstly to suppress and then to come to terms with his experiences in the death camp of Buchenwald. The theme of repressed memory establishes a close link between *L'Ecriture ou la vie* and *La Montagne blanche*, and the title of the later autobiographical work is anticipated in the earlier novel. In *La Montagne blanche* the phrase 'l'écriture ou la vie'[20] occurs in an account of a scene from a (fictional) play written by Juan in which the authors Flaubert, Grillparzer, and Dostoyevsky discuss the necessity of choosing between a dedication to art or an ordinary life with a family and domestic responsibilities (47). Later, it is revealed that one of the friends of Kepela, a fellow Czech émigré, is writing a book called *L'Ecriture ou la mort* (136–7).[21] In *L'Ecriture ou la vie* writing is associated with dwelling on problems of memory and experience, hence with the dreadful, obsessive memories of Buchenwald; so, for much of Semprun's life, *not* writing has appeared as the only way of surviving.

In *L'Ecriture ou la vie* Semprun gives his own response to the classic dilemmas of the Holocaust survivor. He describes the tension between a sense of need and duty to narrate on the one hand and, on the other hand, a reluctance to narrate (since the recollection of trauma entails a repetition of that trauma) coupled with the conviction that the Holocaust anyway cannot be adequately captured in words. The decision to tell the story does not resolve the question of *how* the story can be told. Semprun

---

[18] 'impossible to transmit'. David Rousset, *L'Univers concentrationnaire* (Paris: Editions de Minuit, 1965; 10/18 edn.), 117. Compare Semprun's modification of this view in *L'Ecriture ou la vie*, 136: 'L'autre genre de compréhension, la vérité essentielle de l'expérience, n'est pas transmissible ... ou plutôt, elle ne l'est que par l'écriture littéraire ...' ('The other sort of understanding, the essential truth of the experience, is not transmissible ... or rather it can only be done through literary writing ...').

[19] 'how to speak about it and how not to speak about it?' Elie Wiesel, *Entre deux soleils* (Paris: Seuil, 1970), 249.

[20] 'writing or life'.   [21] 'Writing or Death'.

recounts a discussion held amongst former inmates of Buchenwald shortly after the liberation of the camp on precisely this issue. Most of those participating assent to the view that Buchenwald should be narrated as simply and truthfully as possible: 'Il faut dire les choses comme elles sont, sans artifices!'[22] Semprun argues against this view. He rejects the belief that only unembroidered, factual testimony is adequate, and also the commonplace that the Holocaust lies beyond language. For him, everything can be said, but the truth of experience must be mediated through the artifice of art:

> Pourtant un doute me vient sur la possibilité de raconter. Non pas que l'expérience vécue soit indicible. [. . .] Ne parviendront à cette substance, à cette densité transparente que ceux qui sauront faire de leur témoignage un objet artistique, un espace de création. Ou de recréation. Seul l'artifice d'un récit maîtrisé parviendra à transmettre partiellement la vérité du témoignage. Mais ceci n'a rien d'exceptionnel: il en arrive ainsi de toutes les grandes expériences historiques.[23]

Two important points emerge from this passage: first, Semprun denies that there is anything unique about the difficulty of narrating the Holocaust; and second, his argument presents *fiction* rather than testimony as the only adequate means of encapsulating it.[24] For Semprun, the unimaginable becomes imaginable only through artifice, hence only in art.

One of the consequences of this view is that Semprun's fiction does not attempt to achieve a quasi-testimonial reconstruction of the experience of deportation. In *La Montagne blanche* Juan believes that everything *can* be said about the past (118), but the novel is never explicit about the detail of his experience. This is a text in which the Holocaust forms a crucial point of reference, it is informed at every moment by the memory of the Holocaust, yet it contains no narrative of the Holocaust itself. Juan narrates his experiences on four occasions: to his wife Laurence, to Antoine, to Franca, and on the night of his suicide; but the reader is given only the briefest information about what he says on any of these occasions. On the night of his suicide we are told bluntly that 'il raconta' (300).[25] We are led

[22] 'We should say things as they are, without artifice!' *L'Ecriture ou la vie*, 134.

[23] 'However a doubt comes to me about the possibility of recounting. Not that lived experience is unsayable. [. . .] Only those will reach that substance, that transparent density, who can make of their testimony an artistic object, a space of creation. Or of re-creation. Only the artifice of a mastered narrative will succeed in partially transmitting the truth of the testimony. But there is nothing exceptional about this: it is like this for all great historical experiences'. *L'Ecriture ou la vie*, 23.

[24] This passage is echoed in *La Montagne blanche*, 118–19; on the necessary interminability of Holocaust narrative, see also *L'Ecriture ou la vie*, 23–4. Wiesel argues on the contrary that the Holocaust is unique and not susceptible to literary representation; see *Entre deux soleils*, 248–9: 'Expérience unique, l'holocauste défie la littérature.'

[25] 'he recounted'.

to believe that his account goes on late into the night, but the novel offers only a schematic, paragraph-long summary of the substance of his experience. Suppressing his memories has served like a powerful time bomb to Juan; releasing those memories acts as a prelude to his suicide. So both narrating and not narrating prove to be destructive; and Semprun's novel reproduces Juan's reluctance to tell his story by eliding details of what he describes. *La Montagne blanche* narrates *that* he narrates, but not *what* he narrates. The account of Buchenwald remains a hole in the text, an absent cause, or an abyss into which all else falls. The novel avoids the equally destructive alternatives of narrating or suppressing memory by drawing attention to a silence at its centre. We see the aftershock of Buchenwald, but not Buchenwald itself. We are not invited to share Juan's memories, but rather to realize that there is no simple channel for their direct transmission. Semprun's novel describes an act of self-revelation which is nevertheless withheld from the reader. The whole novel is bound up with the trauma of narration and suppressed memory which leads to Juan's suicide; and, as the rest of this chapter will show, Semprun's aesthetic endeavour consists in the attempt to elaborate a traumatized textuality in response to the traumatized memory which is its subject.

Telling stories

One of the hallmarks of recent French fiction (though by no means unique to it) has been its extreme self-consciousness, its awareness of its own fictional status. Typically, this is openly put on display rather than concealed in the interests of facilitating the reader's suspension of disbelief. In line with this tendency *La Montagne blanche* is structured around a conceit. It opens with discussion of a postcard of Joachim Patinir's painting *The Crossing of the Stigian Lagoon*, sent to Franca and Antoine by Juan; and it closes with Juan committing suicide by swimming to his death in that very painting: 'L'eau du fleuve Styx l'emporta dans ses flots' (310).[26] The reader is not expected to find this, and the rest of the novel, 'realistic' in any straightforward sense; frequent references to real characters and events locate the novel in time and in a particular culture, but barely make the extraordinary coincidences of the plot or the characters' remarkable displays of cultural knowledge any more plausible. Following one of the characteristic moves of recent fiction, the novel displays the artifice of its conventions, even whilst maintaining its dependence upon them.

---

[26] 'The water of the river Styx carried him away in its waves.'

An important aspect of this self-conscious artifice is the deliberate play on the knowledge, responses, and interpretative skills of the reader. The novel plays games, giving clues to information which is nevertheless withheld. Even the fact that Juan is a survivor of Buchenwald is initially revealed only through oblique hints. The first indication is given when he is angered by Nadine's account of a play set in a concentration camp (30). Shortly afterwards, the smoke issuing from a power station chimney makes him feel ill, reminding him of 'la fumée du crématoire, autrefois. | La fumée sur la colline de l'Ettersberg, autrefois, dans une mort antérieure' (39).[27] The allusion will only be clear to those readers who know that Ettersberg was where the Buchenwald crematorium was located. On the following page, we are told that 'La fumée s'étendait sur le paysage, comme autrefois sur la forêt de hêtres' (40).[28] For anyone who knows German, it is easy enough to translate 'forêt de hêtres' into 'Buchen-wald', but otherwise the allusion may be lost. A page later still, we are told of 'la fumée des crématoires sur la plaine d'Oswiecim' (41),[29] which uses the Polish name Oswiecim rather than the more familiar Auschwitz. These references are insistent enough for the point to be clear, but perhaps not quite explicit enough for most of us to catch on straightaway. It is not until p. 92 that Buchenwald is named as such, and not until p. 113 that we learn that Nadine is writing a thesis on the extermination of the European Jews.

The same deferred or partial revelation is adopted in relation to the title of the novel. On p. 96 we are told that Juan is currently working on a text called *La Montagne blanche*, though we are told nothing about it. On p. 128 it is suggested that White Mountain is the translation of the Czech 'Bilà Hora', and that Kepela is frustrated at being unable to remember the number of the tram that went there. Only after p. 200 is it finally made clear that Bilà Hora is where one of the Jewish cemeteries in Prague is located. Kepela had worked there after his expulsion from the Czech Communist Party, and Kafka and some of his family are buried there. As we are reminded in the novel, had Kafka lived he would almost certainly have died in Auschwitz, as did his sisters and his one-time fiancée Milena. So the numerous references to the Jewish cemeteries allude to the themes of anti-Semitism and the Holocaust which are never far from the foreground of the text.

Through such games with the interpretative competence and cultural knowledge of the reader, the text makes hints, gives clues, but holds back from full, unambiguous disclosure. In effect it refuses explicit narration

[27] 'the smoke from the crematorium, in the past. | The smoke over the Ettersberg hill, in the past, in a previous death'.

[28] 'The smoke stretched over the landscape, as in the past over the forest of beech trees'.

[29] 'the smoke of the crematoria over the plain of Oswiecim'.

just as, at a thematic level, Juan holds back from telling his story. In the process, the novel about the sexual intrigues of the artistic élite gradually acquires more sombre overtones, as we are led slowly to realize that more is at stake here than simply who gets to sleep with whom. The day on which the novel ends, 25 April, has a double significance, beyond being the birthday of Franca and the anniversary of Juan's first meeting with Antoine. As the reader is informed (but only on p. 299 of the text), the 25th is 'le Jour de la Déportation',[30] the day which commemorates the Deportation of the French Jews; it is a news broadcast drawing attention to this which prompts Juan's final narrative of his time in Buchenwald. The liberation of Buchenwald also took place in April, on 11 April 1945 to be precise. As he recounts in *L'Ecriture ou la vie*, Semprun returned to France some two weeks after the liberation of the camp. So, the day of the deportation is also the day on which Semprun, and Juan in *La Montagne blanche* begin their new, post-Holocaust life. Since this is the beginning of spring, it is also symbolically the time of the year when life begins afresh. However, this new life is, for Juan as for Semprun, a sort of afterlife. Numerous passages throughout the novel indicate that the survivor is haunted by the idea of his own death, by the thought that he has in fact died along with his comrades at Buchenwald, and that everything that follows is unreal. In some sense, his life came to an end in April 1945: 'comme s'il était mort, trente-sept ans plus tôt, parti en fumée. Comme si sa vie, dès lors, n'avait été qu'un rêve où il aurait rêvé tout le reste, le réel: les arbres, les livres, les femmes, ses personnages' (110).[31]

April, we are told, is a particularly difficult time for Juan, because of the memories that are associated with it; so he finds various ways of surviving this time of year, such as travelling or getting involved in more or less casual sexual affairs. But this year, his affair with Nadine is highly unsuitable. Once again, in this instance, important information is initially withheld, as the first account of the meeting of Juan and Nadine is radically modified later in the novel. In chapter 3, when they first meet, Nadine is sensitive to, and even attracted by, Juan's 'indécente assurance masculine' (44).[32] In a discreet, apparently flirtatious gesture which will be picked up later, he takes her first by the arm ('Il lui retint le bras', 44) and then by the wrist ('Il effleura son poignet', 50),[33] and he jokes about her name, translating 'Feierabend' as 'Soir de loisir' (45) and later introducing

---

[30] 'the Day of the Deportation'.
[31] 'as if he had died, thirty-seven years earlier, gone up in smoke. As if his life, from then on, had been just a dream in which he had dreamt everything else, the real: the trees, the books, the women, his characters.'
[32] 'indecent masculine self-assurance'.
[33] 'He held on to her arm'; 'He lightly touched her wrist'.

her as 'Feuerabend' ('Soirée de feu', 51).[34] In short, in this first account of their encounter Juan appears as little more than an ageing, lecherous old seducer. In chapter 6, however, a very different account of their meeting is given, punctuated by the repeated phrase 'il aurait dû la fuir' (111–14).[35] As a partner in a sexual dalliance to help him overcome the difficult month of April, Nadine is singularly inappropriate: she is Jewish, she discusses Kafka and refers to his friends and family who were killed in the Holocaust, and she is writing a thesis on the extermination of the Jews. She frequently discusses her work with Juan; in effect, he has taken as a lover someone who will constantly remind him of what he most wanted to forget: 'Mais il aurait dû la fuir, l'oublier, fermer les yeux pour ne pas voir son regard, se boucher les oreilles pour ne pas entendre sa voix. [. . .] On ne franchit pas le souvenir terrifiant du mois d'avril aux côtés d'une jeune Juive d'après les massacres mais pétrie dans l'argile friable— inaltérable—de la mémoire collective' (114).[36] The past is catching up with Juan, and his choice of lover looks not only inappropriate, but positively suicidal. Moreover, in details of which the significance is unlikely to strike the reader at first, his past influences his most intimate gestures. On first meeting Nadine, Juan takes her by the wrist, in a gesture which looks merely flirtatious; later in the novel, another explanation is suggested for this action. Just before or just after sex, we are told, Juan caresses Nadine's forearm; this might recall 'l'instant où il l'avait tenue par le poignet, le premier soir, rue de l'Université' (113).[37] But this is not simply an affectionate gesture; Juan is, we are told, caressing her 'à l'endroit précis où aurait pu s'inscrire, entre le réseau délicat des veinules à fleur d'épiderme, le tatouage bleuâtre du numéro matricule d'Auschwitz' (113).[38] Even the structure of the sentence here mimics the delay, and intensifies the shock, in the delivery of information practised throughout the novel: the tender phrase 'entre le réseau délicat des veinules'[39] interrupts the main clause, and makes us suspect, perhaps, that the information about to be delivered will be less brutal than it turns out to be.

Throughout *La Montagne blanche* the reader is expected to work hard, attending to the clues in the text and trying to make sense of them. This search for elusive meaning is mimicked at a thematic level by the frenzy

---

[34] 'Evening of leisure'; 'Evening of fire'.   [35] 'he should have run away from her.'

[36] 'But he should have run away from her, forget her, close his eyes in order not to see her gaze, block his ears in order not to hear her voice. [...] You don't get through the terrifying memory of the month of April at the side of a young Jewish woman from after the massacres yet shaped in the crumbly clay—permanently fixed—of collective memory.'

[37] 'the moment when he had held her by the wrist, that first evening, in rue de l'Université'.

[38] 'at the precise place where could have been etched, between the delicate network of veins on the surface of her skin, the bluish tattoo of the number given at Auschwitz'.

[39] 'between the delicate network of veins'.

of interpretative activity in which the characters of the novel are engaged. In the opening pages of *La Montagne blanche* the question of interpretation is contrasted with the silent, non-interpretative appreciation prompted by art. Franca looks at Antoine's new painting and says nothing: 'Elle ne dit rien. Qu'y aurait-il à dire? Se remplir les yeux de tous ces bleus célestes et maritimes. S'en imbiber; rien d'autre' (17).[40] On the other hand, the postcard sent by Juan to Antoine and Franca appears to be densely enigmatic, requiring elucidation: '[Antoine] l'avait lue. Aussitôt, l'impression l'avait ressaisi, aveuglante mais confuse, d'un langage chiffré; dont il ne connaîtrait pas le code' (19).[41] The brief message demands interpretation: 'Sur quelle référence obscure jouait donc le texte de Juan, aussi bref, elliptique même, parce que sans doute chargé de sens?' (20).[42] Later, Antoine considers the possibility that there may, after all, be nothing to interpret: 'Peut-être avait-il mal lu, mal interprété, du moins. Peut-être était-ce un texte tout à fait innocent' (22).[43] Subsequently, the postcard becomes an object of interpretation for each of the characters in turn: Franca tries to fathom its significance, Nadine wonders why Juan sent it, and Juan (here, the author mystified by his own text) puzzles over why Franca has ostentatiously left it lying around.

The postcard thus becomes a figure of the text itself in that it is elliptic and opaque, teasing its various readers (including its author) with a significance which it does not quite reveal. Semprun's style contributes to the impression that simultaneously something very precise is being sought, and that there is nothing to find. The question of translation is raised on several occasions, and the narrator seems to be searching for an unambiguous idiom with fastidious earnestness: 'Pourtant, le mot était juste, parfaitement ajusté' (55).[44] At the same time, we can also see here a textual playfulness (*juste/ajusté*) which suggests that perhaps what is most important here is the game of language rather than any communicated meaning. When Juan thinks of Proust, the text gets carried away by the play of words: 'Il abandonna Gilberte et Albertine, qui voguaient ou vaguaient, divaguaient même, dans son vague à l'âme' (32).[45] The text is at once playful and obsessively exact, pedantic yet disruptive of its own

---

[40] 'She said nothing. What could there be to say? Fill her eyes with all those celestial and maritime blues. Absorb them; nothing else.'

[41] '[Antoine] had read it. Immediately, he had again had the impression, blinding but confused, of an encrypted language; of which he did not know the code.'

[42] 'On what obscure reference was Juan's text playing then, so brief, elliptic even, because probably loaded with meaning?'

[43] 'Perhaps he had read badly, interpreted badly, at least. Perhaps it was a completely innocent text.'

[44] 'Yet the word was right, perfectly adjusted.'

[45] 'He abandoned Gilberte and Albertine, who were roaming or floating, straying even, in his melancholy.'

meaning; it oscillates between implying that it has something to say which it can convey adequately, or that its significance is beyond full exposition (Juan's memories of Buchenwald are never narrated), or that it has nothing to say, that it is absorbed in its own textual complexities.

This oscillation between exactitude and pointlessness, pedantry and incoherence, is constantly rehearsed in the interminable, sometimes also tiresome conversations of the principal characters. They seem to be locked in a search for sense, as they find apparently significant patterns in the events of the world around them. The novel is set in a number of locations (Zurich, Prague, Merano, Venice); each of these locations serves as a focus for a series of perhaps interlocking incidents in which historical events and the characters of the novel are involved. In Zurich, for example, Kepela is betrayed by his lover Ottla (who has been recording his conversations for the Czech secret police); he then encounters by chance his old friend Josef Klims, who is also the partner of another former lover. Klims takes him to a street where, at different times, a whole series of real people had lived: the German physiologist Lavater, visited by Goethe; the playwright Büchner, who had discussed Lavater in one of his lectures, and recorded the transformation of Revolution into Terror in his play *Dantons Tod*; and Lenin, the leader of the Russian revolution. The characters expend their energies in analysing the connections between these interrelated facts. Yet it remains possible (probable even) that they are mere coincidences, that the search to give them significance is pure fabrication. The characters talk as if everything hangs together in a meaningful whole; but perhaps they are finding significance where there is none.

After the suicide of his father, Kepela realizes that the work of mourning is interminable: 'il sut que toute sa vie serait insuffisante pour aller jusqu'au bout d'un travail têtu, tenace, obsessif, de deuil: jusqu'au bout de la haine, de la lucidité, du nécessaire combat sans espoir et sans trêve' (281).[46] Beneath its blithe, civilized, intellectual surface, the text itself is bound up with this unending, hopeless work of mourning. At all levels it bears the traces of an irreparable loss, which at the semantic level is enacted in the loss of meaning. Thematically, stylistically, and structurally, *La Montagne blanche* is a novel which gestures towards a coherent revelation which is never unambiguously achieved. This loss of meaning can evidently be traced back to the experiences of Juan and of Semprun himself in Buchenwald; but it is also suggested that Buchenwald is itself a symptom, a sign of something deeper, rather than the sole cause of the novel's traumatized textuality.

---

[46] 'he knew that his whole life would not be enough to get to the end of the stubborn, tenacious, obsessive work of mourning: to the end of hatred, of lucidity, of the necessary combat without hope and without truce.'

Crises of identity

Who dies in *La Montagne blanche*? At an immediate level it is the central character of the novel, Juan Larrea; but Juan's identity is far from simple. His name suggests Don Juan, the legendary seducer, whose demise is perhaps announced in the title of chapter 8 of the novel, 'La Fin du libertinage'.[47] Juan Larrea was also the name of a Spanish poet of the 1930s; and in *L'Ecriture ou la vie* Semprun informs his reader that it was one of the names he used in the 1950s whilst working in Spain as a clandestine member of the Spanish Communist Party. Semprun explains that Larrea kills himself so that he need not.[48] Following a pattern also adopted in Semprun's other novels, Juan is a sort of sacrificial *alter ego*, killed off in order to make possible his author's survival.[49]

So Juan is not so much a character as an overdetermined intertext, a substitute for other real or imagined figures. Indeed, in *La Montagne blanche* repetition, substitution, and interchangeability destroy the bases of secure individual identity. Juan's suicide is a repetition of that of Kleist, who also killed himself by drowning; Kleist's suicide figures in one of Juan's plays (see 46), and his name is mentioned for a final time only five pages before Juan's death (305). Juan's act repeats that of Kleist, and the novel becomes obsessed with such repetitions and substitutions. The three principal male characters are astonishingly similar, sharing the same cultural references, artistic taste, and sexual partners. This similarity, whilst providing the foundation for their friendship, also entails a disturbing theft of identity: 'Ça l'agaçait à la fin, que Juan eût investi le même territoire imaginaire que lui. Car ce n'était pas la première fois que ça se produisait: ils semblaient avoir les mêmes obsessions, ils étaient hantés par les mêmes personnages. Mais Merano, quand même, c'était son domaine à lui! Larrea ne pouvait y être qu'un intrus' (60).[50] The female characters are equally interchangeable, their substitutions for one another made more distasteful by the male perspective adopted throughout the novel. Juan takes Nadine as a lover when Franca fails to turn up at a party ('la jeune femme s'était glissée sans le savoir dans cette absence de Franca,' 76);[51] she is the same age as was Franca when she first met Juan and Antoine (304); and she reminds the two men of Mary-Lou,

---

[47] 'The End of Libertinage'.   [48] Semprun, *L'Ecriture ou la vie*, 255.

[49] On this point, see Lutz Küster, *Obsession der Erinnerung. Das literarische Werk Jorge Sempr úns* (Frankfurt am Main: Vervuert, 1989), e.g. 237, 260.

[50] 'It annoyed him in the end, that Juan could have occupied the same imaginary territory as him. Because it was not the first time that it had happened: they seemed to have the same obsessions, they were haunted by the same characters. But Merano, even so, that was his private domain! Larrea could only be an intruder there.'

[51] 'the young woman had slipped without knowing into that absence of Franca'.

the lover they had shared in their twenties. Each figure is a substitute for someone else; but the original term which would give the series of substitutions some fixity is constantly receding. Antoine realizes that in his paintings of Franca he has in fact been reproducing the body of his long-dead aunt Ulrike, with whom he had had an incestuous relationship (268); and that relationship in turn reproduced an incestuous streak recurring throughout the history of his family. Every story, experience, or memory masks another; characters are not self-assured centres of identity, but fractured selves in search of an elusive wholeness.

In *L'Ère du vide*, first published in 1983, Gilles Lipovetsky had announced what he called 'une deuxième révolution individualiste', giving rise to 'de nouvelles valeurs visant à permettre le libre déploiement de la personnalité intime, à légitimer la jouissance, à reconnaître les demandes singulières, à moduler les institutions sur les aspirations des individus'.[52] Published three years later, Semprun's *La Montagne blanche* portrays a dissolution of the individual rather than a new individualism; the unitary self with its own private memories and experiences is depicted as giving way to a disturbing absence of secure selfhood, a sense of interchangeability with others which causes characters to feel invaded in their own intimate identity. Everything is potentially reducible to a repetition of something else. Franca is distressed to think that Juan has stayed in the same hotel with Nadine as he had with her, that they have visited the same pictures in the same gallery in the same order (94–5). Private identity and individual experience are being emptied of their particularity: 'Nadine écrivait des cartes postales. C'est une chose qu'il avait déjà vu faire à toute sorte de jeunes femmes, dans toute sorte d'endroits. [. . .] On les accompagne dans les musées, les rues, les restaurants. On les baise comme d'habitude, par habitude, mais le dépaysement leur fait trouver l'acte inhabituel, plus gratifiant que d'habitude' (195).[53] Juan is 'troublé par le sentiment du déjà vu, de la répétition': 'C'était l'ombre de Franca, sans doute, qui faisait naître cette sensation de déjà vu, déjà vécu. Mais du même coup, c'était la vie elle-même, la vie en général, la vie tout court, qui devenait répétitive. Oiseuse, peut-être même' (197).[54] The sense

---

[52] 'a second individualist revolution'; 'new values aiming to allow the free deployment of intimate personality, to legitimate pleasure, to recognize particular demands, to inflect institutions to fit the aspirations of individuals'. Gilles Lipovetsky, *L'Ère du vide. Essais sur l'individualisme contemporain* (Paris: Gallimard, 1983, 1993; Folio edn.), 10, 12.

[53] 'Nadine was writing postcards. It was something he has already seen all sorts of young women do, in all sorts of places. [. . .] You go with them to museums, streets, restaurants. You screw them as usual, as you usually do, but the change of location makes them find the act unusual, more gratifying than usual.'

[54] 'troubled by the sense of déjà vu, of repetition. [. . .] It was the shadow of Franca, probably, which gave birth to this feeling of déjà vu, déjà vécu [already experienced]. But at the same time, it was life itself, life in general, life and no more, which was becoming repetitive. Pointless, perhaps even.'

of repetition is a form of death, and it foreshadows Juan's later suicide. The self has become an empty vessel to which nothing can happen which is not always immediately *recognized* because it is a re-enactment of something that has already taken place. The loss of meaning in *La Montagne blanche* goes together with a loss of the sense of being the subject of one's own experience; the self who might act, remember, live its own life, has been radically destabilized. The return of the subject discussed in the Introduction to this book is, at least in *La Montagne blanche*, highly paradoxical; it entails a return to something which is fractured, characterized by an essential emptiness, and thus also lost at the very moment it is refound.

Juan locates the fragmentation of the unitary self, secure in its identity and desires, in the experience of Buchenwald. However, Semprun is unusual amongst Holocaust writers in that he does not give the Holocaust unique status, and Buchenwald is depicted as one source of trauma and dissolution amongst others. Antoine's difficulties pre-date the war, and reach back far into the prehistory of his family and of Europe; Kepela's exile is tied to the history of Communist Eastern Europe, with (particularly in his native Czechoslovakia) its successive waves of repression, liberalization, and more repression. Rather than just a series of individual traumas, *La Montagne blanche* depicts a more general European crisis. This is suggested by the references to the philosopher Edmund Husserl's lectures delivered in Prague and Vienna in 1935, published under the title *Die Krisis der europäischen Wissenschaften*; Antoine's mother attends the first lectures in Vienna, and later takes Antoine to hear Husserl in Prague (218, 261). Antoine reads—and the novel quotes—Husserl's lectures on the evening of Juan's suicide (259, 260). In his lectures, which were delivered towards the end of his life, Husserl diagnosed a crisis in the human sciences deriving from the separation of knowledge and meaning. This crisis affects European humanity in its entirety; it entails the breakdown of faith in reason to make sense of human existence: 'At the same time we lose our belief in an "absolute" reason, from which the world receives its meaning, the belief in the meaning of history, the meaning of humanity, in its freedom, that is its ability to create reasonable meaning for its individual and general human existence.'[55] Without this belief, modern humanity is in danger of sinking in the flood of scepticism ('in der skeptischen Sintflut zu sinken'),[56] which could be one way of describing what happens to Juan when he drowns himself at the end of *La Montagne blanche*.

---

[55] Edmund Husserl, *Die Krisis der europäischen Wissenchaften und die transzendentale Phänomenologie* (Hamburg: Felix Meiner Verlag, 1982), 12; my translation.
[56] Ibid. 14. The word *Sintflut* refers to the biblical Flood which Noah escaped by building the ark.

Although he was a long-standing Protestant, Husserl's Jewish origins meant that he was not permitted to teach or publish in Germany after the Nazis took power in 1933. His former pupil Martin Heidegger had dedicated his major work *Being and Time* to him, but had allowed the dedication to be removed from editions published under the Nazi regime. In *La Montagne blanche* the date of the lectures (initially wrongly given as 1936, with 'pas de doute possible' (218),[57] though later corrected) also suggests a connection with the Spanish Civil War, which would lead to the triumph of Fascism in Spain: '—Justement, dit Kepela. La *Krisis* de Husserl et la guerre d'Espagne, ça va ensemble. C'est la fin d'une époque, la fin d'une après-guerre. Ou le début d'une avant-guerre' (218).[58] In Semprun's novel, then, Husserl's philosophical analysis is related to a broader political context: the rise of European Fascism, the stirrings of the Second World War, and the resulting annexation of Eastern Europe to the Stalinist empire. *La Montagne blanche* is a novel deeply immersed in European culture; it contains numerous references to, amongst many others, figures such as Goethe, Kafka, Kleist, Grillparzer, Shakespeare, Baudelaire, Rimbaud, Brecht, Heraclitus, Proust, Musil, Dostoyevsky, Kundera, Beethoven, Schubert, and Veronese. What lies behind this is the nostalgic fantasy of a unified European culture common to all, a shared sense of humanity and values: 'tout le monde faisait les mêmes voyages, jusqu'à la Première Guerre mondiale: c'était la même Europe pour tous' (68–9).[59] The reader is likely to feel more excluded than included by the bewildering display of cultural knowledge in which the characters and the novel indulge. That sense of exclusion is part of the point: something is perceived as having been lost, even if the alleged common heritage was only ever available to an economically privileged class (it can hardly be true that everyone made the same journeys). In Semprun's novel personal trauma is associated with a more general view of Europe itself, which functions as a sort of mythical lost object: 'C'était finalement une histoire européenne que se tramait là, dans cette mémoire lancinante. Une histoire qui concernait surtout le cœur de l'Europe, qui la frappait au cœur' (110–11).[60]

La Montagne blanche revolves around a crisis of meaning and coherence both in the lives of its characters and in European culture more

---

[57] 'no possible doubt'.

[58] '—Precisely, said Kepela. Husserl's *Krisis* and the Spanish war, they go together. It's the end of an era, the end of the post-war period. Or the beginning of the pre-war period.'

[59] 'everyone made the same journeys, up until the First World War: it was the same Europe for everyone.'

[60] 'It was finally a European story that was being woven there, in that troubled memory. A story that concerned above all the heart of Europe, that struck it at the heart.'

generally. It is concerned above all by the loss of an interpretative paradigm which would make sense of recent European history. The political aspect of this loss can be seen by a comparison with Semprun's first novel, *Le Grand Voyage*. That work was generally acclaimed on its publication as one of the first works about the concentration camps to have real literary merit. The novel centres upon the narrator's journey to Buchenwald, with 120 men crammed into a railway car. The narrator, Gérard (this was indeed the name by which Semprun was known in the French Resistance), combines description of the journey with flashbacks to life before Buchenwald and flash-forwards, using a device which has been called 'anticipative memory', which allows the description of scenes from Buchenwald and life after the liberation of the camp.[61] Semprun's narrative technique, which has been extensively compared to that of Proust, establishes an elaborate network of memory and anticipation, dream and reality, which is put here to the service of the author's Socialist commitment: his experience of the horror of reality is directly linked to the hope and necessity for change. The different time-scales are joined together in an unbroken continuity which passes through trauma to potential victory. Most importantly, Nazism does not entail a fundamental disruption in the central character's political commitment and the understanding of history that goes with it. On the contrary, as in *L'Univers concentrationnaire* by Semprun's fellow Buchenwald-detainee David Rousset, Nazism can be readily understood within a Marxist interpretation of Western capitalism: it is the gangrene of an economic and social system, the product of class conflict and therefore a warning to the non-Communist world.[62] Underlying *Le Grand Voyage* is what one critic has called a 'basically sanguine Marxism'[63] which is not overwhelmed by the narrator's personal misfortunes. Indeed, one of the achievements of the book is to maintain the relative independence of private trauma and political belief, so that the former does not undermine the latter. This is not to say that there is no risk of interference: the survival of Fascism in Spain surfaces in the text to indicate the grim knowledge that the experiences of Buchenwald perhaps do not have the sense attributed to them. Also, the narrator remains haunted by his memories of the camp: in an obvious and ironic allusion to Proust's madeleine he describes how eating bread transports him back to the camp. Nevertheless, such moments are not allowed to dominate the text; psychological trauma

---

[61] See Lawrence Langer, *The Holocaust and the Literary Imagination* (New Haven: Yale University Press, 1975), 288.

[62] See Rousset, *L'Univers concentrationnaire*, 119–21.

[63] Sidra Dekoven Ezrahi, *By Words Alone. The Holocaust in Literature* (Chicago: University of Chicago Press, 1980), 169.

leads to no epistemological impairment. The scars left by Buchenwald are private, they are, as the narrator insists, no one else's business. He will narrate only what he wants to narrate; on the other hand the political causes and consequences of the concentration camps belong to the public domain.[64]

When he published *Le Grand voyage*, the process that would lead to the expulsion of Semprun from the Communist Party and his disillusionment with Marxism was already under way. By the 1980s the French Communist Party was in decline, and Marxism had lost much of its postwar status as the most influential political philosophy in the French intellectual world. For Semprun in particular, Marxism had turned foul; its interpretation of history no longer provided a frame to give coherence to historical processes, and the Communist revolution in Eastern Europe had turned to repression. Dialectics, in *La Montagne blanche*, is treated as a tool of intellectual and political terror rather than a means of grasping the unity behind the contradictions of history and experience. The death-like state of repetition has supplanted the forwards motion of the historical dialectic. *La Montagne blanche* also signals the impossibility of keeping private trauma distinct from public significance. This is no longer the work of a basically sanguine Marxist who can understand his own suffering through the lens of a broader political struggle. In its language and structure as well as in the actions of its characters, the text bears the marks of a trauma which affects identity at both private and collective levels.

The European dimension of the novel is indicated by the references to Veronese's painting *The Rape of Europe* which is seen by Kepela and Ottla in the Doge's Palace in Venice, and which provides the title for the penultimate chapter of the novel ('L'Enlèvement d'Europe'). Following the classical story of Zeus adopting animal form to seduce Europe, the painting depicts a bull licking the feet of a dainty (and apparently unperturbed) young woman. Kepela appreciates the collusion of eroticism and violence and views the painting through his own erotic preoccupations: 'Il en avait admiré la composition savante; il avait été touché par la sensualité de la figure d'Europe: le mouvement alangui du corps; l'écartement des jambes faisant plisser le lourd tissu de la robe; l'admirable sein dénudé; le visage pâmé, aux lèvres entrouvertes; l'oeil exorbité qui trahit la montée irrésistible d'un désir panique' (62).[65] Kepela sees in the Veronese's work

---

[64] For further discussion of this, in particular in relation to Semprun's *Quel beau dimanche!*, see Colin Davis, 'Understanding the Concentration Camps: Elie Wiesel's *La Nuit* and Jorge Semprun's *Quel beau dimanche!*', in *Australian Journal of French Studies* 28/3 (1991), 291–303.

[65] 'He had admired its skilful composition; he had been moved by the sensuality of the figure of Europe: the languid movement of her body; the separation of her legs making folds in the heavy

a representation of violent abduction, repeated in the history of the painting itself (270) and throughout the history of Europe; but as Europe is about to be carried away she appears curiously compliant in her own rape: 'Et la garce y trouvera même son plaisir!' (272).[66] Her compliance is every bit as suicidal as Juan's act at the end of the novel.

In the mid-1960s, the title of Semprun's first film with Alain Resnais had announced that 'la guerre est finie';[67] yet in the mid-1980s, for Semprun and more generally in France, the war was still not yet over. The trial in 1987 of Klaus Barbie (the German commander in Lyon) and in the 1990s of the collaborator Paul Touvier and Maurice Papon, a functionary in the collaborationist Vichy government, illustrated beyond doubt that old wounds were not healed, and the struggle for the memory of France was by no means over. France is still periodically discovering and rediscovering that its past contains causes for shame as well as for pride, and there is no single narrative which can persuasively encompass both. Semprun's work, along with that of many of his contemporaries, suggests that a wilfully forgotten past retains the potential to blight the present. The philosopher Theodor Adorno famously announced that after Auschwitz all culture is garbage.[68] *La Montagne blanche* approaches the same view, though with the greatest reluctance. It celebrates European culture, but also undertakes an interminable labour of mourning for that culture, marking its achievements as powerless to save Europe from its own self-destruction. Semprun's characters are trying to preserve the remnants of value which art and literature seemed to promise; but as victims of Nazism or Stalinism they are left with only fragments of their own selves. The novel is, finally, a work about clinging onto the wreckage: of culture, of history, of the self, and of meaning. It is a brave, perhaps desperate attempt to pay homage to a civilized world, a unified culture and a unitary self, which only survive in the 1980s in fantasies of a lost coherence.

fabric of her dress; the admirable naked breast; the swooning face, with her lips slightly open; the bulging eye that betrays the irresistible rise of frightened desire.'

[66] 'And the whore will even find her pleasure in it!'　　　[67] 'the war is over.'

[68] Theodor Adorno, *Negative Dialectics*, trans. E. B. Ashton (London: Routledge and Kegan Paul, 1973), 367.

4 Playing with the postmodern: Jean Echenoz's *Lac* (1989)

The fictional world of *Lac* is immediately recognizable to its readers on two interconnected levels. On the one hand it displays the objects and signs, the fashions and spectacles of contemporary consumer society: characters wear fake designer sunglasses, watch game shows on television, listen to popular music on their walkmans, and shop in bland commercial centres. On the other hand, the characters are also the participants in a spy novel, and enact the rituals of surveillance and secret weapons, double-crossing and amorous intrigues familiar from the James Bond model. Yet the reader's sense of familiarity is always at one remove: the text maintains a humorous and critical distance from both of these axes, signalling itself as a malicious mimic of the originals it imitates and revealing a sensibility which has positioned Echenoz as a postmodern cultural spectator. One of the purposes of this chapter will be to explore what such a position might entail, as well as to examine in more detail the way in which Echenoz exploits the thriller genre and evokes the scenes of contemporary urban life whilst revelling in humour and in the sheer possibilities of play in language.

Lac is Echenoz's fourth novel. His first, *Le Méridien de Greenwich*, was published by Editions de Minuit in 1979, and he has remained ever since with this most intellectual and prestigious of publishers, who also published *L'Amant*. *Le Méridien de Greenwich* offers a late twentieth-century version of a Jules Verne adventure story, complete with a galleon and a desert island; *Cherokee* (1983), winner of the Médicis prize, centres on the activities of a private eye and refers in its title to a jazz composition which is the structuring motif of the text; *L'Equipée malaise* (1986) recounts a hopelessly ineffectual plot to take over a Malaysian plantation, in which an SDF (person living on the streets) emerges as the unlikely hero.[1] By 1989, therefore, the French reader was ready to open an Echenoz novel with an expectation of humour, subversion, and contemporaneity, an expectation which is fully met in *Lac*.

---

[1] Echenoz had also published a short story *L'Occupation des sols* (1988).

The spy novel

The conventions of the spy novel are expertly manipulated for readerly pleasure in *Lac*, whilst simultaneously being held up for our inspection as a familiar comedy routine. The rhythm of the plot varies from chapters in which the narrator appears to have abandoned his own intrigue, to action-packed episodes with *coups de théâtre* of dramatic effect. The opening chapter takes a leisurely and playful approach, failing to communicate any significant detail of the nature of the plot, and lingering instead on a humble participant in the spy game, who, despite glorying in the name of Vito Piranese, is destined to disappear from the narrative at an early stage, resurfacing almost unnoticeably in the last. Much humorous play is made in the opening paragraph of the fact that Piranese has only one leg: thus he puts his leg on every day 'au saut du lit'[2] and enunciates the firm principle that however long the telephone may have been ringing, his leg comes first.

This one-legged spy, who bursts into tears during a surveillance operation when a favourite song of his ex-girlfriend is played on the car radio, clearly does not conform to the James Bond model of the handsome tough hero who always gets the girl. Franck Chopin, who replaces Piranese as the centre of narrative interest from the third chapter on, also makes an unlikely spy. An entomologist engaged in scholarly research on flies, Chopin doubts whether there can be much left to discover about them, and agrees to work for the egregious Colonel Seck largely from a sense of professional discouragement. The plot begins to gather pace when Chopin falls in love with Suzy Clair, whose husband Oswald, ostensibly a civil servant working in the Ministry for Foreign Affairs, has mysteriously disappeared six years earlier in the course of a house move, taking with him a roomful of secret dossiers. Chopin is sent to the luxurious Parc Palace du Lac Hotel, where his mission is to spy on Veber, an Eastern bloc grandee, by means of tiny microphones which he has to implant into the flies and then introduce into Veber's room. The ludicrous nature of this technique, in which 'des mouches' (flies) set about the task of 'mouchardage' (spying), is a source of much entertainment: when Chopin complains that it is outdated, Seck confesses that he's been caught on a bureaucratic hop—all the more high-tech equipment has been already booked out by his colleagues. A long-suffering Chopin sets about his task, impeded not by sophisticated defences but by open windows through

---

[2] 'au saut du lit' might usually be translated as 'first thing in the morning' but literally means 'at the moment of leaping out of bed'.

which the flies escape, by energetically wielded newspapers, and by the difficulties of preventing the flies from coupling. Nothing of any significance has been achieved when Suzy Clair unexpectedly appears at the hotel: her husband, Oswald, turns out to be Veber's assistant, and, after a series of complications in which Chopin is twice kidnapped by Veber's security guards, Colonel Seck arrives to save the day, unaided by Chopin who has omitted to bring a gun. Oswald is eventually exchanged for Seck himself. Veber is destined for liquidation by his own side and Seck will replace Veber. Substitutions and double-crosses abound with few of the characters ending up on the side on which they began.

Was Chopin's first meeting with Suzy Clair accidental? Was the whole operation always designed to engineer the exchange of Seck and Oswald? These questions are never resolved and Chopin reflects in the final chapter that throughout he has been merely a stooge 'myope comme une taupe enfouie dans le sol natal' (188).[3] For much of the plot the reader is kept equally misinformed—mysterious phone calls remain unexplained, conversations are reported taking place without their content being revealed, and Chopin's lack of persistence and percipience leaves us without a privileged insider. Thus when Chopin succeeds in breaking into Suzy Clair's hotel room to ask her to explain her sudden appearance, instead of learning anything new he allows himself to be told that all will be clear in the morning. He spends a blissful hour with her watching television in bed whilst we are none the wiser. When Veber's assistant 'le chiffreur' (encoding assistant) is revealed to be Oswald, we realize that we have been unwittingly acquainted with the missing Oswald for most of the book.

This lack of information is of course partly what allows the *coups de théâtre*: the moments at which Suzy Clair's presence in the hotel is identified, and at which Oswald's identity is revealed are highly dramatic. The torrent of double-crosses and revelations of the last three chapters is as fast-moving as any Eric Ambler or Ian Fleming thriller. Yet much of the pleasure of the narrative is also derived from the comically elaborated spy routines which barely advance the plot at all: the more complex the procedure the characters embark on, the less it appears to achieve. Thus the fake advertising brochures which Chopin finds in his mailbox, and which he has to devote considerable technical efforts to decoding, never do more than set up the next rendezvous with Seck. On his way to one of these meetings Chopin employs 'la procédure classique de dissuasion de filatures par zigzag': leaping in and out of taxis, boarding trains and leaving them just before their departure, doubling in and out of buildings

---

[3] 'as blind as a mole buried in its native soil'.

by different doors Chopin grumbles 'toujours le même cirque' and arrives covered in sweat, convinced that 'tout ça ne sert à rien' (53).[4] Exchanges of identical briefcases at prearranged stops on bus routes, different coloured ribbons strategically placed in telephone boxes, hairs placed across the wardrobe—all these manœuvres feature exuberantly in the narrative, before the decidedly disenchanted spies weary of them. 'On se fatigue même de l'espionnage, très vite,' sighs Chopin (73).[5]

There is also an extended joke centring around the spy drowning in bureaucracy. Veber spends all his time on dossiers and worries whether he has with him the new norms, farcically entitled the Boyadjian-Goldfarb norms. Oswald Clair, the double agent, returns in triumph with a bureaucratic treasure trove:

> —Les normes, fit Maryland. Vous avez pu vous procurer les normes, j'espère.
> —Les trois versions, confirma Clair, avec les corrections de Ratine et le mémorandum Boyadjian. Vous trouverez aussi les protocoles de réunion du groupe Technique et Prévision, et la plupart de leurs rapports au comité de surface. (185)[6]

As we shall see later, this insistence on norms, systems, and surfaces has another role to play in the text, but it also has a comic function, and again one which derives from the genre's own conventions.

The more senior figures, Seck and Veber, correspond more closely to the stereotype of the shadowy senior figure of the Secret Services, at least in some of their tastes: Seck has a military past, makes substantial wins at the gaming table, and drives a large car equipped with coffee, rum, and cigars. His own senior officer, Maryland, smokes a brand of gauloises which cannot be purchased in the shops—it is specially produced for him personally. Veber is partial to oysters with Tokay wine, has an impressive golf handicap and a minimalist smile. However, it gradually emerges that Seck is black and hankers after his native Nigeria, gazing nostalgically at aeroplanes as they pass overhead. He likes lowbrow English pop music of the 1960s, especially Englebert Humpledinck and Roger Whittaker (both names comically mis-spelled in the text), and is pursued by ex-military comrades who badger him into finding them cosy sinecures. Veber remains more shadowy and is protected by two security guards with the unlikely names of Rodion Rathenau and Perla Pommeck who are also a

---

4 'the classic zigzag procedure for shaking off tails'; 'the usual carry-on'; 'it's all quite pointless.'
5 'Even spying gets tedious, pretty quickly.'
6 'The norms, said Maryland. You managed to get hold of the norms, I hope. | All three versions, Clair confirmed, with the Ratine corrections and the Boyadjian memorandum. You will also find the meetings protocol for the Technical and Forecasting group, and most of their reports to the surface committee.'

mix of the apparently stereotypical and the amusingly inappropriate. Rodion was a weakling at school and collapses if anyone uses his school-boy nickname of B12 (a reference to the Second World War bomber aeroplane), whilst Perla has been given anabolic steroids and diverted into security work because she failed miserably in the vamp role seducing minor embassy officials for which she had originally been recruited. In each case Echenoz first demonstrates his—and our—acquaintance with the codes and norms of the genre, before inserting details which fail to fit. Again we can note an interest in codes, and their displacement.

Magical objects

If the bones of the spy novel produce the structure and many of the most recognizable features of the text, there is barely a page of the novel which does not construct the material universe in which the characters conduct their activities. Furniture, telephones, clothing, pictures, interiors, cars, the contents of a handbag, the objects on a desk are noted and described as if by an obsessive interior decorator, or perhaps a boy scout memoriz-ing them for Kim's game. The flotsam and jetsam of an era are collected like features in the catalogue of a museum of culture. Commentators often refer to an ethnological feel to this attention paid to the artefacts of a culture. But why should Echenoz's objects receive so much attention? After all, the world of Balzac's novels is filled with furniture, interiors, clothing and, in the 1950s and 1960s, the new novel famously filled its pages with objects, often described at great length. What has changed, it might be said, is the balance of power between character and object. In Balzac's world the object carries meaning as an indicator of the characters' social milieu, places them for us, reveals their circumstances and their history. In Robbe-Grillet's novels the material world is independ-ent of the characters, coexisting with them but essentially alien to them and carrying no inherent meaning. In Echenoz's fiction the object fre-quently seems to have taken over, to carry meanings which are not within the characters' control but which surround them with cultural injunc-tions which will form their taste, guide their choices. The listing of the contents of Suzy's handbag exhibits both the taxonomic urge, so charac-teristic of the text and so easily assimilated to the idea of an ethnographer of culture, and simultaneously suggests a range of cultural options and subject positions offered by the collection of cassettes which she carries with her: self-improvement in the form of a Teach yourself Russian tape, an astrological tape predicting her future over the next two years;

English pop music; the sound-track of a couple of films; a classical quintet. Passing from one to the other, selecting them at random, Suzy is the epitome of the floating subjectivity summoned into being by first one option, and then another. Consumer culture saturates the text: Suzy writes the copy for a catalogue of luxury accessories for women; Carole takes fashion shoots for a living; Marianne is a television presenter. Advertising images are embodied and satirized within the text. Suzy's doorbell rings: 'Le visiteur était un jeune homme bien bâti sous une brosse courte, une chevalière à chaque auriculaire, une chaînette d'or autour du cou. Inondé d'un after-shave très vert il souriait, respirant la santé comme s'il sortait de la douche, l'oeil mi-clos par une bulle de savon restée dedans' (51).[7] The shower gel advert script is immediately recognizable. Clothes are equally presented as part of a consumer image to which even senior party hacks fall prey. Veber arrives at the Parc Palace du Lac Hotel with two cases of dossiers and *three* cases of clothes. In one of the most action-packed episodes of the novel the narrative pauses to describe his outfit: 'Le secrétaire général portait ce jour-là une veste pied-de-poule sur une chemise rose, cravate et pantalon roi' (166).[8] The unlikely names of the fashion industry are of course also a source of enjoyment here. The status of clothing is given another humorous twist when Chopin suddenly discovers that the unknown lady in the revealing yellow bustier dining with Veber is actually Suzy Clair: 'Chopin se figea, tout son corps d'un coup devint froid: Suzy, Suzy Clair née Moreno elle-même était assise en face du secrétaire général'; when he begins to recover he asks himself: 'qu'est-ce qu'elle fait là, qu'est-ce que c'est que cette histoire, et d'abord qu'est-ce qu'elle fait dans ce truc jaune impossible, qu'est-ce que c'est que ce truc jaune que je n'ai jamais vu?' (125).[9] There is in fact no significance to the bustier in the sense that Suzy is not on a femme fatale mission—but the garment signals a cultural meaning which is beyond Suzy's control.

Like Chopin's interest in the bustier, the question must be posed of how far Echenoz's interest in objects is innocent, following in the wake as it does of the work of a famous French cultural analyst, Roland Barthes.

[7] 'Her visitor was an admirably built young man with a crew cut, a signet ring on each of his little fingers, and a gold chain round his neck. Inundated with a pungent after-shave, he was smiling, radiating good health as if he had just stepped out of the shower, one eye half-closed by a soap bubble still inside.'

[8] 'That day the General Secretary was wearing a houndstooth jacket over a pink shirt, and a royal blue tie and trousers.'

[9] 'Chopin froze, his whole body suddenly chilled: Suzy, Suzy Clair née Moreno in person was seated opposite the General Secretary'; 'what's she doing here, what's this all about, and for a start what's she doing in that impossible yellow item, what's this yellow thing I've never seen before?'

Barthes's *Mythologies* (1957) launched the study of what Barthes called the semiotics of everyday life, that is to say the study of apparently natural cultural objects and the analysis of the cultural message or myth which they impose. Barthes spoke of the work of decipherment of such messages and the struggle it entails against apparently 'innocent objects'. Barthes's targets included the advertising industry, depictions of royalty, a glass of red wine, a plate of steak and chips, children's toys, the popularity of wrestling and, in a later study, the fashion industry.[10]

At this point one might merely see Barthes as a general predecessor to the mode of inspection of everyday objects which Echenoz undertakes, but there is one episode in *Lac* which functions as such a blatant wink to *Mythologies* that it cannot be overlooked, and that is the episode of the car showroom. One of the most famous sections of *Mythologies* is entitled 'La Nouvelle Citroën' in which Barthes analyses the way in which the new Citroën DS 19 functions as an object of such gleaming and seamless perfection that it becomes an 'objet parfaitement magique'.[11] He writes: 'Dans les halls d'exposition, la voiture témoin est visitée avec une application intense, amoureuse: c'est la grande phase tactile de la découverte, le moment où le merveilleux visuel va subir l'assaut du toucher' (142).[12] Chapter 3 of *Lac* opens with a description of the car showrooms on the Champs-Elysées: the men who have stepped inside to shelter from the rain admire the 'très chers modèles que ne pourront jamais s'offrir ces hommes qui ont assez de temps pour tourner autour d'eux' (18). They long to touch the models but dare not: 'entrouvrant une audacieuse portière, ensuite ils n'osent plus la fermer' (19).[13] In both texts the unattainable status of the car is stressed, the potential amorous relation with it suggested, and the role of touch and gaze underlined. But, in the Echenoz text, the demystifying thrust of Barthes's analysis is much less in evidence. Consumer society, which, for the early Barthes at least, was identified as one of the masks of bourgeois ideology, has become for Echenoz in the 1980s and 1990s, a fact of life, a self-sustaining structure. No character from the novel enters the car showroom. It features in the text in its own right, with the same magical and absolute status as the car itself.

---

10 See Andrew Leak, *Barthes: Mythologies* (London: Grant and Cutler, 1994) for a helpful introduction to Barthes's text.

11 'totally magical object', Roland Barthes, *Mythologies* (Paris: Editions du Seuil, 1957), 140. Subsequent references are given in parentheses in the main text.

12 'In the showrooms, the model car is visited with intense, loving care: this is the major tactile phase of discovery, the moment when the visual marvel has to withstand the assault of touch.'

13 'very expensive models that these men who have the time to hang around them could never afford to buy'; 'daringly opening a door that they are then too timid to close'.

A second example of the distance between Barthes and Echenoz can be found in the attention both pay to a particular hairstyle. Barthes famously deconstructed the apparently neutral hairstyle of a campaigning Catholic priest, the abbé Pierre, discovering in his Franciscan cut an archetype of saintliness and charity of such signifying power that his motives could not be questioned. The *sign* of charity, declares Barthes, substitutes for the reality (52). In *Lac*, a very minor character makes a single appearance in the novel, and is accredited with a wonderfully elaborate hairstyle: 'L'ami de Frédéric était un grand jeune homme très maigre et très timide, avec une tête d'alezan coiffée en brosse complexe, queue de canard dans la nuque et sur le front trois mèches brushées en décrochement: sa coupe de cheveux devait constituer un poste à part dans son budget' (85).[14] Anything but neutral, the haircut appears to exist in its own right, almost independently of its owner. Its deconstruction would yield merely its fashionable status.

Fashions, styles, objects proliferate in the text. Most are not presented as sinister, but are displayed and enjoyed as 'magical', as artefacts of a consumer culture in which the characters evolve. Others are accorded a life and sensibility of their own within an animistic vision which has nothing of the scientific about it. Files sit sleepily in their cabinet 'suspendus comme des chauve-souris' (9) and the telephone, one of Echenoz's favourite domestic objects, becomes an 'animal perdu: l'appareil en effet se tapissait dans le coin le plus obscur d'une des chambres, lié par son fil au mur comme par sa laisse à un poteau le chien abandonné, l'été' (31–2).[15] During a house move Suzy Clair's furniture and plants 'se retrouvaient parqués sur le trottoir, se regardant bizarrement, inquiets de ce départ vers l'inconnu' (27–8).[16] Particular attention is paid to the life of a wicker trunk:

> Ayant très peu de famille connue, Oswald ne disposait d'aucun héritage mobilier, et du côté de Suzy seule une grande malle d'osier provenait de la boucherie d'un oncle, promue au rang de table de chevet: après n'avoir connu que l'acide univers de la sciure et du froid, du carreau gras, sans autre perspective que renfermer des linges et des couteaux sanglants tout au long de sa vie d'objet, pour cette malle à présent c'était une chaude retraite inespérée,

---

[14] 'Frédéric's friend was a tall young man, very timid and thin, with a horsy face and a complex chestnut crewcut, ducktail at the back of the neck and three strands styled to stand up over the forehead: his hairdressing bills must have been a separate item in his budget.'

[15] 'hanging upside down like bats'; 'lost animal: the machine was crouching in the darkest corner of one of the rooms, tied to the wall by its wire like a dog abandoned in the summer tied to a post by its lead'.

[16] 'found themselves parked on the pavement, eyeing each other strangely, anxious about their departure to an unknown destination'.

bourrée de confortables vêtements d'hiver, de fourrure et de cachemire, d'angora, maintenant on l'élevait, à dos d'homme, vers les hauteurs de la rue de Rome. (29–30)[17]

This is a lengthy description of an object which will not figure again in the narrative. On one level it provides a humorous displacement of the role of human beings in the universe; on another it serves to contrast with the rest of Suzy and Oswald's furniture which they have purchased together and which all are copies of styles prevalent in the first third of the century. 'Tel était le goût des Clair',[18] notes the narrator, slyly implying that this 'taste' is simply a consumer choice made amongst other ersatz styles available in the shops. So many décors are evoked in the novel that it is impossible not to see them all as mere sets, chosen to promote a particular kind of ambient illusion: amongst a myriad of examples one might choose the décor of Dr Belzunce's consulting room, every detail of which appears to have been selected to bolster the doctor's (admittedly shaky) professional status, or the office of the most important secret agent Maryland, in which everything signals power and discretion. The effect is not one of naturalist illusion but of artificiality. Chopin's hotel room displays the same attention to reproducing a particular style, here a mix of objects chosen to suggest on the one hand 'hôtellerie française traditionnelle (parquet lustré, meubles anciens, gros édredons)' and the other 'confort ultramoderne international (douche pulsatile à modulateur de jet, stores et rideaux télécommandés, circuit vidéo de films pornographiques doux)'(88).[19] The use of parentheses in this description underlines the way in which each object signifies as part of a system of other objects, constituting a code which signals 'French tradition' or 'modern international comfort'. The trunk evoked above escapes this system, but it is no coincidence that it simultaneously carries darker connotations of blood and violence, also to be found in some of the large set-piece décors of public architecture which feature in the novel—such as the shopping centre, and the wholesale market of Rungis—which cast a more disquieting shadow over the text.

[17] 'Oswald had very few known relatives, and hence no family furniture, while on Suzy's side there was only a large wicker trunk which had come from an uncle's butcher's shop and had been promoted to the rank of bedside table: after a life in the acrid world of sawdust and cold, and greasy tiled floors, with no future other than storing linen and bloody knives throughout its career as an object, the trunk was enjoying an unexpected retirement, stuffed full of comfortable winter garments, furs and cashmere, angora, and was now being hoisted by human sweat up towards the heights of the rue de Rome.'

[18] 'Such was the Clairs' taste'.

[19] 'traditional French hostelry (polished parquet floor, antique furniture, thick eiderdowns)'; 'ultramodern international comfort (power shower with adjustable jets, curtains and blinds on remote control, video system with soft porn films'.

Monstrous sets

During one of the slow periods of the plot, Suzy visits a shopping centre to collect the tranquillizers which the doctor-cum-secret agent has pre-scribed her. She finds herself in a totally planned and deeply depressing environment, consisting of 'une esplanade cernée de tours fuligineuses entre lesquelles balance une odeur vive et fade de pourriture plastique' (158).[20] The occasional touches of colour or attempts at ornamentation—the results perhaps, comments the narrator, of the architect's bad conscience—simply serve to underline the oppressive atmosphere. Nature itself is domesticated within this environment by a fountain 'qui vomit sans mollir un étroit ruban d'eau plate' (158). Populated by women carrying shopping bags and men reading the job adverts or the racing page in the paper, 'tous ont l'air fatigué d'affronter, ou de ne plus pouvoir affronter quelque chose' (159).[21] Only the chemist is in good humour as he surveys the likely consumers of his tranquillizers. Suzy picks her way through the rubbish blowing over the esplanade: crumpled bits of wrapping paper, various kinds of tickets, pages from old newspapers, faded hair locks in front of the hairdressers, dead leaves from far away, all these objects, carriers of signs and meanings, are tossed at random, detached from their original context. In the shop windows Suzy decodes the blocks of language painted on the windows or on labels: 'très beau carrelet, superbe thon, promotion sur les langues et sur les cœurs' (160)[22] and, as she leaves the centre, travels through block after block of huge complexes of flats built to be rented out, each cheek by jowl with building sites in which other blocks are going up or being knocked down, she deciphers the lives briefly led in the semi-demolished interiors from the signs of the mark in the wallpaper where a double bed once stood, or the remains of a soap dish still standing in the tiles of what was once a bathroom. The verbs 'décrypte' ('decipher') and 'déchiffre' ('decode') are insisted upon in the text: just as Chopin has to decode his messages from Seck and Veber needs the services of a decoding assistant, so Suzy and the reader are called upon to make sense of the signs and systems of meaning of contemporary life.

However, the shopping centre is a positively comforting environment compared with the two evocations of Rungis, Paris's wholesale market

---

[20] 'an esplanade surrounded by grimy tower blocks; a strong and sickly smell of rotting material in plastic hung in the air between them.'

[21] 'which stubbornly vomits a narrow ribbon of still water'; 'all of them looking tired of coping or not being able to cope with something'.

[22] 'first-class fresh plaice, superb tuna, special offer on tongues and hearts'.

built on the outskirts of the city in the 1960s to replace the old central markets at Les Halles, themselves described in Zola's novel *Le Ventre de Paris* (1873) when they had just been newly built, now converted into a vast shopping and leisure complex. The first time Chopin goes to Rungis for a rendezvous with Seck the description focuses on the huge size of the complex and its organization like a police state, complete with batteries of video cameras, wire fencing, controlled entry, and forests of signs forbidding any commercial operation except the wholesale. Inside the fences, the area is a structuralist fantasy, broken down into sectors dealing with different products linked by a six-lane boulevard. Chopin meets Seck outside the vast offal pavilion: 'là se traite ce qui reste après qu'on a prélevé la viande et recyclé la squelette, ce que l'on récupère entre la chair et l'os, là se trafiquent le cartilage et le viscère, là professe un brain-trust de compétence tripières qui sondent les cœurs et les rognons' (76–7).[23] Echenoz's exuberant humorous word-play is of course present here, but the overwhelming impression remains gothically sinister, as Chopin's meeting is interspersed with glimpses of men in white covered in blood, and of dustbins piled high with bones. The spectre of a war between man and the animals he kills to eat is raised at the end of the chapter describing this first visit, and it closes on an image of human desolation striking in the overall context of the novel, as the sound of Chopin's car engine in the deserted streets is described as sounding plaintive, 'comme un homme gémit seul entre quatre murs nus' (81).[24] The second visit is gorier still as Chopin has to penetrate inside the offal pavilion to find Seck; the elaborate word-play continues as workmen swop figures over 'leurs étals bourrés de bacs de foies, de sacs de cœurs à prendre, séminaires de cervelles et foules de pieds, lignes de langues tirées de l'invisible, poumons à la pelle et rognons à gogo' (104)[25] but this is barely sufficient to counter the sounds of skulls being smashed and our introduction to Monsieur Touré, a specialist in emptying out lambs' brains. Like the shopping centre, the wholesale market is essentially concerned with the circulation of consumer goods; just as the chemist's profits depend on human misery, this market 'of national interest', as it is twice described, depends literally on the butchering of animals. Beneath the surveillance system of the central administrative tower lie the vaults of twenty-four banks.

---

[23] 'the place which deals with everything left after the meat has been removed and the skeleton recycled, everything that can be recuperated in between the flesh and the bones; the place where cartilage and viscera are traded, and where a brains trust of gut experts pronounces and probes hearts and kidneys.'

[24] 'like a man groaning alone inside four bare walls'.

[25] 'Their stalls piled with vats of livers, with sacks of hearts going for a song, seminaries of brains and handfuls of feet, tons of tongues sticking out, lungs by the shovelful, and kidneys galore'.

From the set to the simulacrum and the hyperreal

Echenoz's focus on the planned environments of social life creates a connection with the thinking of Jean Baudrillard, a French social theorist himself influenced by the work of Roland Barthes, and whose name has come to be identified above any other with postmodernism. In *Le Système des objets* (1968), Baudrillard studied domestic objects much as Barthes had studied consumer objects, but insisting less on the single object than on the way in which the modern object of consumption receives its meaning in the context of a system of object signs and of interconnections between systems. Domestic décors become less a matter of individual pieces of furniture than a 'completely produced world'.[26] In *La Société de consommation* (1970) he went on to study forms of social environment, including the new totally planned shopping centre of Parly 2, to which Echenoz's shopping centre would appear to refer. What makes Baudrillard one of the prophets of postmodernism, however, is his insistence on the proliferation and status of signs. A helpful summary of Baudrillard's position is offered by Douglas Kellner:

> For Baudrillard [. . .] postmodern societies are organized around simulation and the play of images and signs, denoting a situation in which codes, models, and signs are the organizing principles of a new social order where simulation rules. In the society of simulation, identities are constructed by the appropriation of images, and codes and models determine how people perceive themselves and relate to other people. Economics, politics, social life, and culture are all governed by the logic of simulation, whereby codes and models determine how goods are consumed and used, politics unfold, culture is produced and consumed, and everyday life is lived.[27]

The work of art itself, from this perspective, is dominated by systems and signs, and by the simulation of forms. We have already seen, in the first section of this chapter, how *Lac* mimics the spy novel, recycling its conventions and codes and exploiting its signs. But this is only the first of many artistic simulations which abound in the text. When Suzy marries Oswald Clair she comes with two nude portraits of herself, painted according to two different sets of conventions: one shows her posing nymph-like beneath the shower, the other places her against an industrial background. Both end up in the hall cupboard since they cannot be integrated into a domestic interior. The cab of a lorry at Rungis is covered in representations of girls in every possible format: 'photos, dessins,

---

[26] See Mike Gane, *Baudrillard's bestiary. Baudrillard and culture* (London: Routledge,1991), 36.

[27] See Douglas Kellner (ed.), *Baudrillard: A Critical Reader* (Oxford: Blackwell, 1994), 8.

fanions, statuettes et décalcomanies de pin up formidables' in one of which a girl 'seulement vêtue de bottes moulantes et d'un boléro frangé, chevauchait dans le sens de la marche une motocyclette Electroglide et le vent de la course entrouvrait le boléro: seins uniques et lèvres éternelles' (108).[28] The link between image and reality is replaced by the interrelation between heavily overworked visual images.

At a more elevated level, a statue by Emile Frémiet outside the Museum of Natural History represents a struggle between a man and a bear, while a more recent one, by Barbedienne, depicts Frémiet sculpting the bear. In the Pré-Catelan, Suzy and Chopin sit in the Shakespeare Garden; *Macbeth* is evoked in the garden by a small patch of heath. The simulacrum reaches ludicrous proportions in the example of the dozen or so paintings of the Parc Palace du Lac Hotel which adorn its own walls, especially as the hotel itself is nothing other than a vast simulacrum. We have already noted the décor of Chopin's bedroom: the dishes on the menu in the restaurant have such elaborately fanciful names that our beleaguered bureaucrat is unable to guess what food they represent. The hotel grounds contain a giant imitation of a game of chess, and the lake is not a real lake, but a manufactured stretch of water covering up a sand quarry. Some of the sand has been retained 'pour inventer une plage' (181) and all the paraphernalia of the seaside has been installed as décor. Everthing has had to be designed in miniature, so that the speed boat is 'un hors-bord nain, racine carrée de chris-craft' (96) tied up to a minuscule jetty. On the other side of the lake is a leisure park which looks more like a lawn: 'ce décor paraissait aussi faux qu'une toile peinte ou qu'une transparence' (182).[29] It is into this décor, and across the fictional lake, that the characters of the fiction *Lac* are spirited away to safety, in a miniature boat.

At this pitch of deliberately displayed artificiality, we are entering the world of the hyperreal, as Baudrillard has termed it, in other words of the simulation which relates only to other simulations, and in which any sense of an originating 'real' has disappeared as reproduction passes from medium to medium and comes to seem more intensely 'real' than any reality. This disappearance of the real is also apparent in the way in which characters construct their identities by appropriating images or models culled from the world of simulation. Rodion Rathenau, himself a stereotype bodyguard, existing within a fiction, reads a spy comic strip and

---

[28] 'photos, drawings, pennants, statuettes and transfers of amazing pin-ups'; 'dressed only in tight-fitting boots and a fringed bolero, sat astride an Electroglide motorbike with the wind blowing open her bolero: unique breasts and eternal lips'.

[29] 'in order to invent a beach'; 'a dwarf outboard motor, a square root of a motorized dinghy'; 'this décor looked as artificial as a painted backdrop or a transparency'.

immediately mentally substitutes himself and Perla for the two main characters. When he succeeds in capturing Chopin he invokes the cinematic model: 'c'est comme au cinéma. Debout contre le mur et les mains sur la tête' (137).[30] Rathenau is being satirized—yet how would the reader, let alone the character, recognize a bodyguard except in terms of representations of bodyguards which they have already met? Echenoz creates an imitation of a bodyguard from the models which are in cultural circulation. Chopin identifies with cinematic heros: he sleeps through most of a film chosen by Mouezy-Eon to while away the time until they can return to the hotel under the cover of dark, but watches Paul being abandoned by woman after woman (as Chopin has been) and turns back to see the unfortunate hero taking a series of physical punishments, as he has just done.

The Frank Sinatra film *Some came running* literally runs in parallel with the action of the novel in chapter 19. After switching from channel to channel (like Suzy with her tapes), Chopin passes directly from an episode of the Mannix detective series, the complications of which recall the plot complications of *Lac*, to the beginning of the 1958 Vincente Minnelli film, which he recognizes: the sight of Sinatra in uniform suddenly inspires Chopin to spring into action. However, by the time Chopin has broken into Suzy's room, Sinatra is back in ordinary clothes and settling into a drinking session. Chopin slides into bed with Suzy, equally abandoning all heroics, and leaves when the credits come up and the announcement of what will be shown next week in the 'rétrospective en cours' (137).[31] This gentle joke also draws attention to the way in which cultural systems interpenetrate each other: although the text is firmly located in contemporary Paris, there is a significant network of references to American cultural icons, to jazz music, and to the culture of the 1950s.[32] Indeed, the oblique references to Barthes's *Mythologies* themselves evoke the culture of 1950s France.

The text overflows with codes, norms, and systems which the characters and reader are called upon to decode or put into play. Chopin decodes not only false brochures and Mouezy-Eon's signals via his paintings but even the sign language used by a deaf and dumb character he comes across in a café: 'rompu aux codes les plus courants, Chopin comprit que l'homme ressassait un problème conjugal, puis celui d'un règlement d'allocation, compliqué par une question de rappel'

---

[30] 'it's just like the movies. Back against the wall and hands above your head.'
[31] 'current retrospective'.
[32] The presence of 1950s and 1960s culture in Echenoz's novels is explored in Jean-Claude Lebrun, *Jean Echenoz* (Paris: Editions du Rocher, 1992).

(94).[33] The free play of the sign, detached from its referent, is embodied by the dot over the letter 'i' which Chopin removes from the fake advertising brochure, drawing attention to: 'le signe typographique qui se décolle, qui se détache et dégringole' (39).[34] Detached from its origin, the sign takes on a life of its own. Is *Lac* then, with its preoccupation with the sign, with codes, with the simulacrum, pure product of the postmodern?

Antidotes and anti-coagulants

The example of the deaf and dumb man above, quietly signing away to himself in his corner, in a soliloquy of domestic problems, underlines the extent to which Echenoz contemplates his contemporary subjects with a humorous and sympathetic eye. Stumbling through the world of signs and consumer images, the anxieties, foibles, and imperfections of an array of characters come strongly, if briefly, to life. Mouezy-Eon fakes a vehicle breakdown in the course of his rescue of Chopin; the breakdown, and the objects he disposes to mimic the event, are pure simulacrum, but as he works his mind is on his son, evoked in the briefest of details: 'son fils unique, conseiller fiscal en instance de divorce à Laval: pas sûr que Jean-François supporte sans mal cette séparation. Pour sa part, Mouezy-Eon n'avait jamais tellement sympathisé avec Jocelyne' (150).[35] These characters will never reappear in the text but the situation is immediately recognizable. The hotel chamber maid whose husband William unaccountably wants to give up his job; the amorous couple in the hotel ground whose illegitimate desires are hampered by a dog; the girl glimpsed crossing the road whose parcel turns out to be a baby—a sense of an endless cast of vibrant lives inhabits the text. Many of the characters are caught up in romantic complications of one kind or another: Frédéric, a minor character who helps Suzy to track down Oswald encapsulates the droll pathos with which such complications are characteristically treated: 'Vous en connaissez beaucoup, des types qui passent leur vie à chercher le mari de la femme de leur vie?' (64).[36] Chopin's love story with Suzy, which

---

[33] 'familiar with the most common codes, Chopin understood that the man was turning over in his mind a marital problem, then a difficulty over the payment of a benefit, complicated by a reminder issue.'

[34] 'the typographical sign which comes unstuck, detaches itself and rolls away.'

[35] 'his only son, a financial adviser in the middle of a divorce in Laval: Jean-François might not cope well with the separation. Mouezy-Eon himself had never really got on well with Jocelyne.'

[36] 'Do you know many blokes who spend their lives searching for the husband of the woman of their life?'

appears doomed after Oswald's reappearance, is suddenly ressucitated as a possibility on the last page of the text, underlining a discreet romanticism which is never very far from the surface.

In the same vein the text exhibits a seam of retro nostalgia, largely relating to the 1950s culture mentioned earlier. The James Bond novels and films themselves are products of the 1950s and 1960s; many of the features recycled in the novel, therefore, such as the platinum blondes with red lipstick and prominent busts of Piranese's fantasy, or the chrome Colt Diamondback with which Colonel Seck saves the day, themselves carry nostalgic connotations. Music, films, architecture, and cars of the period are also evoked; to the examples already mentioned could be added Suzy's memories of herself as a child in the back of her parents' purple and cream Aronde car on Sunday afternoon outings, the music of Nat King Cole, Gerry Mulligan, Fred M. Wilcox's film *Forbidden planet*, the American cartoons *Woody Woodpecker* and *Loopy the Loop*. A degree of sentimentalism connected with the animal and natural world joins the features of the text which work against the more nightmarish vision of a postmodern proliferation of signs without referent. The humanization of animals which has an oyster retreating in terror as Veber reaches out his hand towards it, or Chopin's caged flies watching a television programme about butterflies in China 'comme en prison les types regardent les filles des plages de la Californie' (119) are matched by a zoological approach to human behaviour which devotes a paragraph to Chopin's method of peeling a banana, a description of Oswald 'gonflant ses lèvres en signe d'acquiescement mesuré' (68) or by a reference to Perla Pommeck growing up in a 'biotope aisé' (95).[37] Unexpected comparisons between the contemporary world and the natural universe often provide a sudden change of tack which situates the Baudrillardean universe within a much broader Darwinian perspective; thus an ambulance turns on to 'le périphérique intérieur qu'elle remonta comme un saumon le cours de la Garonne' (145). Suzy and Chopin's sexual discovery of each other is juxtaposed with Chopin's observation of his flies: 'c'était toujours intéressant pour Chopin d'observer à la loupe un bref coït avant de jeter au couple une miette de couenne' (37).[38]

Humour and word-play have been mentioned at almost every turn of this discussion, and the constant stream of inventive possibilities in language is a strong antidote or, as Barthes conceived of it, an

---

[37] 'like male prisoners watching Californian girls on the beach'; 'pursing his lips in a sign of measured agreement'; 'comfortably-off biotope'.

[38] 'the inner ring road which it negotiated like a salmon swimming up the Garonne'; 'Chopin was always interested to be able to observe through his magnifying glass a brief coitus before throwing the couple a bit of rind.'

'anti-coagulant' to the automatisms, the frozen blocks of language which Echenoz catalogues. Sitting in a café Chopin hears the endless repetition of the phrase 'Bienvenue, docteur Bong' emitted by a pinball machine, an automatism first noted and then humorously replayed in a new context several chapters later when Chopin is injected by the bodyguard and loses consciousness: 'Chopin bascula dans le coma. Bienvenue, docteur Bong' (137).[39] The highlighting given to fragments of frozen language simply by selecting them for recording within the text itself is often sufficient to comically underline their inherent absurdity: Suzy's son Jim wears a green tracksuit with the words 'Carolina Moon' inscribed in yellow along his thigh whilst reading a child's comic entitled 'Super géant Piscou'. The television game show he watches uses phrases so worn as to be comic simply in their appearance in a literary text: 'FORMIDABLE, FABIENNE, C'EST MAGNIFIQUE, ET VOICI MA PREMIÈRE QUESTION' intones the presenter and then, inevitably, a moment later comes 'AH, FABIENNE, JE SUIS DÉSOLÉ' (63).[40] The literal possibilities of frozen fragments of language are often humorously alluded to: even in the grim commercial centre visited by Suzy the humorous potential of a sign signalling a special offer on hearts and tongues is self-evident, and we have also seen the same phenomenon at work in the gruesome descriptions of Rungis. But much of the word-play is delighted in with no dark shadow: the workers at the mirror factory behind Suzy's flat carry 'de longues psychés sans se regarder dedans' (50); the flat in which Chopin is briefly held prisoner 'semblait avoir été abandonné en catastrophe par une secte de cynophiles dix-septiémistes aux abois' (152);[41] Chopin sits by the minuscule lake in a 'transatlantique' (116)—the word for a transantlantic liner but also for a deckchair. Unexpected comparisons abound to create humour: the hotel employee who succeeds in manœuvring a huge female guest into her coat 'comme s'il montait une tente en même temps qu'il langeait un nourrisson' (122). Chopin goes about putting handcuffs on Veber 'comme si c'était un cathéter et des compresses qu'il brandissait au lieu des menottes et du Kolibri' (177).[42] Play with names in the text reaches delirious proportions, from the borrowing of the names of famous artists—Chopin, Piranese, Clair—to the creation of cartoon like names—Rodion Rathenau, Perla Pommeck. The name of Maryland, the top boss, inevitably evokes

---

[39] 'Chopin slipped into a coma. Welcome, Dr Bong.'
[40] 'That's fantastic, Fabienne, that's marvellous, and here is my first question'; 'Oh, Fabienne, I'm so sorry.'
[41] 'long swing mirrors ('psyché') without looking at their own reflection in them'; 'seemed to have been abandoned in a hurry by a sect of seventeenth-century specialist dog lovers at bay.'
[42] 'as though he were putting up a tent at the same time as changing a baby's nappy'; 'as though he were brandishing a catheter and compress instead of handcuffs and a Kolibri'.

chicken, and the extraordinary name of Mouezy-Eon evokes a Queneau character, Mounnezergues.[43] Play is a striking feature of the text and one which we need now to examine in the narrative modes and structures of the text's own proceedings.

The modes of the self-conscious text

The novel draws attention to its own functioning in numerous ways. The use of the spy novel conventions is one aspect of this; another is the series of images which function as a *mise-en-abyme* of the novel. In chapter 2 Vito takes a long bus journey through Paris, described as a kind of 'safari photographique [. . .] l'heure étant idéale pour observer toutes sortes de salariés lâchés sur les trottoirs pour y chasser leur nourriture, parfois y déployant leurs parades amoureuses' (12).[44] The idea of the snapshot taken from a moving bus, and the strongly implied zoological perspective, fits well with the observation of fragments of everyday urban life and cameos of characters described above. The snapshot image is taken up again in a more extreme form when Chopin is locked in the flat on the edge of the ring road. The window looks out onto a wall designed to cut down the noise of the traffic, and the wall has glass portholes of a metre or so width. Approaching the window Chopin fills his time trying to guess the make of the passing cars 'dont il voyait filer des bribes par le hublot percé dans le mur antibruit, éclairs de couleur fugitifs, illisibles comme des photos floues' (144).[45] Here the position of the observer of contemporary life is much more constrained in every sense, and the target rather than the observer is moving. In yet another *mise-en-abyme*, Mouezy-Eon, being driven through the outskirts of Paris, takes out his sketch pad and begins to draw 'de petits croquis instantanés de tel ou tel point de vue du paysage qui défilait. Chopin se demandait comment il parvenait à choisir ses sujets dans ce décor: sous l'apparente diversité de la banlieue, toutes les choses y semblaient affectées du même poids, du même goût, nulle forme sur nul fond ne faisait sens, tout était flou' (188).[46] In all these

---

[43] This is noted in William Cloonan's perceptive chapter on Echenoz's writing in *The Contemporary Novel in France* (Gainesville, Fla.: University Press of Florida, 1995), 201–14 (204). Cloonan sees this reference as signalling a debt in Echenoz's fiction to Oulipo, a group founded at a colloquium on Queneau in 1960 which sees literature as above all a ludic exchange between author and reader.

[44] 'photographic safari [...] the time of day being ideal for observing all sorts of workers let out on to the pavements to chase their food, sometimes exhibiting their amorous displays'.

[45] 'which he saw snatches of going past the porthole in the anti-noise barrier, fugitive flashes of colour, unreadable like blurred photos'.

[46] 'instant little sketches drawn from one point of view or another of the scenery going past. Chopin wondered how he managed to choose his subjects in this landscape: beneath the

examples the idea of a rapid series of instant images is present, like the drawings for a cartoon film, or the projection of photographic images on to the cinema screen, and there is a marked lack of confidence in any coherent overall meaning.

Form is never invisible in this text and filmic techniques are often ostentatiously employed as part of a narrative process which constantly seeks an active recognition on the part of the reader. When Chopin looks through the wall above, trying to identify the makes of cars, he succeeds with only one, an ambulance hurtling along the hard shoulder. The narrative then immediately shifts to the inside of the ambulance and sails away with its occupants, abandoning Chopin by this visual link familiar from the cinema. We have no choice but to follow. Even more explicitly filmic techniques are imported into the text in the penultimate chapter when, at a moment of tension, Colonel Seck finds himself challenged by Veber:

> le colonel hésite; ne sachant que répondre, un nouveau blanc se fait jour dans son dispositif. Arrêt sur image: agitées par le vent d'Orient dominant, les branches des arbres proches viennent régulièrement frapper les fenêtres, contrefaisant le bruit du moteur de l'appareil de projection. L'action reprend son rythme lorsque la porte de la suite s'ouvre à nouveau. (174)[47]

Here we have not just an incursion into the filmscript but a self-conscious script which draws attention to itself as film by mimicking the sound of the projector. The concept of the sound-track is also widely used in the text. Characters turn on radios or play their own music in all sorts of circumstances, whether it is Seck searching out English pop music of the 1950s and 1960s on his car radio, Suzy listening to Gerry Mulligan while she works or the pianist in the hotel bar playing 'September Song'. More complex sound-tracks occur when the muffled street sounds coming through the windows in Suzy's flat create a monstrous piano effect, the left hand keeping up a continuous low sound while the right improvises high notes consisting of car horns or breaking glass from the mirror factory, all mixing in with Gerry Mulligan. The ring of the telephone completes the effect. Other recognizably classic cinematic sound effects occur when Chopin has to listen to the noises of Veber's body over his microphone: 'mastication, déglutition, rares hoquets, un claquement de

---

apparent diversity of the suburbs, every object seemed to have been touched by the same force, the same taste, no form made any sense against a background, everything was blurred.'

[47] 'the Colonel hesitates; unsure what to answer, a new blank appears in his system. Freeze frame: blown by a strong easterly wind, the branches of the nearby trees make regular tapping noises on the window, imitating the noise of a projector running. The action starts up again when the the door of the hotel suite reopens.'

langue sonnant ainsi qu'un disjoncteur' (120), or when he himself hurries up the hotel stairs, listening to 'le bruit de son corps comme un orchestre en marche, grosse caisse du cœur, cymbale cloutéee du souffle et maracas des articulations' (135).[48] In these examples a complex of contrasting sound effects emerges, preventing a harmonious whole, and mirroring the disjointed effects of Chopin peering through the holes in the anti-noise barrier. Perhaps the most striking effect of all with dislocated sound, however, is the scene in which Chopin sits by the lake; an accordionist is playing and the notes take off across the waves in the lake 'se grimpant les unes sur les autres selon le parcours aléatoire du vent, les notes n'arrivaient pas forcément à Chopin dans l'ordre prévu par la partition' (117).[49] Here again the text draws attention to its own variance from the model it ostensibly sets out to imitate, whether the model is the spy story or the contemporary world it depicts and necessarily distorts.

Conclusions: Lac(k)?

The title of *Lac* is clearly mischievous: there are two lakes in the story (Lake Geneva and the imitation lake at the Parc Palace du Lac Hotel), neither of which is central to the plot. The hotel lake does, however, suggest a kind of model for the text itself, in that it is a downsized simulation of a real lake, just as the text is a simulation of the spy novel and a downsized model of the more self-important novels of earlier eras. The French word 'lac' is furthermore a homophone of the English word 'lack' and it has been suggested that this bilingual pun is a central motif in the novel: thus, Vito lacks a leg, Suzy lacks her husband Oswald, the French lack information they need about Veber's operations, and, more seriously, humanity at the end of the twentieth century lacks 'genuine ideals or self-knowledge'.[50] It is difficult to resist the pun, given Echenoz's interest in Anglo-Saxon culture and the presence of so many anglicisms in the text itself, and it is also true that 'lack' as a concept is much used by twentieth-century thinkers from Freud and Lacan to Baudrillard. Is Echenoz doing much more, however, than jokily exploiting the literal meaning of this twentieth-century watchword? The text's familiarity with fashionable ideas is

---

[48] 'chewing, swallowing, occasional hiccups, a clicking of the tongue sounding like an electric circuit breaker'; 'the noise of his body like a walking orchestra, the drumming of his heart, the muffled cymbals of his breathing and the maracas of his joints.'

[49] 'piling one on top of another according to the random direction of the wind, the notes did not necessarily reach Chopin in the order laid down by the score.'

[50] See Cloonan, *The Contemporary Novel in France*, 212.

manifest and its thorough immersion in contemporary culture self-evident, but, as I have argued in this chapter, the vision of a postmodern world in which all is driven by signs and simulation is undercut by humour, by an unashamedly romantic, even sentimental and nostalgic vein, by a series of connections set up between the natural universe and human behaviour, and by a recognition that there is an underside of violence which we may indeed care about beneath the seductive surface of consumerism. Above all, *Lac* is marked by a vitality, by an exuberant pleasure in language and its possibilities, and by a concern with readerly pleasure which bodes well for the future of the French novel.

5 Friendship and betrayal: Hervé Guibert's
A L'ami qui ne m'a pas sauvé la vie (1990)

Hervé Guibert died of an AIDS-related illness combined with the effects of a suicide attempt in a Paris hospital in December 1991.[1] Although Guibert had won critical acclaim for a series of fictional and other texts published throughout the 1980s, it was *A l'ami qui ne m'a pas sauvé la vie* (1990), an account of the eight-year period of his life in which he had been HIV positive, which propelled him into the forefront of public consciousness. Like Duras before him, he made a celebrated appearance on 'Apostrophes', on 16 March 1990, alongside fellow AIDS sufferers historian Jean-Paul Aron and novelist Guy Hocquenghem, which produced soaring sales of his book and media star status.[2]

Discussion of AIDS had been gradually developing in France over the decade since the identification of the virus in 1981; by the late 1980s a number of grass-roots organizations were campaigning for sufferers' rights, an agency commissioned by the Socialist government was promoting preventive measures and attempting to combat the social rejection of high-risk groups, and the Front National had launched its own homophobic campaign.[3] In 1991 France had the highest number of AIDS-related deaths in Europe, and the highest number of HIV positive individuals.[4] Nevertheless, public discussion of the subject remained muted, not least because of the association with homosexuality and the central place which heterosexual sex occupies in French culture.[5] Whilst it is true that by the end of the 1980s anti-homosexual legislation in France had disappeared, and that a number of the most important French writers and intellectuals of the twentieth century were generally known to be homosexuals—Proust, Gide, Cocteau, Barthes, Foucault— homosexuality was not perceived as being at the centre of their work. As Christopher Robinson shows in his helpful account of twentieth-century French gay and lesbian writing, it was not until the 1970s, the decade in which the gay rights movement took off, that the literary

[1] See Jean-Pierre Boulé's helpful study Guibert: *A l'ami qui ne m'a pas sauvé la vie* (Glasgow: University of Glasgow French and German publications, 1995), 2 n. 4.

[2] See ibid. 2.

[3] See Robert Harvey, 'Sidaïques/Sidéens: French Discourses on AIDS', *Contemporary French Civilisation*, 16/2, 308–35.

[4] Ibid. 311–12.   [5] See Harvey's comments on this subject.

stereotype of the homosexual as outlaw, haunted by crime, sickness, and evil began to be displaced.[6] The AIDS crisis unfortunately reawakened these sterotypes and the gay community was thus ambivalent about highlighting the virus as a gay issue. However, Guibert unambiguously practises a 'gay signature', placing in his text a discourse of gay sex alongside a chronicle of the progress of the AIDS virus in his body.[7]

Issues of sexuality and the writer's experience of his illness, together with the way in which the medical establishment, the international drugs companies, and others have sought to manage and profit from the disease are clearly crucial to the textual universe of *A l'ami qui ne m'a pas sauvé la vie*, but these issues also act as a window onto other questions: the question of the meaning and status of friendship, signalled in the title, and explored through a variety of figures who enact with Guibert complex rituals of solidarity and betrayal; the issue of writing the self in a dialectical relationship with death, and of writing both self and others in a world in which public confession is rife, and where 'others' include well-known figures, such as his friend the philosopher Michel Foucault; and finally, the issue of time, the time dictated by the progression of the virus, monolithic and unpredictable, and the time of writing which seeks to break up that progress, darting back and forth in a series of feints and mirages. It is logical, however, to begin with the AIDS narrative.

An AIDS chronicle

Guibert was clear that his text is a novel, though the fictional dimension may be above all a margin of manœuvre which both prevents the absolute identification of his characters with people in his circle, and permits him to loosen the straitjacket of documented facts. Unlike Duras, writing her own story at many years' distance, Guibert is using his recent and current life as material, with events overtaking the writing process in the same way in which Serge Doubrovsky's novel *Le Livre brisé* is overtaken by the death of his wife, about whom he is writing. Doubrovsky coined the term 'autofiction' to describe his writing enterprise, and it is also a useful term in relation to Guibert's texts, as well as to Annie Ernaux's work, discussed

---

[6] Christopher Robinson, *Scandal in the Ink. Male and Female Homosexuality in Twentieth-Century French Literature* (London: Cassell, 1995), 96.

[7] The phrase 'gay signature' is taken from the book of the same name in which the editors offer a helpful gloss on the way in which the concept of signature usefully replaces that of identity. See O. Heathcote, A. Hughes and J. Williams (eds.), *Gay Signatures. Gay and Lesbian Theory, Fiction and Film in France, 1945–1995* (Oxford: Berg, 1998).

here in Chapter 6. 'Autofiction' suggests a less grandiloquent genre than that of autobiography, and implicitly recognizes that textual self-construction is not a matter of simple documentation, but engages with the realm of the imagination. Nevertheless, the AIDS narrative does appear to bring a strongly documentary element to the text, in the recording of the progress of the disease in Guibert's body, with supporting facts and figures, in the detailing of the treatments undertaken and their effects, and in offering a series of textbook explanations of various stages of the disease, often voiced by one of the many medical experts who appear in the text. It is particularly at these moments of explanation that the way in which the text functions as an education of the reader becomes apparent. We become familiar in the course of the text with the illnesses symptomatic of the virus, we become accustomed to T4 counts and levels of P24, we are made to confront the full list occupying ten lines of text of the side-effects of AZT: the text succeeds in bringing into literary discourse a language of AIDS which we might more normally encounter in a medical context.

In the opening chapters of the text, the history of Guibert's own relation to the virus is not approached chronologically; however, in a typical writing manœuvre, we are suddenly reminded, in chapter 18, that there are two AIDS narratives: the narrative of his illness up to the moment at which he began writing, and the deterioration of his condition as he writes. After the revelation in chapter 18 that he is waiting for further test results, a brutally telescoped chronology is given in the following chapter: in 1980 he had hepatitis, in 1983 an abscess in his throat, in 1987 shingles. In 1988 he is confirmed as HIV positive but, after three months of believing he is condemned to die, he is led by his friend Bill to believe that he will be cured by a new miracle drug to which Bill has access. Writing in early January 1989, he is still uncertain about this possibility, but has learned in the last month that the crucial T4 count is continuing to fall, and that he must now consider taking AZT, a highly toxic drug which attacks the bone marrow and freezes the production of red and white blood cells, but which should give him up to another eighteen months of life. The results he awaits at the start of the writing process eventually prompt him to begin his AZT treatment in March, only to halt it again in October. Here the narrative falls silent.

Intermingled with the charting of the progress of the symptoms and the textbook explanations are a series of striking metaphors which work to represent the nature of the virus in a quite different way. In chapter 4, for example, Guibert sets out the current levels and significance of his T4 count, introducing a set of medical terms and a precise list of dates and numbers, and then switches into an analogy with an electronic game:

Avant l'apparition du sida, un inventeur de jeux électroniques avait dessiné la progression du sida dans le sang. Sur l'écran du jeu pour adolescents, le sang était un labyrinthe dans lequel circulait le Pacman, un shadok jaune actionné par une manette, qui bouffait tout sur son passage, vidant de leur plancton les différents couloirs, menacé en même temps par l'apparition proliférante de shadoks rouges encore plus gloutons. Si l'on applique le jeu du Pacman, qui a mis du temps à se démoder, au sida, les T4 formeraient la population initiale du labyrinthe, les T8 seraient les shadoks jaunes, talonnés par le virus HIV, symbolisé par les shadoks rouges, avides de boulotter de plus en plus de plancton immunitaire. (13–14)[8]

Drawing on the American game's construction of a dog-eat-dog world, this boldly visual image captures in stark terms Guibert's sense that a remorseless war is being waged in his body—it conveys his sense of loss of control and associates the virus with a futuristic and evil universe, an association which reappears on a number of occasions in the text. The populist nature of the image—Pac-Man was one of the earliest video games and became a craze in the early 1980s—is an indicator of the desire to open up the AIDS narrative to a wide audience, and the American origin of the game darkly heralds the later suggestion, formulated by Bill, that 'le sida aura été un génocide américain. Les Américains ont précisément ciblé ses victimes: les drogués, les homosexuels, les prisonniers' (251).[9] In the telescoped chronology of events given in chapter 19, referred to earlier, there is also a strong suggestion that either Guibert or his lover Jules caught the virus from an American partner, just as it is implied that Muzil (Foucault) caught the virus in San Francisco.

Only a few pages later, in chapter 6, another set of metaphors is employed to make the point that AIDS is not an illness as such but 'un état de faiblesse et d'abandon qui ouvre la cage de la bête qu'on avait en soi, à qui je suis contraint de donner pleins pouvoirs pour qu'elle me dévore' (17).[10] This time stressing Muzil's intuition, confirmed by medical research, that the virus originated with African monkeys, AIDS is described as an illness brought about by sorcery. The metaphor of the

---

[8] 'Before the appearance of AIDS, an inventor of electronic games had already portrayed the way the virus behaves in the blood. On the screen of a game for adolescents, the blood was a labyrinth in which the Pac-Man circulated, a yellow munchie controlled by a lever which gobbled up everything it met, stripping the various passageways of their plankton, and itself under threat from even greedier munchies. If you consider the AIDS virus in terms of the the Pac-Man game, which held its popularity for some time, then the T4s would be the original population of the labyrinth, and the T8s would be the yellow munchies, pursued by the HIV virus, symbolized by the red munchies and their insatiable appetite for immunological plankton.'

[9] 'AIDS will turn out to have been an American genocide. The Americans targeted their victims very precisely: drug addicts, homosexuals, prison inmates.'

[10] 'a state of weakness and surrender which uncages the beast within us all, and which I must give free rein to devour me'.

caged animal within, unleashed by black magic, conveys a sense of primeval fatality and of autodestruction. Both images are savage and break away sharply from the objective tone of the facts and figures. Two other modes of apprehending the virus are embedded in the narrative. One is a startlingly affirmative approach, deriving from the fact that AIDS is 'une maladie à paliers, un très long escalier qui menait assurément à la mort mais dont chaque marche représentait un apprentissage sans pareil' (192).[11] From this perspective, the virus offers its victims the opportunity to savour life; in an almost existentialist sense, the sufferer becomes more conscious of his own fate: 'le sida, en fixant un terme certifié à notre vie, six ans de séropositivité, plus deux ans dans le meilleur des cas avec l'AZT ou quelques mois sans, faisait de nous des hommes pleinement conscients de leur vie, nous délivrait de notre ignorance' (193).[12] However, it is precisely this certainty which Bill's promise undermines. Running counter to this idea of existentialist control is another more dominant trope focusing on the *modus operandi* of the virus as decoy and delusion. Describing the promised new drug, Bill explains that the virus works by dividing itself 'pour mettre en jeu un processus de leurre [. . .] C'est l'enveloppe du virus qui fait office de leurre: dès que l'organisme décrypte sa présence, il envoie ses T4 à la rescousse, qui, massés sur l'enveloppe et comme aveuglés par elle, ne détectent pas le noyau du virus, qui traverse incognito la mêlée pour aller infecter les cellules' (276).[13] The virus is said to enact a bullfight ritual, in which the envelope plays the part of the red cape, the virus nucleus that of the sword, and the human body becomes the exhausted animal. The drug works by allowing the body to see through this diversion and reactivate its immune system. An image is again thrown up here which dramatically encapsulates the working of the virus and connects it to ancient savage rituals, as well as to the performative gender parade which the bullfighter, in his elegantly feminized dress, inevitably suggests.

The trope of the decoy is not however confined to the virus—it spreads into the forces designed to combat the condition. One obvious example is that of the wonder drug itself—for Guibert, it will prove a mirage, hovering on the horizon of the text but never materializing. Another example is that

---

[11] 'an illness with stages, a very long staircase leading certainly to death but of which each step represents a unique opportunity for self-discovery'.

[12] 'in putting a fixed term on our lifespan, six years of seropositivity, plus two years at best with AZT, or a few months without, AIDS made us fully conscious of our lives, and freed us from ignorance.'

[13] 'running a decoy operation [...]. It's the viral envelope that functions as a decoy: as soon as the body detects its presence, T4 cells are sent to the rescue and, massing on to the viral envelope, they behave as if they were blinded by it, incapable of detecting the virus nucleus which slips incognito through the fray to set about infecting other cells.'

of the 'double blind' procedure used by medical research to test drugs, in which neither patient not researcher knows whether a given patient is receiving the drug or a substitute. Before Guibert hears of Bill's new drug, Doctor Chandi suggests he joins the trials for another drug (in itself an illusion since Chandi suspects it, rightly, to be ineffective), and explains the research procedure. Fascinated by the idea of the procedure, Guibert nevertheless refuses to submit himself to a game of illusion in which the stakes are so high as to risk the sanity of its participants. Doubles and delusions spread to all corners of the text, and we will be returning to the theme, most particularly in the consideration of writing, perhaps the most crucial snare of all.[14]

Running alongside the chronicle of the symptoms is the account of the way in which the condition is managed by a series of doctors and medical institutions. The sections which focus on this account are some of the most difficult for the reader to deal with as the anguished and humiliated narrator recounts the indifference, incompetence, and cupidity which he encounters within the medical establishment. The account of his visit to the Claude-Bernard Hospital which occupies the whole of the longest chapter of the text is placed early in the narrative (chapter 18) and functions as a paradigm for the institutionalized violence to which the narrator feels subjected. The three preceding chapters recount in turn his dealings with three different doctors, each of whom fails to identify the virus (about which, it should be said, almost nothing was actually known at the time) and diagnoses another condition with confidence. The heavy irony and surreal dimensions of these accounts prepare the Claude-Bernard visit, which is nevertheless more lurid and accusatory in tone. The memory of the visit fills the narrator with terror: he narrates in detail the nightmare of his journey in a weakened state through a strike-bound Paris to the hospital, and his discovery that the hospital is in the last stage of closure. Instead of a state-of-the-art clinic he finds a décor in which 'tout était désert, pillé, froid et humide, comme saccagé' (56),[15] a phantom hospital which reminds him of his visit to Dachau.

The highly public nature of the way in which patients are handled in the hospital leaves him cowering in a corner, dreading recognition; the

---

14 Other false doubles and illusions include Guibert's newly born nephew, whom his sister decides to call 'Hervé Guibert' (see 72–3); the delayed results which leave Guibert 'entirely ignorant of what he already knows' (71); the striptease spectacle in which the lights come up and the men, briefly selected to take part in a sexual ritual, suddenly become weary workers again (67–8).

15 'the whole place was deserted, pillaged, cold and damp, as if it had been vandalized.' The comparison to Dachau is one of a number of references in the text which suggest a relation, perhaps of an indirect kind, between the AIDS narrative and the holocaust narrative, discussed in Chapter 3. See also the reference in chapter 4 (13) to Resnais's famous documentary film on the concentration camps, *Nuit et brouillard* ('Night and Fog').

quantity of blood removed fills so many test tubes that he feels like an animal in an abattoir, and is convinced that it is being taken without his permission for use in research rather than simply for the necessary tests. Absurdist and surreal humour abound, a coping strategy which leads him to transform the nurses squashed into a small space and frenetically repeating the same mechanical gestures into circus acrobats, and to laugh at the idea that he could die in one of the hospital's deserted and inter-minable corridors without ever being found. The barely controlled hys-teria which drives the account and surfaces particularly in the absurdist elements and in the extreme comparisons (Dachau, the abattoir) partly derives from the fact that the narrator is still waiting at the time of writing for the test results of that visit, but it is also clear that his own doctor's failure to give him the right information beforehand, and the failure of both the doctor and the nurse he deals with to realize that he is sensitive to their every remark, leave him feeling reduced to the status of pathological body. The surrealist vision of the institutional tends to reoccur in the narrative at moments of particular anxiety and tension: thus when he visits the Vatican chemist in Rome in an urgent attempt to find a drug for a new symptom, he describes a futuristic décor, worthy of Kubrick's *Clockwork Orange*, in which nuns sell perfume and priests hand out aspirins and condoms. When he decides to acquire the drug which could permit him to end his life a kindly lady chemist orders it specially for him, sells it to him joyfully and sends him smilingly on his way 'd'un air radieux et solonnel, comme si elle eût été une employée d'une agence de voyages qui venait de me vendre un tour du monde, et me souhaitait bon vent' (261).[16] This last example shows how even an act of well-intentioned kindness can take on quite a different meaning within the context of a fatal illness, and within the social and institutional structure which places control of an individual's death in the hands of others.

The narrator's comings and goings between Paris and Rome further produce a sense of the cultural relativity of the experience of illness and its treatment: the Spallanzani Hospital in Rome is less impersonal than the Claude-Bernard, but the laxity of Italian procedures leads to a mix-up in the patients' blood. When he finally decides to begin on AZT treatment, his French doctor prescribes twice as much of the drug as the Italian doctor, who states frankly that too little is known about the drug or its effects for there to be any authoritative view of how or when it should be taken. The French doctor describes this as dangerous talk, preferring to maintain a screen of infallibility.

---

[16] 'with a radiant and solemn air, as if she had been an assistant in a travel agency who had just sold me a world tour and was wishing me bon voyage.'

At the level of the doctors themselves, Dr Chandi, the French doctor recommended initially to Guibert by Bill, emerges as a largely positive figure, tirelessly organizing appointments and help for his patient and gently leading him to a consciousness of each new stage of his illness. However, even he is suspected by the narrator of working hand in hand with Bill and the international drugs companies. AIDS is shown to be a career opportunity for medical practitioners and researchers, and to represent the possibility of making vast fortunes. Bored by his professional activities, Bill is attracted by the idea that 'il n'y avait plus rien de vraiment intéressant à entreprendre aujourd'hui que la lutte contre le sida' (187), but he is also keenly aware that the development of a new vaccine is 'le moyen de faire vraiment fortune' (187).[17] When a new vaccine does appear to be emerging, Bill tells the narrator that the great danger is that the 'capitalist adventurers' will gain control of it, forcing the price up to as much as a thousand dollars for a dose that can only save the world if it costs ten dollars. At a less avaricious level, Guibert also sketches in a cruel portrait of those for whom AIDS became a social ladder, including Foucault's companion, fictionalized as Stéphane, for whom Foucault's death opens up a new career in the creation of an organization combatting AIDS. The in-fighting which occurs between the trio fronting the organization is portrayed with malicious humour: one of the trio remarks to the narrator 'Nous avons deux fléaux à combattre, le sida et Stéphane' (140) whilst another friend comments that 'Stéphane se pendrait sans doute de désespoir le jour où l'on trouverait un remède contre le sida' (141).[18]

The satirical awareness displayed of the social and institutional structuring of the phenomenon of AIDS can in part be read as a bow to Foucault, whose work on the history of the clinic as institution and the history of sexuality is alluded to in the text.[19] On another level, it also acts as a tonic element counteracting the manifestations of physical decline and suffering in the narrative. The entry of the pathological body into literature is not new—many readers will be familiar with narratives of tuberculosis and plague—but it is nevertheless true that, for the 1980s and early 1990s, AIDS had a particularly dread status, and the exposure of the

---

[17] 'there was nothing more crucial to tackle today than the fight against AIDS'; 'the way to make a serious fortune.'

[18] 'We're fighting two battles, one against AIDS and one against Stéphane'; 'Stéphane will probably commit suicide in despair the day a cure for AIDS is discovered.'

[19] Lawrence Schehr discusses interestingly the way in which Foucault's thinking is both cryptically present in the text and simultaneously challenged by it. See L. Schehr, 'Cippus: Guibert', in *Alcibiades at the Door. Gay Discourses in French Literature* (Stanford, Calif.: Stanford University Press, 1995), 155–96.

body in this context involves special taboos. When procedures break down in the Italian hospital and Guibert has to carry his own blood down for analysis there is a sense, as Jean-Pierre Boulé remarks, in which this event is an analogy for the way in which Guibert carries his body to us as readers.[20] The narrator complains about the fact that he is forced to exhibit to Bill all the details of his physical condition—'devoir répondre à tout moment du taux de ses T4 qui dégringolent, c'est pire que de montrer ce qu'on a dans la culotte' (264–5)—but, in the narrator–reader relation, he is essentially displaying at will rather than being forced into admission.[21] The narrator's control and management of this display makes it bearable and less likely to create the indignant public reaction which met, for example, Simone de Beauvoir's exposure of Sartre's ageing and incontinent body, in *La Cérémonie des adieux* (1981). However, the narrative of *A l'ami qui ne m'a pas sauvé la vie* goes beyond most texts displaying the pathological body in that it combines this with the display of the sexual body, and one engaging in acts which lie outside the norms of heterosexual literary discourses. Two sets of taboos are thus engaged with simultaneously. As Michael Worton writes, in relation to Guibert's texts, the status of the male body in Western contemporary society is already problematic—it becomes even further problematized when it is represented not as a sign of male power, of mental and physical health, but rather as a site of illness and of erotic pleasure.[22] The two are sometimes combined, as in the painful scene in which the narrator tries to re-enact with his partner Jules their former sexual pleasures, but the knowledge of their common fate turns their activities into a macabre ritual. The reader is pinned down in this scene by a paralysing sense of horror at the way their fate prevents even this intimate act from creating a sense of union between the partners, accompanied by an uncomfortable sense (no doubt varying with the reader) that the violence and the detail of the acts described are themselves outside the norms of high literary discourse. Other episodes in the text make it abundantly clear that both Jules and the narrator consider themselves free to engage in sexual relations entered into purely for physical pleasure. Given that these relations are almost certainly the cause of their illness, the text appears to offer a direct challenge to the potentially homophobic readerly response.

---

[20] Boulé, Guibert: *A l'ami qui ne m'a pas sauvé la vie* (1995), 22–3.

[21] 'having to come clean at any moment on the level your T4s have plunged to is worse than being asked to drop your trousers.' See Boulé's discussion of 'Writing the body' in his *A l'ami qui ne m'a pas sauvé la vie*, 9–25.

[22] See Michael Worton, 'En (d)écrivant le corps, en imaginant l'homme: le "vrai corps" de Guibert', in Ralph Sarkonak (ed.), *Le Corps textuel de Hervé Guibert* (Paris: Lettres Modernes, 1997), 63–77, 67.

Masters and timelords

'Pauvre petit Guibert, ex-maître du monde' (233):[23] thus the narrator describes himself at the close of chapter 73, a chapter in which he seems to bow his head and metaphorically lay down his arms in double defeat before the literary style of the Austrian writer Thomas Bernhard, and the level of his T4 count, which the narrator now brings himself to admit has fallen to the point at which his options are fast disappearing. Earlier, Guibert's textual self-construction repeatedly suggests that he considers himself to have a special relationship with destiny: on the one hand he presents himself as a pariah figure, the devil besides whom everyone avoids sitting on the train and whom the sombrero-sporting tourists drunk on tequila in a Mexican plane appear especially invented to torture; on the other he believes himself to be one of the elect, a figure whom destiny has cast as AIDS victim only to allow him a unique and miraculous escape. There is an irresistible parallel with the Romantic poet— Chatterton, seeking solace from a brutal materialist world in poetry and, eventually, suicide, or the albatross figure of the Baudelaire poem, made fun of by ordinary mortals but becoming king of the skies in flight. In a way the text is above all the story of the loss of this illusion of salvation of the elect.

One important element of the illusion is the series of relationships which he enjoys with illustrious and powerful figures of his time: Muzil/ Foucault and Bill, at the top of the hierarchy, the film actress Marine/ Isabelle Adjani one rung down, and, in the background, figures such as the television presenter Christine Ockrent. In the event both Bill and Marine turn out to be false gods, bearing gifts which melt away when Guibert has most need of them; only Muzil does not disappoint Guibert and maintains the profile of the timelord, untouched even by the disease which destroys him. The question of whether Guibert himself betrays Foucault by recounting details of his death and his sexual practises was one much commented on at the time of publication, and was raised by the interviewer Bernard Pivot in Guibert's appearance on 'Apostrophes'. The obsessional desire to know the intimate details of the life of public figures has been much scrutinized in the 1990s, in the wake of public interest in the life of the royal family, in Britain, and in the Clinton– Monica Lewinsky affair in the United States. Can Guibert be said to be simply cynically feeding this desire? The textual construction of the narrator's relationship with Muzil suggests that he cannot. When Jules

---

[23] 'Poor little Guibert, ex-master of the world'.

cuts off the narrator's golden locks, converting him without warning from a cherub to a deathshead, Muzil's reaction is described at length:

> Je suis heureux que le geste de Jules fît que je n'eus pas à cacher à Muzil vivant ma vraie tête d'homme de bientôt trente ans, car il eut ce jour-là, après avoir lutté en lui-même contre un mouvement d'effroi et de recul, la générosité, à force de concentration, d'admettre cette tête enfin vraie, et de déclarer qu'au fond il la préférait à la tête qui avait fait qu'il m'avait aimé, ou plus précisément qu'il la trouvait plus juste, et plus adéquate à ma personnalité que ma charmante tête d'angelot bouclé. Il se déclarait finalement ravi du sacrifice de Jules, et il en tapait de joie dans ses mains, voilà comment était Muzil, cet ami irremplaçable. (94)[24]

Muzil's generosity here, in concentrating on how to integrate this new image of Guibert into what he knows of him, instead of focusing on the disappointment and even betrayal expressed by others in Guibert's circle, is only one of the many gifts which Guibert describes him bearing. Muzil is indeed an 'irreplaceable friend' for the narrator, and his embodiment of this key value in the text's universe has an important function, acting as the counterweight to the friend of the title who cannot be counted upon. At the same time Muzil is also an avatar of the illness and death which awaits the narrator; Muzil's death takes place four years before the narrator is confirmed as HIV positive, but already, as the latter consigns the details of Muzil's sufferings to his notebook he has 'une certitude qu'en plus de l'amitié nous étions liés par un sort thanatologique commun' (105).[25]

Muzil's fate throws up a huge shadow on the wall which Guibert is aware he cannot match. A few months before his death Muzil gives Guibert a copy of Marcus Aurelius's *Pensées*, explaining that the work begins with a series of thanks 'à ses aînés, aux différents membres de sa famille, à ses maîtres, remerciant spécifiquement chacun, les morts en premier, pour ce qu'ils lui avaient appris et apporté de favorable pour la suite de son existence' (78).[26] Guibert cannot match Muzil's strength in not telling his companion of his illness, and in maintaining an apparently

---

[24] 'I'm glad that Jules's act meant that I did not have to hide from Muzil while he was still alive my real face, the face of a man about to be thirty, because that day, after he had struggled against his own impulse to recoil in fright, he had the generosity to make himself concentrate on it and to accept it as finally my real face, and to declare that actually he preferred it to the face which had first appealed to him, or more accurately that he found it truer and better suited to my personality than my charming little curly-haired cherub face. He declared himself to be in the end delighted by Jules's sacrifice, clapping his hands with pleasure over it, that's how Muzil was, a friend like no other.'

[25] 'a feeling of certainty that we were linked not only by friendship but by a common thanatological destiny.'

[26] 'to his elders, to the different members of his family, to his teachers, thanking each one individually in turn for what they had taught him, beginning with the dead, and for the way they had changed his future for the better.'

stoic serenity. However, at the time of the gift of the Marcus Aurelius book, Muzil expresses his intention to put on paper what he himself has learned from Guibert, suggesting here a reciprocity in the relationship, despite Muzil's fame and status, which distinguishes it sharply from Guibert's relationships with his other 'maîtres'. Perhaps, as some commentators suggested at the time of publication, Foucault was perfectly well aware that Guibert would create a fictional existence for him; though Guibert records his friend's recoil from his public identity, his invention of pseudonyms and his avoidance of other diners' eyes in restaurants, Foucault admired Guibert's writing, his self-textualization, and knew that his own life would soon be being represented by biographers whose accounts could not carry the affective charge of Guibert's.[27] The responsibility of the friend to select and present his or her own image of the dead is underlined through Guibert's insistence on his admiration of Christine Ockrent's choice of a clip of Foucault laughing, shown on the news headline on the evening of his death, a clip which both warms Guibert's heart and undermines necrological norms, just as Guibert's inclusion of Foucault's sexual pleasures undermines our expectations of an account of the life of a great thinker.

If Muzil is the ultimate timelord, the master who teaches Guibert but who, in his humility, also receives, Bill is constructed as a 'friend' who cannot bear the obligations of friendship, a man who must always be in charge of any social relation, using his money and power to intervene in a web of friendships, 'fonçant avec sa Jaguar pour kidnapper l'un d'entre nous et l'inviter à dîner dans quelque grand restaurant' (197).[28] The initiatory stage in the relationship between Bill and the narrator, situated fifteen years earlier, precisely enacts one of these projected kidnappings, as Bill casually approaches the 18-year-old Guibert in the drugstore Saint-Germain and invites him to Africa. 'Vous savez, ce n'est pas du tout compliqué d'aller en Afrique' (189),[29] proffers Bill, proposing to take Guibert along in the light aeroplane which he flys himself. This Saint-Exupéry like vision of the man in his flying machine impresses the young Guibert enormously—and yet, at the last moment, having had the necessary vaccinations and made his preparations, Guibert walks away, beginning a power struggle between himself and the older man of which the miracle drug offer enacts the final stage.

The vocabulary used to present Bill in the chapters in which he first announces the miracle drug is suffused with heroic, salvatory lyricism:

---

[27] See for example Raymond Bellour, 'Trompe-la-mort', *Magazine littéraire* (Apr. 1990), 54–6.
[28] 'charging in with his Jaguar to kidnap one of us and invite us out to dinner in a grand restaurant'.
[29] 'Going to Africa is perfectly easy, you know'.

Bill makes his announcement at a last supper scenario, dispensing hope to the lost as a man closely involved in a discovery 'qui allait sauver l'humanité de son plus haut péril contemporain' (187). The narrator counts himself as a 'phénomène du destin' (189) simply because he is close to Bill and Bill himself, 'n'était-il pas, davantage que moi, un de ces phénomènes stupéfiants du destin, un de ces monstres absolus du sort, qu'ils semblent tordre et sculpter à leur guise?' (190). As a child Bill is said to have overcome polio 'par un seul effort de sa volonté ou par un miracle du hasard [. . .] comme un enfant s'assied sur un lion furieux' (190).[30] Lion-tamer, saviour, master of the skies and of destiny, Bill appears as the ultimate fantasy hero, straight from the pages of a boy's adventure story. This swashbuckling fantasy reaches its climax when Guibert imagines Bill making a romantic bid for freedom from the research system and the 'capitalist adventurers' in America, whose operations leave no place for friendship: 'Mais moi j'aimerais que Bill assomme Mockney pour lui voler son vaccin, et me l'apporte dans le coffre-fort glacé de son petit avion de fonction, celui qui faisait la navette entre Ouagadougou et Bobodioulasso, et qu'il s'abîme avec l'avion et le vaccin qui m'aurait sauvé dans l'océan Atlantique' (242).[31] Instead, Guibert is faced with betrayal: Bill chooses to save Eduardo instead, Eduardo who is barely in need of treatment and whose claim on Bill is sufficiently weak to allow Bill to savour to the full his status as *deus ex machina*. Guibert announces grimly to Dr Chandi that 'Bill est un fantoche [. . .] ce ne sera jamais un héros' (281).[32] This realization punctures more than Guibert's idealization of his 'friend'— it brings to an end the last illusion that a miraculous escape from an imminent death can be managed, and brings with it the end of the narrative. Only two slender fragments of the text follow: one, chapter 99, enacts a revenge by proxy scenario in which Bill, having picked up in his Jaguar a young man running barefoot along the motorway finds himself pursued and harassed by a new outsider figure, who refuses to be contained and satisfied by the crumbs Bill is prepared to offer. The closing fragment addresses Bill directly: 'Jusqu'où souhaites-tu me voir sombrer? Pends-toi Bill!' (284). This final act of interpellation of Bill, combined with a rejection of him, is an important closing act, signalling the end of the illusions

---

[30] 'which would save humanity from its greatest contemporary peril'; 'phenomenon of destiny'; 'wasn't he, even more than me, one of those stupefying phenomena of destiny, one of those absolute monsters who seem able to twist and shape destiny at will?'; 'a single effort of will or by a miracle chance [. . .] like a child who sits on the back of an enraged lion'.

[31] 'But I want Bill to knock Mockney's brains out, steal his vaccine and fly it to me in the cooler of his little company plane, the one he used to fly between Ouagadougou and Bobodioulasso, and I want the plane to crash with Bill and the vaccine that would have saved my life into the Atlantic Ocean.'

[32] 'Bill is all show, [. . .] he'll never be a hero.'

referred to above and opening the way forward for the direct addressing of the title of the text. It is rare for a title to emerge so strongly from the very end of a narrative but in this case it seems inconceivable that the title could have pre-dated the writing process. 'J'ai enfin retrouvé mes jambes et mes bras d'enfant' (284) writes the narrator in the closing sentence but, in a spirit contrary to the biblical story in which Christ warns Peter that he will need God when he becomes old and infirm, Guibert finds his moral and psychological independence at the very moment of his physical weakness.[33]

Writing time

The question of the title returns us to the question of writing and to the form of the text. In a later work Guibert refers to *A l'ami qui ne m'a pas sauvé la vie* as a letter, and one to which many readers replied.[34] However, the title has an unusual—perhaps unique, notes Ralph Sarkonak[35]— status in appearing to be a dedication promoted to the rank of title, an amalgam well suited to the notion of 'autofiction'. To this ambiguity can be added the uncertain identity of the 'friend', at least until the end of the narrative, and the apparent paradox of directing a narrative at a friend who has failed the writer.[36] However, as suggested above, it can be read as a statement of strength rather than as an act of aggression. The text is divided into one hundred sections, many of which are only two or three pages in length; the reading experience is less that of a novel than that of reading a volume of correspondence, or, given the interest exhibited in the text in visual images, of turning the pages of a photograph album. This fragmented structure allows frequent switches between narration

[33] 'How far do you want to see me go down? Take a running jump Bill!'; 'At last I have rediscovered the arms and legs I had as a child.' There is an echo here of Michel, the protagonist of Gide's *L'Immoraliste* (1902), who comes upon Christ's words to Peter just as he is recovering his strength after a serious illness and turning away from God.

[34] See *Le Protocole compassionel* (Paris: Gallimard, 1991) in which he refers to *A l'ami qui ne m'a pas sauvé la vie* as 'une lettre qui a été directement téléfaxée dans le cœur de cent mille personnes' ('a letter faxed straight to the heart of a hundred thousand people'). The later book carries the dedication: 'A toutes celles et à tous ceux qui m'ont écrit pour *A l'ami qui ne m'a pas sauvé la vie*. Chacune de vos lettres m'a bouleversée' ('To all those who wrote to me about *To the friend who did not save my life*. Every one of your letters moved me deeply').

[35] See his detailed analysis of the question in 'Du para- au métatexte: *A l'ami qui ne m'a pas sauvé la vie*', in *Le corps textuel de Hervé Guibert* (Paris: Lettres modernes, 1997), 155–85.

[36] I have explained in the preceding section that I take the friend to be Bill. Sarkonak proposes other possible candidates: Jules, Muzil, the body of readers, the book itself. See Sarkonak, 'Du para- au métatexte', 160.

of episodes from the past and a focus on the writing present. Time does not move forward in a linear drive; the narrative is above all a 'reordering of time', a desperate and doomed attempt to subvert the time of the virus which moves on inexorably towards death.[37]

The first seventeen chapters roam back and forth over the years since 1981 in which the narrator first heard of AIDS, dip back towards 1977 when he met Muzil, and return to the writing present in late December of 1988 and the beginning of January 1989. However, this leisurely approach is suddenly interrupted by the announcement in chapter 18 that the narrator, writing on what he initially records as being 4 January, has only another seven days to wait for his latest set of results, and that that is the date he had set for completion of the narrative of his illness to date. The race between writing and the progression of the virus becomes starkly evident as the narrator launches headlong into the long account of his visit to the Claude-Bernard hospital, and the brutal chronology of AIDS time in chapter 19, discussed earlier. At the end of this chronology of symptoms and signs, of sexual encounters and of prayers to ward off the inevitable, he notes: 'c'est cette chronologie-là qui devient mon schéma, sauf quand je découvre que la progression naît du désordre' (19). The time of writing is not the time of the virus progression, though each inform and inhibit the other: 'Ce livre qui raconte ma fatigue me la fait oublier, et en même temps chaque phrase arrachée à mon cerveau [. . .] ne me donne que davantage envie de fermer les paupières' (70).[38] Writing cannot win outright, even though Guibert boldly asserts his investment in writing rather than in living, and writing must therefore become a series of feints, teases, and illusions, a theme noted earlier. Each episodic chapter may start off in an entirely new direction, in a new time frame. Each may pick up the threads of an earlier chapter, like a conversation temporarily interrupted.

There are numerous structural feints and devices, beginning with the apparently perfectly planned number of one hundred chapters, which self-evidently do not in fact enact a balanced linear narrative with an opening, a development, and a concluding phase. Is the central narrative thread the development of the virus, or the development of Guibert's consciousness of the virus, or the current development of the virus, or the history of Guibert's illusion, as suggested above? If the latter, it might

---

[37] The phrase 'the reordering of time' is Lawrence Schehr's: see his excellent chapter on Guibert in *Alcibiades at the door. Gay discourses in French literature*, referred to in n. 19.

[38] 'that's the chronology which I'm using as my outline, except when I see that progress arises from disorder'; 'This book which narrates my fatigue makes me forget it, and at the same time every sentence that I wrench from my brain [. . .] only makes me want to close my eyelids even more.'

be noted that once the confession that he is awaiting new results is made, the narrative recounts first Marine's betrayal (chapters 26 onwards) then the final stages of Muzil's illness (chapters 31 to 41) before beginning, in chapter 59, on the narrative of Bill's betrayal which occupies the rest of the narrative. Some commentators have suggested that there is an evident narrative development at the midway point, since it is in chapter 49 that Guibert has his positive HIV results confirmed, and in chapter 50 that he sets about the practical arrangements he needs to make as a result of knowing that his death will follow in the space of a few short years at most.[39] However, a case could equally be made for identifying chapters 23 and 73 as key turning-points, if his current state of consciousness is taken to be the driving force of the narrative, rather than the history of his condition, since chapter 23 is the point at which the writer confesses that he is awaiting the results which will tell him if he is entering the final AZT phase, and chapter 73 marks the point at which he confesses that he has the results, and that they are not good. However, even these points mark not the moments at which the narrator becomes aware of these facts but the moment at which he resolves to tell the reader—thus the focus of the narrative becomes the moment of writing, the relationship with the reader, rather than the actual dates dictated by others. Here the notion of writing as taking control of time is apparent. There are several false endings to the narrative: the narrator tells us in chapter 23 that he had intended to complete the narrative of his illness by the time he receives his results, an intention which is not achieved, except in so far as that by chapter 73, he is narrating as past time a period which was originally writing time (in other words, narrating events taking place after 26 December 1988, the day on which he begins writing). In chapter 78 he describes himself as finishing his book (in March 1989), but the narrative continues and actually terminates in October 1989. Writing is again control.

Within this overall schema of control, writing can be manic. When Guibert contemplates committing suicide he considers how he would pass the time between swallowing his digitaline and death—in listening to music? masturbating? Instead he awaits his 'natural' death writing books: 'continuer à écrire des livres, et à dessiner, tant et tant et en veux-tu en voilà, jusqu'à la déraison' (235). The compulsive delirious writing stream evoked here is related to his desire to write 'tous les livres possibles [. . .] et de dévorer ces livres presque simultanément dans la

---

[39] See in particular F. Reymondet, 'La fin: issue fatale, issue narrative dans *A l'ami qui ne m'a pas sauvé la vie* d'Hervé Guibert', *Dalhousie French Studies*, 39/40 (1997), 181–91.

marge rétrécie du temps, et de dévorer le temps avec eux, voracement' (74).[40] Although most of the chapters are brief, the elaborate construction and length of sentences within them sometimes appear as an expression of this desire to write without end, to pile on clause after clause in a display of showmanship defeating natural breathing and escaping standard syntax. The incursion of strongly surrealist visions has already been mentioned, but there are also many realist scenes located in familiar Parisian or Italian streets and restaurants. The desire to write all possible books fills this single book, as does the desire not only to write but to paint and to draw and take photographs. Chapter 24 explores at some length his response to a reproduction of a painting by Antonio Mancini, entitled 'Dopo il duello' ('After the duel'), with at its centre a young man in despair, dressed in black, a bloodstained shirt and sword at his feet. Guibert writes: 'Le tableau n'avouait pas l'anecdote de son sujet pour le murer, comme j'aime toujours, sur une énigme: le jeune modèle était-il l'assassin de la victime emportée hors du tableau? ou le témoin? était-il son frère? son amant? son fils?' (76).[41] At one level this uncertainty over the young man's identity mirrors the possible assassin concealed within Bill's status as friend, and even Guibert's own guilt at the idea he may himself have unwittingly infected others; at another, Mancini, interned in a psychiatric hospital by the family of the young male model for his painting, joins the cortège of doomed artists and writers with whom Guibert both identifies and struggles as predecessors. His desire to attempt to reproduce (badly) the painting, over and over again, is reminiscent of his desire to write a parody of another doomed artist, the Austrian writer Thomas Bernhard whose death had preceded the beginning of the writing of *A l'ami qui ne m'a pas sauvé la vie* by a matter of months. Guibert describes Bernhard's incantatory style as infecting his own writing, in an imitation of the way the HIV virus is infecting his body. Just as Mancini's painting is an enigma, Bernhard's style is said to be a monstrous inflation of its own subject; the slippage between style and substance fascinates Guibert, and points us again towards the idea of writing as simultaneously revelation and disguise.

As he approaches his death he describes himself as collecting objects and drawings like 'le pharaon qui prépare l'aménagement de son tombeau, avec sa propre image démultipliée qui en désignera l'accès,

---

[40] 'continuing to write books, and to draw, more and more, as much as you can take, to the point of insanity'; 'all the books that could be written [...] and to devour those books almost simultaneously in the reduced margin of time, and to devour time with them, voraciously'.

[41] 'The painting did not reveal the story behind its subject but cloaked it, just as I always like, in an enigma: was the young boy the murderer of the victim whose body had been carried out of the picture? Or his second in the duel? Was he his brother? His lover? His son?'

ou au contraire le compliquera de détours, de mensonges et de faux-semblants' (229).[42] One of the objects in this collection is the photograph which he takes in Lisbon of five translucid wax heads of small boys, sold as votive offerings for relatives of children struck down by meningitis. Guibert arranges them for his photograph on the balcony of his hotel room in front of a panoramic view of the city without at first realizing that the five heads could be taken to represent the 'Club des 5', the sombre group formed by Jules, Berthe, the two children and himself, all likely to be victims of the AIDS virus. The mix of splendour and vulnerability of the image is disturbing, and no serene outcome is suggested as the narrator struggles and fails in hasty desperation to find a suitable church in which to place the heads and invoke the prayers of others for them. In this episode he seeks the prayers of strangers, just as he had sought the prayers of Japanese monks in Kyoto with a coded wish, after employing his best artistic efforts in copying out a holy text . The text of *A l'Ami qui ne m'a pas sauvé la vie* is similarly addressed, beyond its title, to unknown readers.

Readers

Readers are crucial to the writing scenario sketched out above, in which Guibert confesses or displays to the reader in his own time what is being inexorably displayed to others such as doctors or Bill, according to a schedule and formula which is not that of his own making. But the question remains of which reader. Does the text construct a particular reader? Lawrence Schehr suggests that there is a real risk that the AIDS text brings about 'the loss of the textual space, the loss of the text itself in favour of a sympathy that blinds the reader to what he or she is reading'.[43] Here no reader other than a sympathetic one, a potentially HIV positive reader, is posited. The huge and favourable public response which Guibert received to his text certainly supports this view, but there remains a question of whether we read as a metaphoric brother-in-arms.[44] It seems rather to me that the text generates sympathy in readers who do not feel themselves at risk (as most of the general reading public for French texts, rightly or wrongly, probably felt themselves to be in 1991 and probably continue to do so). The use of the medical voices, noted above, to convey the general

---

[42] 'the pharaoh deciding how his tomb will be arranged, with multiple copies of his own image indicating the opening, or, on the contrary, deciding to complicate entry with detours, lies and pretences'.

[43] Schehr *Alcibiades at the door*, 162.

[44] A term suggested by fellow novelist Patrick Grainville in his review of the novel in *Le Figaro*, 14 Mar. 1990, 34.

information about the virus, together with the use of strong visual im-
agery which conveys the psychological state of the narrator, seems clearly
directed at those who know almost nothing of AIDS, and who are drawn in
to the narrative by the very illusion that Guibert may be saved which is
announced in such paradoxical form in the first sentence: 'J'ai eu le sida
pendant trois mois' (9).[45] As the narrative proceeds, there is, as many commentators at the time of publication noted, a detective story element, in
which the curiosity of knowing what can be meant by the opening declaration is reinforced by the desire to know what the results of the next test will
be. Perhaps guilt at this curiosity is a driving force in sympathy: the French
gay press, unable to participate in this comfortably safe curiosity, was
notably less sympathetic to the text than the mainstream newspapers.[46]

Discourses of death are certainly always difficult for the reader to
handle, and reading today we are likely to feel uncomfortably addressed
from beyond the grave. Yet there is an exhilarating sense to the narrative
which goes far beyond curiosity and guilt. In one of the many marvellous
images thrown up in the course of the narrative, Guibert explores the
fantasy of his erstwhile friend Dr Nacier to create a 'mouroir design', a
clinic which would exploit AIDS by providing a highly expensive hi-tech
context in which a long and ghastly death could be converted into a first-
class trip to the moon. This fantasy shares many of the futuristic features
exhibited elsewhere in the text as targets of Guibert's ferocious irony. But
Muzil also becomes a party to this fantasy, and reshapes it according to his
own desires, converting it into a cultural palace of music and painting,
which would be a place not to die in, but to pretend to die in. Behind one
of the paintings would be a secret door, through which Muzil would
slip out into a back yard, dead in the eyes of the world but in reality free to
reinvent his identity. In writing, Guibert fashions his own 'mouroir
design', a place of culture and painting like Muzil's vision, in which
Mancini, Bernhard, and others are present, but which is not a place
enabling a quiet exit. It is, rather, a place of exhibition, but not, as one
might expect, so much an exhibition of suffering and the sick body, as an
exhibition of what matters in life and death for Guibert, an exhibition
which may prompt the reader to ask what value we put on friendship,
on writing, on what we have learned from others, or may prompt us to
ask what we value at all, how we would spend the last few months after
sentence. In that sense, we may all be readers-in-arms.

---

[45] 'I had AIDS for three months.'

[46] *Gai Pied* does describe the book as 'sublime', but the author of the article strikes a defensive note
and includes a number of criticisms of Guibert which contrast oddly with reviews in papers such as
Le Monde and *Libération*. See Hugo Marson, 'Le sida à Apostrophes', *Gai Pied*, 16 Mar. 1990, 52–4.

6 Love stories: Annie Ernaux's *Passion simple* (1991)

Il n'y a rien de plus impossible à raconter qu'une histoire d'amour.[1]

Aspects of love

The great nineteenth-century novelist Stendhal began his treatise on love, *De l'amour* (1822), with the blunt claim that 'Il y a quatre amours différents'.[2] These four types of love are, he goes on to explain, *l'amour-passion*, *l'amour-goût*, *l'amour-physique*, and *l'amour de vanité*.[3] All amorous experience can be explained in terms of one of these categories; love is not a random, free, radically individual emotion, but rather repetitive, rule-bound, rationally analysable and predictable: 'Tous les amours qu'on peut voir ici-bas naissent, vivent et meurent, ou s'élèvent à l'immortalité, suivant les mêmes lois.'[4]

Stendhal's endeavour to theorize, and so at once to promote and to contain, love is not in itself unprecedented. On the contrary, from the codifications of medieval courtly love to the seventeenth-century *carte de Tendre*[5] and beyond, writers have played with—or preached—the possibility of systematizing lovers' behaviour within explicit rules and repeatable models. More specifically, Stendhal is a pupil of the eighteenth-century *Idéologues*, proponents of a science of man according to which all mental operations might be apprehended following a rational methodology. What is at stake here, in part, is the power of observation and reason: humankind, in even its most intimate and private emotions, is seen to be essentially unified, reacting (even when appearances suggest otherwise) according to shared patterns which can be dispassionately chronicled and rationally explained.

---

1 'There is nothing more impossible to recount than a love story.' Benoîte Groult, *Les Vaisseaux du cœur* (Paris: Grasset, 1988; Livre de Poche edn.), 143.

2 'There are four different types of love'. Stendhal, *De l'amour* (Paris: Gallimard, 1980; Folio edn.), 27.

3 'love-passion', 'love-inclination', 'physical love', 'vain love'.

4 'All loves that can be seen here on earth are born, live and die, or are raised to immortality, according to the same laws.' Stendhal, *De l'amour*, 29–30.

5 The *carte de Tendre* (map of Tenderness) appeared in Madeleine de Scudéry's novel *Clélie* (1654–60); in the form of a map, it purported to teach the ways to win or lose a woman's love.

A key concern for such approaches is to understand how individual variations may occur within the general laws which are observed. In response to this difficulty, Stendhal suggests a refinement of his theory which explains diversity but also threatens to shatter the whole project of categorization. An individual's specific experience of love is coloured by one of six temperaments (sanguine, bilious, melancholic, phlegmatic, nervous, athletic) and one of six political systems (Asiatic despotism, absolute monarchy, aristocracy, federal republic, constitutional monarchy, revolution).[6] These refinements already mean that the four types of love must be divided into 144 specific variants; but Stendhal adds two factors which complicate the taxonomy even further: differences of age and individual particularities.[7] Even if the question of age introduces a relatively restricted number of new variants, the individual particularities (a phrase which Stendhal repeats but refrains from glossing) allow a potentially limitless explosion of possibilities: if, for example, weight, eye colour, and shoe size may all influence our experience of love, the four categories into which all love divides do not prevent the possibility that no two occurrences are ever the same. The categorization proves to be fluid and perhaps even epistemologically useless, a discursive stance rather than a tool of cognition.

There can be no doubt that Stendhal sensed the fragility of his own taxonomical system. Immediately after describing the four types of love, he acknowledges that more categories may be required, perhaps even as many as there are people capable of love: 'Au reste, au lieu de distinguer quatre amours différents, on peut fort bien admettre huit ou dix nuances. Il y a peut-être autant de façons de sentir parmi les hommes que de façons de voir.'[8] Moreover, De l'amour is far from the dry work of systematic categorization that may have been implied so far. It is rather, in the words of one commentator, 'a notebook, a collection of thoughts, memories, anecdotes, epigrams, patches of analysis'.[9] The work is 'an erratic miscellany',[10] pained, wistful, fragmentary, and elusive. Like Stendhal's novels, De l'amour seems to recall an ordered, coherent, intelligible universe whilst also gesturing towards a more postmodern sensibility characterized by play, dispersion, and non-totalizable particularities.

Stendhal's work marks a moment when it still seemed possible to define love in terms of a restricted set of repeated responses. The strain

---

6 Stendhal, De l'amour, 145–6.

7 Ibid. 146–7.

8 'Besides, instead of distinguishing between four different types of love, one might easily acknowledge eight or ten nuances. There are perhaps as many different ways of feeling amongst men as there are ways of seeing'. Ibid. 29.

9 Michael Wood, Stendhal (Ithaca, NY: Cornell University Press, 1971), 33–4.

10 Wood, Stendhal, 34.

of French thought which has been described as poststructuralist or postmodern has focused rather on what cannot be generalized or contained within rigid patterns or rules, escaping classification and resisting intellectual mastery. This attitude has two consequences for the love story. First, when the focus shifts away from grand, public universal issues and back onto individual, unrepeatable, private emotions, the love story reacquires the intellectual and artistic prestige denied it for some time. Love is no longer a trivial issue of what can be dismissed as 'literature for women', even though the rehabilitation of the love story has to some extent coincided with the rise to prominence of writing by women. Marguerite Duras's *L'Amant* (1984) has been one of the most successful and widely studied French novels of the last two decades. Since the publication of Duras's novel, the new respectability of writing by women about love has been confirmed, for example, by Benoîte Groult's *Les Vaisseaux du cœur* (1988), the dark fables of sexual initiation of Marie Redonnet such as *Rose Mélie Rose* (1987), and by the principal subject of this chapter, Annie Ernaux's *Passion simple* (1991).

The second consequence of this shift in the intellectual landscape, however, has been the necessity of renovating the philosophical and aesthetic paradigms through which love is analysed and described. The title of Roland Barthes's *Fragments d'un discours amoureux* (1977) anticipates key aspects of Ernaux's work: it presents a series of fragments rather than a unified theory, it is a *discours amoureux* rather than a *discours sur l'amour*.[11] There is for Barthes no metalanguage separate from the lover's discourse in which love can be dispassionately dissected and theorized; and the traditional subjects of analyses which aim for universality ('we', 'one', 'Man', 'Woman') are replaced by the resolutely non-universal first-person pronoun.[12]

Six years after Barthes's *Fragments d'un discours amoureux*, the critic, psychoanalyst, and novelist Julia Kristeva spelled out the literary and intellectual stakes of this re-evaluation of love in her *Histoires d'amour* (1983). She begins with an apparently casual observation: 'Aussi loin que je me rappelle mes amours, il m'est difficile d'en parler.'[13] However, this difficulty of speaking is not simply the consequence of coyness or embarrassment; it derives from the very nature of the subject. In love, identity and language are put to the test:

---

11 'amorous discourse'; 'discourse on love'. See Roland Barthes, *Fragments d'un discours amoureux* (Paris: Seuil, 1977), 9.
12 See ibid. 7.
13 'As far back as I can recall my loves, it is difficult for me to speak of them.' Julia Kristeva, *Histoires d'amour* (Paris: Denoël, 1983; Folio edn.), 9.

> En effet, dans le transport amoureux, les limites des identités propres se perdent, en même temps que s'estompe la précision de la référence et du sens du discours amoureux (dont Barthes a si élégamment écrit les *Fragments*). Parlons-nous de la même chose lorsque nous parlons d'amour? Et de laquelle? L'épreuve amoureuse est une mise à l'épreuve du langage: de son univocité, de son pouvoir référentiel et communicatif.[14]

Love, in Kristeva's account, is essentially individual rather than the repetition of what others have known before; it is something permanently new, a revolution or cataclysm in which subjectivity is put at risk and language fails to communicate. And as it fails to attain the status of a theoretical metalanguage, the lover's discourse is confronted with its own inadequacy and becomes literature: 'Impossible, inadéquat, immédiatement allusif quand on le voudrait le plus direct, le langage amoureux est envol de métaphores: il est de la littérature.'[15]

The modern love story, then, inevitably poses the questions of the subjectivity of the lover, the nature of narrative, and the sense of experience. These are precisely what are at stake in Ernaux's *Passion simple*.

Ernaux and *le repli sur soi*

Annie Ernaux was born in 1940 in Normandy.[16] Through her first three novels—*Les Armoires vides* (1974), *Ce qu'ils disent ou rien* (1977), and *La Femme gelée* (1981)—she acquired a reputation as a feminist author by depicting the social, economic, educational, and sexual pressures on girls and women, and the difficulties of escaping from the ingrained patriarchy of French society. Her two subsequent books, *La Place* (1983) and *Une femme* (1987), form a diptych in which a narrator writes in turn about her father and her mother, combining in each case a personal memoir with an informal sociological study of the lives and deaths of ordinary people. These books also examine the narrator's own sense of class betrayal: her success in the educational system is presented as one of the causes of her estrangement from her parents and their provincial world. This betrayal

---

[14] 'In effect, in the rapture of love, the limits of proper identities are lost, at the same time as becomes blurred the precision of the reference and meaning of amorous discourse (of which Barthes so elegantly wrote the *Fragments*). Are we speaking about the same thing when we speak of love? And what is this thing? The test of love is a testing of language: of its univocity, of its referential and communicative power'. Kristeva, *Histoires d'amour*, 10.

[15] 'Impossible, inadequate, immediately allusive when one would want it to be the most direct, the language of love is a flight of metaphors: it is literature.' Ibid. 9.

[16] For a general introduction to Ernaux's work, see Elizabeth Fallaize, *French Women's Writing. Recent Fiction* (London: Macmillan, 1993), 67–74.

is inevitably exacerbated by the literary form of the texts in which it is described. Ernaux's novels are the kinds of works which the working-class figures of *La Place* and *Une femme* could not have written and would not have read.

Ernaux's next novel, *Passion simple* (1991), apparently represented a new departure. It is much simpler in form than her earliest writing and has none of its anger; and on the surface it does not share the sociological ambitions of *La Place* and *Une femme*. There isn't really any story here. The novel is written from the perspective of a woman who has been having an affair with a married man and organizing her entire life around the possibility that he might call. The opening line of the narrator's account (following a brief introductory section which will be discussed later) more or less summarizes the whole of the text: 'A partir du mois de septembre l'année dernière, je n'ai plus rien fait d'autre qu'attendre un homme: qu'il me téléphone et qu'il vienne chez moi' (13).[17] The feminist commitment of Ernaux's earlier work seemed to some readers to have been abandoned. Her narrator subordinates her life entirely to waiting for a man. Moreover, she behaves unapologetically like a stereotypical love-struck girl as she reads the horoscope, listens to sentimental songs, buys clothes solely for her lover to see and rejects the possibility of getting on with her career. The narrator depicts herself and her life as entirely bound up with her passion for her lover.

The momentous political and historical events going on during the period described in the novel barely impinge on the text. Although the narrator's lover comes from an (unnamed) Eastern European country, the fall of the Communist regimes plays no role in their relationship; the Gulf War of 1991 is briefly mentioned in the final section of the novel, but it is accorded less space and significance than the narrator's last meeting with her lover. The narrator describes how she can recall world events only in as far as they are related to her love; the fall of the Berlin Wall or the execution of Ceauşescu in Romania barely impinge.[18] *Passion simple* thus enacts what sociologists have called *le repli sur soi*, a withdrawal of interest from the public and the political coupled with a widespread cynicism about the validity of political programmes.[19] This *repli sur soi* can be traced against the different stages of the Mitterrand presidency through the 1980s. In 1981 Mitterrand's election as President was quickly followed by the election of the first Socialist government in France's Fifth

---

[17] 'Ever since the month of September last year, I have no longer done anything except wait for a man: for him to telephone and come to me.'

[18] Ernaux, *Passion simple* (Paris: Gallimard, 1991; Folio edn.), 61. Subsequent references are given in the text.

[19] On *le repli sur soi*, see John Ardagh, *France Today* (London: Penguin, 1995), 21.

Republic. This new regime was greeted by a wave of popular enthusiasm, parallelled perhaps by the public response to the Blair victory in Britain in 1997. However, whilst Mitterrand survived as President, the French left was defeated in 1986 and nearly annihilated in the elections of 1991, the year in which *Passion simple* was published. Hope for and belief in radical social change through political reform had largely evaporated, leading writers and other voters to search for their pleasures in more private, intimate, or passionate relations.

Problems of narration

If *Passion simple* can be seen to reflect a withdrawal from overt political and sociological concerns, the novel is a reflection on some of the aesthetic issues which have dominated French fiction over the last forty years. In form and theme the novel seems simple, perhaps even lightweight: a collection of thoughts, reflections, and recollections all concerned with the narrator's experience of sexual obsession. The very title, *Passion simple*, draws attention to the simplicity both of the experience narrated and of the manner in which it is represented. Readers familiar with the canonical 'great works' of French fiction will be struck both by the brevity and apparent lack of ambition of Ernaux's novel, when compared, say, with the hubris of Balzac's attempt to chart the whole of contemporary society in his *Comédie humaine*, or Proust's monumental investigation (running to thousands of pages) into identity and memory in *A la recherche du temps perdu*. With fewer than seventy pages of text, Ernaux's novel hardly bears comparison with such landmarks. However, the works of Balzac and Proust are no less products of their time than *Passion simple*, and they reflect epistemological and aesthetic ambitions (art providing the locus of privileged insight into social and psychological realities, and even holding out the promise of personal salvation) which have lost their currency. This chapter will argue that Ernaux's *Passion simple* contains, and its organization is governed by, a very subtle reflection on the problems of writing fiction in the wake of the immodest ambitions of a Balzac or a Proust.

A closer point of reference for modern discussions of literary form is provided by the *nouveau roman*. In their heyday in the 1950s and 1960s the *nouveaux romanciers* put at the centre of their work problems of narration which they (sometimes over-polemically) argued had most often been occluded in earlier fiction. They emphasized how the novel is a highly artificial construct, supported by all sorts of questionable ideological and aesthetic conventions. There is, they suggested, no such thing as a 'natural' way of telling a story, all narratives impose a sort of distorting lens on the world. Since the 1960s the *nouveaux romanciers* have declined in influence. Moreover, for many readers they were aesthetically challenging but in practice uninteresting to read; their sub-versions of readerly expectation were too overt or too disrespectful of literary conventions (plot, characterization) which, however artificial, nevertheless sustain much of the pleasure of reading for most readers most of the time.

As discussed in the Introduction, whilst more recent French fiction has largely turned its back on the foregrounding of aesthetic experimentation practised by the *nouveaux romanciers*, this does not entail a reversion to naïve, unself-questioning forms of writing. On the contrary, most often it represents the endeavour to combine an insight into the artificial, con-ventional nature of fiction with a set of themes and concerns which the *nouveaux romanciers* often neglected. There can be no question for recent novelists of taking the conventions of narrative for granted and regarding fiction-writing as an essentially straightforward activity. Ernaux's fiction is a case in point. Her earliest novels might seem to be an outpouring of anger whilst her later ones appear simple to the point of seeming artless; her *Journal du dehors* (1993) records disjointed, incon-sequential incidents, and *'Je ne suis pas sortie de ma nuit'* (1997) is a diary charting the death of the narrator's mother. But we shouldn't be taken in by this. Ernaux's writing enacts a radical aesthetic programme as it focuses on areas of experience which were most often omitted from the texts given status by the literary establishment. In particular, Ernaux charts the lives and experiences which are often banal, repetitive, and uneventful, and therefore given no place in texts that foreground great public events, adventures, politics, or actions on a grand historical scale. In this respect, Ernaux follows in the line of her fellow Normandy novelist Flaubert, whose *Madame Bovary* (1856) describes the life and death of a bored provincial housewife. And Ernaux goes a stage further than Flaubert in the cultivation of ordinariness: her housewives may share the frustration of Emma Bovary, but their stories will not be relieved by the pleasures and disappointments of adultery or the drama of suicide.

In *La Place*, considering how she might write about her father, the nar-rator asserts bluntly that 'le roman est impossible';[20] art is an appropriate means to portray the simplicity or complexity of an ordinary life. For Ernaux, however, this necessitates a reappraisal of fictional goals rather than the abandonment of literature altogether. Ernaux confronts the

---

[20] Ernaux, *La Place* (Paris: Gallimard, 1983; Folio edn.), 24.

incommensurability of stories and lives expressed in Sartre's *La Nausée* (1938) by the blunt 'Mais il faut choisir: vivre ou raconter'[21] (see Ch. 2 p. 55), or more recently by the insistence of Duras's narrator in *L'Amant* that 'L'histoire de ma vie n'existe pas'.[22] The phrase from *L'Amant* is echoed in Ernaux's *Une femme* by the insistence that 'ma mère n'a pas d'histoire',[23] and again at the end of *Passion simple* when the narrator asks herself and her reader: 'où est mon histoire?' (74).[24] Lives cannot truthfully be recounted in the form of stories, because lives are not plot-driven, they do not have the coherence, the formal, end-directed neatness which characterizes stories.

Ernaux comes closest to formulating the aesthetic project behind her fiction in *Une femme*. Her narrator describes her desire to write something which is neither simply a memoir, nor a biography, nor a sociological study, but which combines all of these; her text should be 'à la jointure du familial et du social, du mythe et de l'histoire',[25] or as she says later, 'quelque chose entre la littérature, la sociologie et l'histoire'.[26] She insists that the book is 'de nature littéraire', but she also wants it to be 'd'une certaine façon, au-dessous de la littérature'.[27] The ambivalence of a work which is both literature and *beneath* literature captures the difficulty of Ernaux's endeavour. In describing her mother, her narrator wants simultaneously to describe 'les traits personnels de caractère', to enable 'la découverte d'une signification générale', but also to preserve something irreducibly private, to write of her mother's actions 'sans leur donner de sens'.[28] The book aims to be both literary and non-literary, to preserve the privacy of memory whilst setting it down for others to read, to respect the individuality of the mother whilst making her a representative specimen in a quasi-sociological study. The tensions in such a project illustrate the difficulties of connecting private experience to the domain of public meanings. Does one person's life fit into more general patterns of significance, or is it entirely unrepresentative, unavailable to analysis in terms of social, historical, or cultural patterns? As the narrator of *La Place* attempts to discover 'la trame significative d'une vie dans un ensemble de faits et de choix', she becomes aware that she is losing 'la figure

---

[21] 'But you have to choose: to live or to tell stories'. Sartre, *La Nausée* (Paris: Gallimard, 1938; Folio edn.), 62.

[22] 'The story of my life does not exist.' Duras, *L'Amant* (Paris: Minuit, 1984), 14.

[23] 'my mother does not have a story.' Ernaux, *Une femme* (Paris: Gallimard, 1987; Folio edn.), 22.

[24] 'where is my story?'

[25] 'at the juncture of the familial and the social, myth and history'. Ernaux, *Une femme*, 23.

[26] 'something between literature, sociology and history'. Ibid. 106.

[27] 'of a literary nature'; 'in a certain way, beneath literature'. Ibid. 23.

[28] 'the personal character traits'; 'the discovery of a general significance'; 'without giving them meaning'. Ibid. 52.

particulière de mon père'.[29] Likewise in *Une femme*, the sociological ambitions of the narrator conflict with her desire to preserve what is unique and unshareable about her mother. In *La Place* and *Une femme* Ernaux hesitates between the search for general significance in private experience and the desire to protect the individual from a general and generalizing gaze. In her next work, *Passion simple*, Ernaux refuses more resolutely the assimilability of experience and its narrative to any pre-existent patterns that might be found in it or imposed on it.

Pillow talk

There is little point in giving a summary of *Passion simple* because very little actually happens. A woman waits for her lover and writes a book about it. However, the project realized in the book might also be expressed in more ambitious terms: it sets out to examine the nature of passion and the problem of how to depict it in narrative fiction. Since the 1960s an impressive array of women writers (including for example Monique Wittig, Hélène Cixous, Chantal Chawaf, Jeanne Hyvrard) had been engaged in the search for a literary language adequate to the task of expressing female desire. The term *écriture féminine* (feminine writing) was adopted to describe the most radical and formally innovative practices which attempted to break away from patterns of writing and thought conceived as inherently male. But, like the *nouveau roman*, *écriture féminine* was never likely to appeal to a broad popular audience. It is hard, therefore, to underestimate the impact of Marguerite Duras's *L'Amant* when it was published in 1984. Duras's enigmatic and cleverly staged appearance on 'Apostrophes', the highly influential literary television programme hosted by Bernard Pivot, helped give the novel a wide public airing; and its critical success was consecrated by the award of the Prix Goncourt, France's most prestigious literary prize. Duras's novel showed unequivocally that the enquiry into female desire and the nature of writing could occupy the best-seller lists as it had also occupied the works of some of the most demanding avant-garde thinkers and writers. Ernaux's *Passion simple* is a work written in the wake of *L'Amant*, and specific similarities to Duras's book suggest that the connection is entirely conscious: in both works, a female narrator recounts scenes from her affair with a foreign lover whom (for different reasons in each case) she

---

[29] 'the significant thread of a life in a collection of facts and choices'; 'the particular figure of my father'. Ernaux, *La Place*, 45.

cannot marry; photographs play an important role in both works, and even the final phone call from the lover at the end of *Passion simple* recalls that from the Chinese lover in *L'Amant*.

Passion simple is, then, a modern love story. We know the barest details about the two protagonists. She has sons at university and a job (probably as a teacher). He is married and comes from some unnamed Eastern European country; he is temporarily based in Paris and not interested in intellectual or cultural matters; later he leaves Paris to return to his home country. Concerning his appearance we know only that he liked Saint-Laurent suits, Cerruti ties, and to be told that he had some resemblance to the actor Alain Delon. And that's about it concerning the personal details of the lovers. We are told even less about the important stages of their affair: how they met, how they became lovers and so on. Such details, the essential ingredients of the love story, play virtually no role in Ernaux's novel. Rather than a chronological narrative or a nostalgic evocation of a lost love, this is a text about passion, memory, anticipation, and the experience of loss. The appearance or identity of the lover are virtually irrelevant, and it is suggested that it would be an intolerable violation of his privacy to reveal more about him: 'Il n'a pas choisi de figurer dans mon livre mais seulement dans mon existence' (33),[30] the narrator tells us. This is love story reduced to its bare minimum. The lover is referred to only as A. (the same initial used to refer to the wife-figure in Alain Robbe-Grillet's *La Jalousie* (1957), one of the best-known examples of the *nouveau roman*); and the narrator refuses to explain or analyse her love:

> Quant à l'origine de ma passion, je n'ai pas l'intention de la chercher dans mon histoire lointaine, celle que me ferait reconstituer un psychanalyste, ou récente, ni dans les modèles culturels du sentiment qui m'ont influencé depuis l'enfance (*Autant en emporte le vent*, *Phèdre* ou les chansons de Piaf sont aussi décisifs que le complexe d'Oedipe). Je ne veux pas expliquer ma passion—cela reviendrait à la considérer comme une erreur ou un désordre dont il faut se justifier—mais simplement l'exposer. (31-2)[31]

The narrator bluntly refuses to explain her love by reference to her recent or distant past, or by recourse to the cultural models which form our understanding and expectations of love: *Gone with the Wind*, in which a woman spurns and then loses the love of her handsome but feckless

---

[30] 'He did not choose to figure in my book, but only in my existence.'

[31] 'As for the origin of my passion, I do not intend to search for it in my distant past, such as a psychoanalyst would make me reconstruct, or in my recent past, nor in the cultural models of feeling that have influenced me since childhood (*Gone with the Wind*, *Phèdre*, or the songs of Piaf are as decisive as the Oedipus complex). I do not want to explain my passion—that would come down to regarding it as an error or a disorder requiring justification—but I want simply to show it.'

suitor; Racine's play *Phèdre*, in which a married woman is wracked by guilt when she conceives a passion for her stepson; or the pained songs of love and loss made famous by the singer Edith Piaf. Rather than explaining her love, the narrator alludes to the title of the novel in her wish *simply* to present it, to make it present once again ('simplement l'exposer').

And just as she will not explain, neither will she recount the affair as a sequential narrative:

> Je ne fais pas le récit d'une liaison, je ne raconte pas une histoire (qui m'échappe pour la moitié) avec une chronologie précise, 'il vint le 11 novembre', ou approximative, 'des semaines passèrent'. Il n'y en avait pas pour moi dans cette relation, je ne connaissais que la présence ou l'absence. (31)[32]

The narrator rejects the fundamental terms—*récit, histoire, chronologie*—which underpin the possibility of narrative representation, but which perhaps thereby also force the formless continuum of experience into pre-established patterns and meanings. Only retrospectively and inauthentically can significant and identifiable stages be found in the course of a life. This is stressed once again later in *Passion simple*, as the narrator is beginning to get over the affair after the departure of her lover: 'je ne peux rendre compte de l'exacte transformation de ma passion pour A.' (67).[33]

So, the narrator either refuses to give important details, or claims that she herself has forgotten them, or never knew them, or that they lie beyond her understanding. In this respect, once again, *Passion simple* makes one of the fundamental moves of twentieth-century French fiction: any assumption on the reader's part that the narrator will have a privileged, authoritative insight into his or her narrative must be discarded. The narrator's aspiration to superior understanding is subverted or, as in the case of *Passion simple*, flatly rejected. She is in no better position to organize and interpret her experience than we are; she is a participant, and one whose ignorance and lack of understanding are equal to our own. She refuses to fit her affair into pre-existing narrative models (*Gone with the Wind*, *Phèdre*, the songs of Piaf, Freud's oedipal triangles); instead, through the very form in which she describes her love, she aims to preserve it in all its contingent unintelligibility, as something which is simply a given, to be accepted and experienced rather than analysed and explained. In this respect she reflects one of the commonplaces of postmodernity: there is no reliable, overarching interpretative

---

[32] 'I am not narrating a liaison, I am not telling a story (half of which escapes me) with a chronology which is precise, "he came on the 11 November", or approximate, "weeks passed". There was none of that for me in this relationship, I knew only presence or absence.'

[33] 'I cannot account for the exact transformation of my passion for A.'

or narrative structure which can be imposed on experience to give it form and intelligibility.[34]

Lovers and strangers

One of the consequences of this refusal to explain is that the peculiar hold that the affair exercises over the narrator remains enigmatic. She herself stresses that there is nothing particularly interesting or remarkable about her lover. What we do learn of him suggests that he may be closer to being a boorish, selfish heavy drinker than the dream lover of romantic fiction. The little we know of him makes it possible to read the text as both individual and typical: it presents the particular experience of one woman, but it also says something about love as it is commonly encountered, as opposed to how it is presented in more idealized or dramatic cultural models. Love, here, is something banal, ordinary, but also strange, inexplicable, radically transforming the life of the person in love.

This entails an effective reversal of a still-powerful model of romantic love. One of the characteristic moves of Western literature is to figure Woman as Other, that is, to represent femininity as mysterious, ungraspable, and alluring to the male by token of its very otherness. At one point in *Passion simple* the narrator visits the spot where Beatrice was first seen by Dante, who would go on to transform the girl into a literary paragon of idealized, unattainable femininity (49). In one of the founding moves of French feminism, Simone de Beauvoir's *Le Deuxième Sexe* (1949) takes issue with this identification of Woman as Other, arguing that it inevitably places women in the role of object, whilst the knowing or desiring subject is always implicitly male. In an inversion of this model, it is the female narrator of *Passion simple* who occupies the role of speaking and desiring subject, whereas the male lover remains fundamentally unknown and unknowable.[35] The narrator knows nothing about his feelings for her: 'Je ne savais pas de quelle nature était sa relation avec moi' (34).[36] All she can tell for certain is whether or not he is in a state of desire by looking to see if he has an erection: 'La seule vérité incontestable était visible en regardant son sexe' (35).[37] The fact that he is foreign serves to make

---

[34] See Lyotard's definition of postmodernity, quoted in the Introduction, as 'l'incrédulité à l'égard des métarécits' ('incredulity regarding metanarratives'), from *La Condition postmoderne. Rapport sur le savoir* (Paris: Minuit, 1979), 7.

[35] This reversal is indicated perhaps by the use of the initial A. which, as indicated in the text above, in Robbe-Grillet's *La Jalousie* referred to the wife-figure, whereas in *Passion simple* it refers to the male lover.

[36] 'I did not know the nature of his relationship with me.'

[37] 'The only incontestable truth was visible if I looked at his penis.'

him even more elusive and unintelligible, because the narrator cannot assume that he acts according to cultural models that are the same as her own (36). They are also separated by language ('je ne parlais pas sa langue,' 36),[38] and French words do not have the same force for him as they do for her: 'Il ne connaissait pas de mots français obscènes, ou bien il n'avait pas envie de les utiliser parce que ceux-ci n'étaient pas pour lui chargés d'interdit social' (21).[39]

Consistently, then, the narrator emphasizes the distance that separates the lovers rather than the amorous bond that unites them. This enables her to abandon the Romantic cliché of a perfect union or fusion between lovers; the distance between sexual partners remains essential to the experiences of love and desire:

> Puis j'ai admis que cette situation m'épargnait l'illusion de croire à une parfaite communication, voire fusion entre nous. [...] J'avais le privilège de vivre depuis le début, constamment, en toute conscience, ce qu'on finit toujours par découvrir dans la stupeur et le désarroi: l'homme qu'on aime est un étranger. (36)[40]

The narrator is playing on the word *étranger*: her lover is (contingently) a foreigner and (necessarily) a stranger. In Plato's *Symposium*, love is described as the search for a lost wholeness undertaken by subjects who have had part of their own identities severed from them.[41] This fable of lost unity has had an immeasurable influence on Western depictions of love, yet for many modern writers it entails a misapprehension of the nature of desire. In line with an investigation which has been undertaken in the work of an imposing range of post-war French thinkers (Sartre, Lacan, Levinas, Deleuze, for example), *Passion simple* presents desire not as the search for a missing 'other half' who will make the lover whole; rather, it is desire for that which, in the desired person, is irreducible to my own familiar world and understanding. In the words of Emmanuel Levinas, whose work revolves around the relationship between self and Other, 'Le Désir est désir de l'absolument Autre'.[42]

---

38 'I did not speak his language.'

39 'He didn't know any obscene French words, or else he didn't want to use them because they didn't have a social taboo for him.'

40 'Then I acknowledged that this situation saved me from the illusion of believing in a perfect communication, indeed fusion, between us. [...] I had the privilege of living from the start, constantly, in full consciousness, what one always ends by discovering in stupor and disarray: the man one loves is a stranger/foreigner.'

41 See Plato's *Symposium*, in *The Collected Dialogues*, ed. Edith Hamilton and Huntington Cairns (Princeton: Princeton University Press, 1961), 542–5.

42 'Desire is desire for the absolutely Other.' Emmanuel Levinas, *Totalité et infini. Essai sur l'extériorité* (The Hague: Martinus Nijhoff, 1971; Livre de Poche edn.), 23.

Desire, then, is a relation to otherness, an encounter with something radically alien which calls into question the constitution of my own world and challenges the very nature of who I am.[43] At the end of *Passion simple* the narrator sums up her affair and what she has learned from it; this entails a disappropriation of her sense of selfhood and a redrawing of the boundaries of her own identity and her own possibilities of experience:

> Et que tout cela commence à m'être aussi étranger que s'il s'agissait de l'expérience d'une autre femme ne change rien à ceci: grâce à lui, je me suis approchée de la limite qui me sépare de l'autre, au point d'imaginer parfois la franchir.
>
> J'ai mesuré le temps autrement, de tout mon corps.
>
> J'ai découvert de quoi on peut être capable, autant dire de tout. Désirs sublimes ou mortels, absence de dignité, croyances et conduites que je trouvais insensées chez les autres tant que je n'y avais pas moi-même recours. A son insu, il m'a reliée davantage au monde. (76)[44]

Storytelling

The narrator's love story has no beginning or real end, it is constituted by an interminable waiting for something which may or may not happen, for a lover who may or may not call. Just as her love is for a partner who remains elusive, her own experience, and hence her own story, marks a break with familiar patterns of behaviour by which we structure our world and make it intelligible to ourselves. The probing of structures also requires a questioning of the literary forms which perpetuate such structures. This apparently simple little work is in fact centrally concerned with the problem of its own narrative; it is densely self-referential,

---

[43] The same discovery of the essential otherness of the lover is signalled in Groult's *Les Vaisseaux du cœur*, 235: 'J'ai longtemps pensé dans ma jeunesse que s'aimer, c'était fusionner. Et pas seulement dans la brève et banale union des corps, ni même dans un orgasme mystique. Je ne le pense plus. Il me semble aujourd'hui qu'aimer, c'est rester deux, jusqu'au déchirement. Lozerech n'est pas, ne sera jamais mon semblable. Mais c'est peut-être ce qui fonde notre passion' ('For a long time in my youth I thought that being in love was fusion. And not only in the rapid and banal union of bodies, not even in a mystical orgasm. I no longer think that. It seems to me today that being in love is remaining two, to the point of heartbreak. Lozerech is not, will never be, like me. But that is perhaps what lies at the basis of our passion').

[44] 'And the fact that all that is beginning to be as foreign to me as if it were the experience of another woman does not change this: thanks to him, I have approached the limit which separates me from the other, to the point of imagining sometimes being able to cross over. | I measured time differently, with all my body. | I discovered what one may be capable of, which is as much as saying of everything. Sublime and mortal desires, absence of dignity, beliefs and actions which I found ridiculous in others so long as I didn't adopt them myself. Unknown to him, he gave me closer ties to the world.'

foregrounding the narration and reception of the text, and the significance of the narrative act itself. The narrator constantly refers to literary works, films, and other cultural media which have moulded her experience of love. *Gone with the Wind*, *Phèdre*, Dante's Beatrice, and the songs of Piaf have already been mentioned. She also refers to Grossman's *Vie et destin* (15) and Tolstoy's *Anna Karenina*, flicks through a work entitled *Techniques de l'amour physique* (23), mentions the magazines *Nous deux* (9, in the epigraph from Barthes) and *Marie-Claire* (26), Oshima's film *Empire of the Senses* (28) as well as Pialat's *Loulou* and Blier's *Trop belle pour toi* and *La Femme d'à côté* (39), an American television soap opera (33), Michelangelo's statue of David and Courbet's painting 'L'Origine du monde' (50), and the stereotypical representations of women in television and magazine advertisements (53).

Through such references, *Passion simple* suggests that the cultural representations to which we are exposed inform the way we experience and conceive the world. She imagines that if her lover can identify their affair with a relationship represented on film, it will seem 'plus belle, en tout cas justifiée' (39).[45] The mediation of experience through culture is a central notion throughout Ernaux's writing, as it deals with the ways in which people are influenced by culturally embedded ideas of who they are and how they should behave. This is suggested in part by the very title of Ernaux's novel *Ce qu'ils disent ou rien*: people are either what they are made through the words of others, or they are nothing at all. *Passion simple* is quite explicit in its ambition to offer to the reader a new model of a love story, one which may then rival other models mentioned by actually influencing the ways in which love may be experienced: 'Je me demande si je n'écris pas pour savoir si les autres n'ont pas fait ou ressenti des choses identiques, sinon, pour qu'ils trouvent normal de les ressentir. Même, qu'ils les vivent à leur tour en oubliant qu'il les ont lues quelque part un jour' (65–6).[46] In these two sentences, the initial modest aim of finding out about others ('pour savoir') escalates and transmutes. The work becomes an act of self-justification for behaviour outside normal patterns ('pour qu'ils trouvent normal'), and then hopes to influence the future experience of its readers ('qu'ils les vivent à leur tour'). Language and culture, it is implied, play a constitutive role in who we are and what we feel; so, when new ways of narrating the love story are explored, the reader's understanding of love may be changed. The possibilities of experience are enlarged when the limits of narrative are extended.

[45] 'more beautiful, in any case justified'.
[46] 'I wonder if I am not writing in order to know if others haven't done or felt identical things, or else, so that they might find it natural to feel them. Even so that they might live them in turn, forgetting that they once read them somewhere.'

So, *Passion simple* is an account of an affair, but also an autobiography of the narrative act itself, a highly dense reflection on the role and nature of narration. The narrator starts writing after the departure of her lover in order to hold on to the affair as it slips away from her. Towards the end of her account, she reaches the point where she describes the inception of the narrative itself as she quotes her opening words: 'J'ai commencé de raconter "à partir du mois de septembre je n'ai plus rien fait, qu'attendre un homme", etc., deux mois environ après le départ de A., je ne sais plus quel jour' (60).[47] The narrator quotes her own text, comments on technical aspects of it such as her use of imperfect and present tenses, and tells us the reasons why the text is written. In the process, she highlights the curious and poignant discrepancy inherent in her endeavour to preserve experience in writing. On the one hand, the text cannot hope to capture an affair depicted as elusive and senseless; the gap between writing and lived experience remains unbreached: 'Le temps de l'écriture n'a rien à voir avec celui de la passion' (61).[48] On the other hand, and at the same time, writing serves as a way of remaining within the experience, of struggling against its dissipation. So, the constitutive tension of the text lies in its depiction of writing as an attempt to preserve an experience which it can nevertheless not hope to represent faithfully and directly. In this respect, the account of passion in *Passion simple* has important parallels with *Une femme*, in which writing functions for the narrator as a way of clinging on to her dead mother but also consecrates an irreversible sense of loss.

The analysis of the writing subject's personal investment in the act of narration is pushed further to include the publication and future reception of the text. The meaning of the narrative is depicted as being as unstable as the meaning of the affair which the text records. Once published, the work is fundamentally changed. At the moment of writing, it is private, available to the narrator alone. However, when she considers beginning to type out her illegible handwritten text, the narrator is aware that its meaning is transformed: 'Tant que j'étais dans la nécessité d'écrire, je ne me souciais pas de cette éventualité. Maintenant que je suis allée au bout de cette nécessité, je regarde les pages écrites avec étonnement et une sorte de honte, jamais ressentie—au contraire—en vivant ma passion, pas davantage en la relatant. Ce sont les jugements, les valeurs "normales" du monde qui se rapprochent avec la perspective d'une publication' (69).[49]

---

[47] 'I started to recount "since the month of September, I have no longer done anything except wait for a man", etc., around two months after the departure of A., I no longer know what day it was.'

[48] 'The time of writing has nothing to do with the time of passion.'

[49] 'As long as I felt the necessity to write, I wasn't concerned with that eventuality. Now that I have come through that necessity, I look at the written pages with astonishment and a sort of shame that I never felt—on the contrary—whilst living my passion, nor in relating it. The "normal" values of the world get closer with the prospect of publication.'

And she envisages being asked by future interviewers the predictable question: 'est-ce autobiographique?' (70).[50] A further twist is added to the complexity of the narrative: not only does the text fail to preserve an elusive experience, but its publication further severs its author from the intimacy of writing; making an experience available to others exacerbates its loss. *Passion simple* thus marks the inevitable tension between the essential privacy and uniqueness of experience (and of writing), and any endeavour to share, communicate, explain or make intelligible to others.

Beginnings and endings

The text's first and most important attempt at self-representation occurs right at the beginning of the work, in a brief section preceding the narrator's account of her affair. She describes the experience of watching an erotic film on Canal+, a subscription channel which non-subscribers such as the narrator can only receive in a scrambled form: 'Mon poste n'a pas de décodeur, les images sur l'écran étaient floues, les paroles remplacées par un bruitage étrange, grésillements, clapotis, une sorte d'autre langage, doux et ininterrompu. [. . .] L'histoire était incompréhensible et on ne pouvait prévoir quoi que ce soit, des gestes ou des actions' (11).[51] The play on the word *décodeur* is of crucial importance here. It refers literally to the device which makes it possible for subscribers to unscramble the broadcasts of Canal+, and by extension to the conceptual key which would make it possible to decode otherwise partially or largely unintelligible messages. Without a decoder, the broadcast or story does not make sense, it is both unintelligible and unpredictable in terms of available interpretative codes. So the erotic film watched by Ernaux's narrator, like the love story she is about to narrate, is defamiliarized; one of the best-known and most popular types of narrative in the Western tradition, the love story, thus appears as scrambled and deeply strange. The predictable patterns and models are disturbed, and we are left with something both familiar and incomprehensible. This is love, but not as our culture knows it.

The pornographic nature of the film seen by the narrator is also important. She makes out the male's erect penis as it enters the female lover and later as it ejaculates on the woman's stomach. Such explicit,

---

[50] 'is it autobiographical?'

[51] 'My set does not have a decoder, the images on the screen were vague, the words replaced by a strange noise, crackling, lapping, a sort of other language, gentle and uninterrupted. [. . .] The story was unintelligible and you couldn't foresee any of the gestures or actions'.

non-feigned sexual acts are traditionally excluded from public representations, and are rarely seen outside private homes or specialist clubs and cinemas. Indeed, it is possible that the narrator is misconstruing what is going on in the film, since the details she records should not be visible through the screen block. Perhaps it is all in her own mind. Whatever the case, the point here is the same: vast, important, and even common areas of erotic experience are denied open expression in a culture which prefers to promulgate idealized Romantic fantasies of utterly fulfilling yet strangely non-sexual love. And one of the crucial areas which are thereby excluded is female sexuality, erotic relations as seen from the female perspective in which the woman is voyeur (of the film) and participant (in her own sexual encounters). The narrator's summary of the experience encapsulates the effect that her own text aims to replicate: 'Il m'a semblé que l'écriture devrait tendre à cela, cette impression que provoque la scène de l'acte sexuel, cette angoisse et cette stupeur, une suspension du jugement moral' (12).[52]

The disturbance witnessed on the screen has a double equivalent in the novel. The text contains no explicit sexual descriptions, so private erotic experience is not made available to the public gaze. At the same time, the novel aims to achieve a more general aesthetic disturbance as it rejects the whole history of Western love stories with their predictable patterns and structures. From the beginning, then, the text warns us that there will be no direct, unmediated representation of love or sexuality; the text aspires to the status of an undecoded, partly unreadable pornographic image. By discarding the familiar themes and narrative paradigms of the love story, the text suggests that there is no 'natural' or truthful representation of love, only a garbled set of half-perceived experiences and memories that don't quite add up to a consistent narrative. The love story doesn't make sense; and the partial, teasing, fragmented, non-linear manner in which Ernaux's protagonist narrates her love story does not allow the reader the illusion of coherence or ready intelligibility.

The disruption signalled at the beginning of the novel is matched by the disruption of its ending. In a sense we know from the beginning how the story will end: the lover will leave the woman, she will grieve for him and eventually get over it, aided by writing about the affair (the therapeutic role of writing is itself something of a cliché). However, the departure of the lover and the decision to write about the relationship turn out to be a false ending, as the text disrupts even the minimal pattern that it has allowed itself. A final section is added, dated February 1991: 'Je pourrais

---

[52] 'It seemed to me that writing should aim for that, that impression provoked by the scene of the sexual act, that anguish and that stupor, a suspension of moral judgement.'

m'arrêter à la phrase qui précède et faire comme si rien de ce qui se produit dans le monde et dans ma vie ne pouvait plus intervenir dans ce texte' (71);[53] but, the narrator adds, 'Il me paraît plus important d'ajouter ce que la réalité est venue apporter que de modifier la place d'un adjectif' (71).[54] She then narrates a sort of epilogue in which her lover rings up during a brief trip to Paris. This final telephone call again recalls Duras's *L'Amant*, at the end of which, years after their affair, the lover calls the narrator whilst (like the lover of *Passion simple*) on a trip to Paris. Verbal echoes and even the clipped style reinforce the connection between the passages from *L'Amant* and *Passion simple*:

Il lui avait téléphoné. C'est moi. Elle l'avait reconnu dès sa voix. (*L'Amant*, 141)[55]

Le premier dimanche de la guerre, le soir, le téléphone a sonné. La voix de A. [. . .] Lui disait 'c'est moi, c'est moi' avec lenteur. (*Passion simple*, 72)[56]

The final sentence of *L'Amant* reports the lover's words to the narrator: 'Il lui avait dit que c'était comme avant, qu'il l'aimait encore, qu'il ne pourrait jamais cesser de l'aimer, qu'il l'aimerait jusqu'à sa mort' (142).[57] These words serve to give the novel a wistful, poignant conclusion and raise questions of the sort, 'What might have been? Where did it all go wrong?' In its way, then, the phone call rounds off the novel quite effectively. The final telephone call in *Passion simple* allows no such finality. The narrator meets her lover once again, but it is as if this 'ending' had never happened: 'J'ai l'impression que ce retour n'a pas eu lieu. Il n'est nulle part dans le temps de notre histoire, juste une date, 20 janvier' (74).[58] Something has happened, yet it is also as if nothing has happened. And in this sense, this non-event, this non-ending, perfectly summarizes the affair as a whole: 'Pourtant, c'est ce retour, irréel, presque inexistant, qui donne à ma passion tout son sens, qui est de ne pas en avoir, d'avoir été pendant deux ans la réalité la plus violente qui soit et la moins explicable' (75).[59]

---

[53] 'I could end with the preceding phrase and act as if nothing of what is happening in the world and in my life could any longer intervene in this text.'

[54] 'It seems to me more important to add what reality has brought than to change the place of an adjective.'

[55] 'He had telephoned her. It's me. She recognized him from his voice.'

[56] 'The first Sunday of the war, in the evening, the telephone rang. The voice of A. [. . .] He was saying "It's me, it's me", slowly.'

[57] 'He had told her that it was as before, that he still loved her, that he would never be able to stop loving her, that he would love her until he died.'

[58] 'I have the impression that this return did not take place. It is nowhere in the time of our story, just a date, 20 January.'

[59] 'Yet it is this return, unreal, almost non-existent, which gives my passion all its meaning, which is to have no meaning, to have been for two years the most violent and least explicable reality.'

Conclusion

In *Passion simple* Ernaux confronts a set of narrative problems arising from the difficulty of representing the most ordinary and intimate experiences. Her narrative is an exercise in studied inconsequentiality; it adopts a structure, or to be more precise a structurelessness, which mimics the structurelessness and opacity of the experiences it describes. There is no story as such, no sequential narrative of beginnings and endings, no chronological progression from the first encounter to the final parting. The text drifts, like the mind of its narrator, through the disorder of desire, memory, and experience. The story never quite gets told, the narrator never quite succeeds in seeing her own experience from some final perspective which might make it all seem coherent and meaningful. Ernaux's boldest aesthetic move, then, is to make ordinariness and inconsequentiality both the subjects of her novel and the keys to its aesthetic performance.

Passion simple came as a surprise to some of Ernaux's readers because it upset their notion of what a feminist author should be writing. In her dependence on her lover and her willingness to let her life revolve around her passion for a man, Ernaux's narrator does not behave as some might think she should. At one point, she acknowledges that what she is doing is reproducing the most stereotypical actions of the woman waiting for a man: 'Je ne pouvais pas regarder la télévision ni feuilleter des magazines, toutes les publicités pour parfums ou fours à micro-ondes ne montrent que ceci: une femme attend un homme' (53).[60] These are precisely the kind of culturally potent and ideologically loaded images of woman which Ernaux's fiction depicts as exercising such a powerful destructive influence on her female characters; yet here the narrator is enacting them herself, apparently without complaint. In the liminary text, which describes the aim of achieving 'une suspension du jugement moral' (12),[61] the narrator attempts to pre-empt and disarm any disapproval the reader may feel; on the other hand, later in the book she recognizes that, once published, it is susceptible to 'les jugements, les valeurs "normales" du monde' (69).[62] So the text anticipates and perhaps even elicits our disapproving response.

This attempted evacuation of all moral and judgemental criteria from the text is perhaps one of the factors which make it most surprising

---

[60] 'I couldn't watch television or flick through magazines, all the advertisements for perfume or microwave ovens show only one thing: a woman is waiting for a man.'

[61] 'a suspension of moral judgement'.

[62] 'the judgements, the "normal" values of the world'.

and most unusual. Questions of whether the narrator's actions are right or wrong, justified or eccentric are, it is implied, simply irrelevant. They belong to a process of evaluation and sense-making which the whole text sets out to resist, both thematically and aesthetically. Stendhal began *De l'amour* by limiting love to four different types but then nuanced the categorization to the point that it began to look redundant. More than a century and a half later, Ernaux's *Passion simple* belongs to a strain of writing and thought which has broken almost entirely with the endeavour to understand and predict human behaviour by showing how individuals replicate more general patterns and possibilities. The human is valued not because it is rule-bound or governed by reason, but because it constantly frustrates the expectations codified by legislators of the psyche. The meanderings of desire and the vagaries of love are thus not marginal concerns; they are crucial aspects of the endeavour to chart a certain postmodern experience, in which intensity and uniqueness are more important than rules and paradigms. The most impressive achievement of *Passion simple* is that it rewrites the story of love with a deceptive simplicity and accessibility. It shows the passion of its title to be neither simple nor simply narratable. On the contrary, it requires a sustained reflection on the limits and function of narrative, and the development of a literary form capable of narrating a love story without recourse to readily available patterns.

Less overtly militant than some of Ernaux's previous fiction, *Passion simple* sets up an implicit defence of erotic passion, however politically incorrect the forms might be which it adopts. Indeed, the knowledge that she is behaving against her best interests or against her political convictions may positively contribute to the intensity of the narrator's experience. In the final lines of the novel, she describes her conception of luxury: 'Il me semble maintenant que c'est aussi de pouvoir vivre une passion pour un homme ou une femme' (77).[63] Such luxury, it is suggested, is both banal, ordinary, available to all, and also life-transforming, valuable and worth affirming even though not ideal and far removed from the models of fulfilment or tragedy that literature has led us to expect.

---

[63] 'It seems to me now that it is also to be able to live a passion for a man or a woman.'

Conclusion   **Modesty and disenchantment**

In one of the introductory texts to the short stories collected in *La Douleur* of 1985, Marguerite Duras instructs the reader without apparent irony, 'Apprenez à lire: ce sont des textes sacrés.'[1] This claim of special, sacred status for the literary text echoes the self-importance of the literary avant-garde which had been dwindling from the 1970s onwards. Far more characteristic of fiction's self-presentation during the Mitterrand presidency is a self-ironizing modesty, or an admission of its failure to be 'literature' in any grand, privileged sense. Duras's claim that 'ce sont des textes sacrés' fits awkwardly with, for example, Daniel Pennac's *Au bonheur des ogres*, also published in 1985. Malaussène meets a potential publisher who rapidly deflates his fantasies of literary greatness: '— Ecoutez, monsieur Malaussène, ce n'est pas un livre, ça, il n'y a aucun projet esthétique, là-dedans, ça part dans tous les sens et ça ne mène nulle part. Et vous ne ferez jamais mieux. Renoncez tout de suite, mon vieux, là n'est pas votre vocation!'[2] Since Malaussène's novel is also to some extent the text we are reading, this comment inevitably rebounds on *Au bonheur des ogres* as a whole. The same can be said of Patrick Modiano's novel of 1985, *Quartier perdu*. Modiano's protagonist is the author of second-rate spy fiction; when told by his Japanese publisher that what he writes cannot be described as literature ('—Ce n'est pas de la littérature, monsieur Guise. C'est autre chose'), he replies tamely: '—Je suis tout à fait de votre avis.'[3] For different reasons, Annie Ernaux displays a similar lack of confidence about the literary status of her work in *Une femme* of 1987; 'Mon projet est de nature littéraire,' she begins, but then insists: 'Mais je souhaite rester, d'une certaine façon, au-dessous de la littérature.'[4] And by giving *A l'ami qui ne m'a pas sauvé la vie* a title which looks more like a dedication or an address, Guibert appears to be presenting his text as a

---

[1] 'Learn to read: these are sacred texts'. Marguerite Duras, *La Douleur* (Paris: POL, 1985), 134.

[2] '—Listen, Mr Malaussène, this isn't a book, there is no aesthetic project in it, it goes off in all directions and it leads nowhere. And you will never do any better. Give up immediately, old chap, that isn't your vocation.' Daniel Pennac, *Au bonheur des ogres* (Paris: Gallimard, 1985; Folio edn.), 266–7.

[3] '—This isn't literature, Mr Guise. It's something else,'; 'I entirely agree with you'. Patrick Modiano, *Quartier perdu* (Paris: Gallimard, 1985; Folio edn.), 20.

[4] 'My project is of a literary nature [. . .] But I wish to remain, in a certain way, beneath literature.' Annie Ernaux, *Une femme* (Paris: Gallimard, 1988; Folio edn.), 23.

personal letter rather than as a work that can readily be classified under the more prestigious rubric of novel or autobiography.

In each of these cases, the text holds back from claims about its own literariness. It knocks itself off the literary pedestal; a hierarchical opposition between the literary and the non-literary is implicitly accepted, but the texts in question situate themselves at the wrong side of the divide, denied the special status still claimed by Duras. Modesty, of course, is a double-edged sword: if it helps make literature less élitist and more accessible, it also becomes less ambitious, less exorbitant in its aspirations and perhaps also in its achievements. Jean-Claude Lebrun, in a survey of French writing in the 1980s, makes a similar point: when the charge can no longer be made against some of the best French writing that it is too opaque for a broad audience, it can be accused on the contrary of being lightweight, superficial, too absorbed in the commonplace to challenge and extend the reader's understanding of the world.[5]

John Ardagh illustrates this response in a generally bleak account of French writing in the 1980s when he describes how literature in France has lost its 'human universality'.[6] He may have a point, but he is blaming writers of the 1980s for not achieving what many of them do not seek to achieve. The grand literary projects of Proust, the surrealists, the committed writers of the 1940s and the 1950s, or the post-war avant-garde all depend on an implicit faith in the powers of literature which is now corroded in the acid of postmodern irony. Disenchantment entails stripping away the discourses of salvation, revelation, edification, or enlightenment through which authors have dignified their work. Instead, authors are reluctant to make exorbitant claims about the stakes and capabilities of fiction. This does not mean that authors such as Duras, Semprun, or Guibert do not take what they are doing very seriously indeed, nor that their treatment of death, desire, identity, and memory is in any way trivial. But many of the younger novelists do not share the confidence of previous generations of authors that the novel is a privileged site where understanding of the self and the world are acquired. Modiano has described the novel as an anachronism, despite his continuing commitment to it.[7] So, in many cases the return to storytelling to which the Introduction refers may also entail a modesty about the storyteller's art and powers. Events are often inconsequential and disconnected, without even provisional pretence of broader significance. The perfect illustration of this is

[5] Jean-Claude Lebrun, 'Die Zeit des Erzählens', in *Intertextualität und Subversivität. Studien zur Romanliteratur der achtziger Jahre in Frankreich*, ed. Wolfgang Asholt (Heidelberg: C. Winter, 1994), 215.

[6] John Ardagh, *France Today* (London: Penguin, 1995), 27.

[7] Patrick Modiano, in Jean-Louis Ezine, 'Sur la sellette: Patrick Modiano ou le passé antérieur', *Les Nouvelles littéraires*, 6–12 Oct. 1975, 5.

Echenoz's novel of 1993, *Nous trois*. The text describes a series of dramatic events: an exploding car, an earthquake, an expedition into outer space. These events hardly seem to strike the principal characters as out of the ordinary; but at the end a normally suave and self-confident womanizer is paralysed when the woman he loves telephones to arrange a meeting. Having remained sanguine as he circled around the earth in a space ship, he cannot now even decide which shirt to wear.[8]

Modiano, whose novels constantly rehearse the senselessness and incoherence of experience, can be related to this trend; but its supreme representative is Jean-Philippe Toussaint. In a series of novels beginning with *La Salle de Bain* of 1985, Toussaint has perfected his own blend of inconsequentiality mixed with a dash of anguish. The emblematic self-referential encounter occurs in *Monsieur*, published in 1986. The central character, known only as Monsieur, meets Anna Bruckhardt at a party. The pair hit it off immediately: they talk all evening without asking each other any question, without exchanging the slightest piece of information. Their conversational mode is the alternation of anecdotes: 'ils se racontaient des anecdotes, plutôt, à chacun leur tour, qui, à mesure qu'ils les accumulaient, devenaient de plus en plus insignifiantes, se rapportant à des gens que l'autre ne connaissait pas et que, eux, ils connaissaient à peine.'[9] From time to time another guest wanders into the kitchen where the pair are talking 'pour voir ce qui s'y passait';[10] but the guest leaves as he had come, since, as we are helpfully informed, 'il ne s'y passait rien'.[11]

This guest, excluded from a conversation of which he cannot see the point, or rather from a conversation of which he cannot see that it has no point, represents the reader here. We are invited (the guest is *un invité* in French, of course) to witness the text's own dialogue with itself, in which no information is shared and no edification is offered. The conversation in the kitchen ends with 'une anecdote peu édifiante qui les mettait en joie'.[12] The text's pleasure here is its own withdrawal into itself, with the expulsion of sense and coherence, and to the exclusion of the reader except as uninvited guest witnessing the proceedings with uncomprehending bemusement. The distance that has been travelled in the paring down of literary language is illustrated when the conversation in the kitchen ends with the one sentence paragraph, 'Ce fut tout'.[13] When

---

[8] Jean Echenoz, *Nous trois* (Paris: Minuit, 1992).

[9] 'they told each other anecdotes, rather, each taking turns, which, as they went on, became more and more insignificant, relating to people that the other did not know and that they barely knew.' Jean-Philippe Toussaint, *Monsieur* (Paris: Seuil, 1986), 94–5.

[10] 'to see what was happening there'.   [11] 'nothing was happening there'.

[12] 'an unedifying anecdote which gave them great pleasure'. Toussaint, *Monsieur*, 95.

[13] 'That was all'. Ibid. 96.

the penultimate chapter of Flaubert's *L'Education sentimentale* ends with the brief paragraph 'Et ce fut tout',[14] the phrase is loaded with understatement and irony, as the unconsummated affair between Frédéric and Madame Arnoux peters out in nostalgia and Romantic delusion. The simple phrase carries much more than its weight. In Toussaint's novel, on the other hand, it simply describes the end of an anecdote. Flaubert's layers of meaning are transformed into a bland explicitness, hiding nothing, barely encouraging any labour of interpretation.

Narrative, in even its casual, everyday forms, has generally served as a means of organizing material into some sort of coherent unity. In the 1960s the enquiries of the sociolinguist William Labov into the narrative abilities of adolescents and preadolescents revealed that even the most untutored narrators recounting the simplest narrative sequences habitually endow an incident with some purpose or point: 'Pointless stories are met [in English] with the withering rejoinder, "So what?" Every good narrator is continually warding off this question; when his narrative is over it should be unthinkable for a bystander to say, "So what?" '[15] Today, the presumption of coherence in narrative can no longer be made, and the texts we have been discussing sometimes do not endeavour in the slightest to ward off the question, 'So what?'; on the contrary, they seem positively to invite such a question, to cultivate the bewilderment that would produce it; they resolutely resist the temptation to retrieve the trivial by assigning it a place in a coherent pattern, by giving apparent purpose to the pleasure of reading. In these novels the event is merely an incident, the story no more than an anecdote, and the anecdote merely a *fait divers*. Everything is as in the sketches described on the penultimate page of Echenoz's *Lac*: 'nulle forme sur nul fond ne faisait sens, tout était flou.'[16]

This attitude to narrative entails a wholesale revision of self-justifications conventionally sought by the French literary avant-garde. From the surrealists to the *nouveaux romanciers* and the *Tel Quel* group, the avant-garde has been empowered by the claim that forms of writing were bound up with ways of conceiving the world and understanding experience: change the former and the latter will also be transformed. The title of Robbe-Grillet's essay reprinted in *Pour un nouveau roman* captures this nicely: 'Nouveau roman, homme nouveau'.[17] Cast off the conventions of

---

[14] 'And that was all'. Gustave Flaubert, *L'Education sentimentale*, (1869; Paris: Garnier-Flammarion, 1969), 441.

[15] Quoted in Jonathan Culler, *The Pursuit of Signs. Semiotics, Literature, Deconstruction* (London and Henley: Routledge and Kegan Paul, 1981), 184; quoting William Labov, *Language in the Inner City. Studies in the Black English Vernacular* (Philadelphia: University of Pennsylvania Press, 1972), 366.

[16] 'no form or background made sense, everything was hazy'. Echenoz, *Lac* (Paris: Minuit, 1989), 188.

[17] 'New novel, new man'. See Alain Robbe-Grillet, *Pour un nouveau roman* (Paris: Minuit, 1963), 113–21.

literary tradition, and bourgeois society will come crashing down. The experimental writing of the 1960s was bound up with the aim of restructuring the world; the refusal of syntax presented itself euphorically as a revolutionary act. This constitutes the most recent version of the persistent Romantic faith in the special powers of literature, which goes together with the desire of authors to be the unacknowledged, or in some cases the acknowledged, legislators of humankind. Duras's claim that 'ce sont des textes sacrés' may indicate that the Romantic tradition still survives, albeit with weakened prestige. Recent fiction is more typically characterized by its conversion to modesty; no relation can be presumed between the story and an incomprehensible real, or between the *fait divers* and some distant domain of general truths. The novelist-protagonist of Modiano's *Quartier perdu* explains his decision to write fiction without reference to vocation, mission or ambition: '—Quand j'ai commencé il y a vingt ans la série des *Jarvis*, il ne s'agissait pas pour moi de faire de la bonne ou de la mauvaise littérature, mais de faire tout simplement quelque chose. Le temps pressait.'[18]

Is the modesty of recent French fiction explained by the fact that it has much to be modest about? Does it condemn the writer to be banal or inconsequential, with little to communicate beyond a self-absorbed fascination with his or her navel? Modern French thought and writing, particularly when it has been labelled as postmodern, has often been repudiated as disastrously relativistic: because it refuses all recourse to universal principles, it is alleged that it undercuts the possibility of any shared values. However, from within the postmodern perspective the issue is not to escape, to make the now implausible leap into universality, but to elaborate strategies of coexistence whereby traditionally disenfranchised groups can finally find a voice alongside one another, without any one perspective or set of values attempting to supplant other positions. And if, for many, universality is off the agenda, this does not mean that our only contacts with one another must now be trivial. Throughout this book we have tried to show that French literature has continued through the Mitterrand years to deal with issues of the greatest urgency: the liquidation of the still-traumatic legacy of France's colonial and wartime past, the Holocaust, the terrible spectre of AIDS, the labyrinths of desire and personal identity, the attempts to give value and meaning to life through the stories we tell ourselves and each other. The aim of the writers we have discussed is not to measure themselves against their

---

[18] '—When I began to write the Jarvis series twenty years ago, it wasn't a question for me of making good or bad literature, but quite simply of doing something. Time was pressing.' Modiano, *Quartier perdu* (Paris: Gallimard, 1984; Folio edn.), 20.

great literary forebears, but to find the words and forms to accommodate the experience of their own times.

There is a common, lazy response to modern writing which consists in decrying it on the grounds that there is as yet no consensus about the modern 'great authors' who share the uncontestable stature of Flaubert, Stendhal, or Proust. But perhaps this lack of consensus is a sign of the strength rather than the weakness of recent French fiction. Too many names vie for our attention, not too few. Moreover, the modesty we have described may not be a failure of ambition so much as an acute grasp of the contemporary situation. The authors we have discussed in this book, along with many others, have been able to arouse broad popular interest as well as academic attention. For them, writing for a disenchanted world entails the difficult labour of finding the stories which will help us negotiate a path through the unfathomable Real. Recent fiction anticipates the establishment of as yet unformulated strategies of survival which perhaps lay the foundation for a viable future. In this respect, disenchantment is not a dead end but a way forward.

Further reading and viewing

Introduction

A vast number of books have now been devoted to an assessment of Mitterrand's presidency, and of his 'era'. Julius Friend's *The Long Presidency. France in the Mitterrand years 1981–1995* (Oxford: Westview Press, 1998) offers a good starting-point and a balanced treatment of Mitterrand's successes and failures. Two books by Alistair Cole, *French Politics and Society* (Hemel Hempstead: Prentice Hall, 1998) and *François Mitterrand. A Study in Political Leadership* (London: Routledge, 1994) provide judicious political analysis. *The Mitterrand Years. Legacy and Evolution*, a collection of essays edited by Mairi Maclean (Basingstoke: Macmillan, 1998), includes a number of helpful essays relevant to the concerns of this introduction—on culture, history, the economy—as well as a useful overview. David Looseley's *The Politics of Fun. Cultural Policy and Debate in Contemporary France* (Oxford: Berg, 1995) is indispensable reading for an understanding of Socialist cultural policy. Jill Forbes's *The Cinema in France. After the New Wave* (London: Macmillan, 1992) and Phil Powrie's *French Cinema in the 1980s* (Oxford: OUP, 1997) offer a stimulating set of readings of films of the period. Several collections of essays on recent French fiction have been published; the essays deal mainly with individual authors, though some also attempt to sketch more general trends. See Michal Tilby (ed.), *Beyond the Nouveau Roman. Essays on the Contemporary French Novel* (New York: Berg, 1990); Joseph Brami, Madeleine Cottenet-Hage, and Pierre Verdaguer (eds.), *Regards sur la France des années 1980. Le Roman* (Saratoga: Anma Libri, 1994); William Thompson (ed.), *The Contemporary Novel in France* (Gainesville, Fla.: University Press of Florida, 1995); Jan Baetens and Dominique Viart, *Etudes contemporaines 2: Etats du roman contemporain* (Paris-Caen: Lettres modernes-Minard, 1999). Readers of German might usefully consult Wolfgang Asholt, *Der französische Roman der achtziger Jahre* (Darmstadt: Wissenschaftliche Buchgesell-schaft, 1994) and Wolfgang Asholt (ed.), *Intertextualität und Subversivität. Studien zur Romanliteratur der achtziger Jahre in Frankreich* (Heidelberg: Universität-sverlag C. Winter, 1994). Claude Prévost and Jean-Claude Lebrun's *Nouveaux territoires romanesques* (Paris: Messidor/Editions sociales, 1990) gives a lively and informative account of some recent fiction. Extracts from French novelists in English translation together with valuable background material can be found in Charles Porter (ed.), *After the Age of Suspicion. The French Novel Today, Yale French Studies* (1988) and Elizabeth Fallaize, *French Women's Writing. Recent Fiction* (London: Macmillan, 1993).

1. Marguerite Duras's *L'Amant* (1984)

Two other novels by Marguerite Duras have close intertextual relationships with *L'Amant*: *Un Barrage contre le Pacifique* (Paris: Gallimard,1950), written and published during the French war in Indo-China, before the French defeat, gives a less confessional version of the relationship between the girl and the lover, and is more conventionally narrated; *L'Amant de la Chine du Nord* (Paris: Gallimard, 1991), reworks the material in a more extended form. *La Douleur* (Paris: POL, 1985), the work immediately following *L'Amant*, groups together a number of texts dealing with the German Occupation. The film *Les Enfants* (1985), which she wrote and directed with Jean Mascolo and Jean-Marc Turine, also closely follows on from *L'Amant* and includes an incestuous brother–sister relationship. The film made of *L'Amant* by Jean-Jacques Annaud, released in 1992, of which Duras was highly critical, can be viewed in relation to Wargnier's *Indochine* (1991) and Claire Denis's *Chocolat* (1988). The critical literature is very extensive. There are a number of feminist studies of the text, including a chapter in Leah Hewitt's *Autobiographical Tightropes* (Lincoln, Nebr.: University of Nebraska Press, 1990). In French Christiane Blot-Labarrère's *Marguerite Duras* (Paris: Seuil, 1992) offers a helpful introduction to Duras's work, whilst in English Leslie Hill's *Marguerite Duras. Apocalyptic Desires* (London: Routledge, 1993) is a stimulating and comprehensive study of Duras's fiction and films.

2. Pennac's *Au bonheur des ogres* (1985)

To date, Pennac has published six novels in the Malaussène series, *Au bonheur des ogres* (1985), *La Fée carabine* (1987), *La Petite Marchande de prose* (1989), *Monsieur Malaussène* (1995), *Des chrétiens et des maures* (1996), and *Aux fruits de la passion* (1999), as well as a one-man play, *Monsieur Malaussène au théâtre* (1996). He has also published a number of books for children, a further novel, *Messieurs les enfants* (1997), and an entertaining defence of the rights of the reader (which includes the right not to read), *Comme un roman* (1992). At the time of writing, there is no comprehensive study of his work. The chapter on Pennac gives some examples of the use of elements of detective fiction in post-war film and fiction. Particularly interesting novels in relation to *Au bonheur des ogres* are Patrick Modiano's *Rue des boutiques obscures* (1978) and Didier Daeninckx's *Meurtres pour mémoire* (1984), both of which deal with mysteries originating in the Second World War. Mathieu Kassovitz's staggering film *La Haine* (1995) is well worth watching in conjunction with the Malaussène novels for their shared view of the poverty, disaffection, and simmering violence of the Parisian suburbs.

3. Jorge Semprun's *La Montagne blanche*

The Holocaust serves as a background to most of Semprun's writing, but is dealt with most directly in the novel *Le Grand Voyage* (1963) and the memoirs *Quel beau dimanche!* (1980) and *L'Ecriture ou la vie* (1994). Semprun's fictional treatment of the after-effects of the Holocaust may be compared with that of Elie Wiesel, who—like Semprun—was in Buchenwald at the time of its liberation, and who went on to win the Nobel Peace Prize in 1986. Wiesel spent some time in France after the war, and his fiction is written in French even though he is now an American citizen. See in particular his early testimonial text *La Nuit* (1958) and his later novels *Le Cinquième Fils* (1983), *Le Crépuscule, au loin* (1987) and *L'Oublié* (1989). For studies of the reassessment of the war years in French fiction, see Alan Morris, *Collaboration and Resistance Reviewed. Writers and the 'Mode Rétro' in Post-Gaullist France* (New York: Berg, 1992) and, with specific reference to writing by women, Claire Gorrara, *Women's Representations of the Occupation in Post-'68 France* (London: Macmillan, 1998).

The essential film on the Holocaust is Claude Lanzmann's unsurpassable documentary *Shoah* (1985). Interesting depictions of French behaviour during the war are given in two films by Louis Malle, *Lacombe Lucien* (1974) and *Au revoir les enfants* (1987). The extent to which the representation of the war is a continuing issue in France can be seen by contrasting the heroic portrayal of Resistance in Claude Berri's *Ils partiront dans l'ivresse* (1996) with the more sceptical treatment in Jacques Audiard's *Un homme très discret* (1995). For a sympathetic and sophisticated account of the problem of testimony, particularly as encountered by Holocaust survivors and in Holocaust fiction and film, see Dori Laub and Shoshana Felman's *Testimony. Crises of Witnessing in Literature, Psychoanalysis, and History* (New York: Routledge, 1992); and Sidra Dekoven Ezrahi's excellent *By Words Alone. The Holocaust in Literature* (Chicago: University of Chicago Press, 1980) analyses many of the issues involved in Holocaust narrative on the basis of a wide range of texts.

4. Jean Echenoz's *Lac* (1989)

Echenoz published two further novels after *Lac* in this period: *Nous Trois* (1992), which combines the hero's pursuit of a mysterious blonde with a trip to outer space, and *Les Grandes Blondes* (1995), which makes an incursion into the world of contemporary French television production. Echenoz is sometimes seen as part of a 'minimalist' stable at the publishing house Editions de Minuit which includes Jean-Philippe Toussaint (*La Salle de bain*, 1985 and *L'Appareil-Photo*, 1988), Christian Oster (*Volley-Ball*, 1989), and Patrick Deville (*Cordon-Bleu*, 1987 and *Longue Vue*, 1988). An earlier work worth reading in relation to Echenoz (and to much writing of the period) is Georges Perec's *La Vie mode d'emploi* (1978). This encyclopaedic novel of contemporary life, which only plays with the grandiose ambition of its title, presents the mix of fascination with objects, storytelling, and delight in the ludic also evident in Echenoz's work. On the cinematic side, there are obvious links to be made between Echenoz's work and the 'cinéma du look', the films of a new generation of directors in the 1980s which privileged style over plot. In particular, the elements of pastiche and irony in Luc Besson's *Subway* (1985), set in the Paris metro, and its questioning of grand values, make it an interesting intertext to *Lac*.

5. Hervé Guibert's *A l'ami qui ne m'a pas sauvé la vie* (1990)

Guibert went on writing other narratives up to his death, some of which were published posthumously. *Le Protocole compassionnel* (1991) and *L'Homme au chapeau rouge* (1992) are often considered as forming a triptych with *A l'ami qui ne m'a pas sauvé la vie*. Jean-Noël Pancrazi's *Les Quartiers d'hiver*, a sombre, beautifully written elegiac novel published the same year as Guibert's text treats the subject of the impact of AIDS on the gay community in a much more indirect way than Guibert. Monique Wittig's *Virgile, Non* (1985) is one of the best-known lesbian texts of the period: this witty and poetic narrative rewrites Dante's account of a journey through hell not with Virgil, but with a female guide called Manastabal. Autofiction is explored in Serge Doubrovsky's *Le Livre brisé* (1989), in which the writing of the text is, like Guibert's text, interrupted and transformed by events taking place during the writing process. Two films preceding *A l'ami qui ne m'a pas sauvé la vie* in which the actress Isabelle Adjani (Marine) appears are Besson's *Subway* (1985) and Nuytten's *Camille Claudel* (1988). Cyril Collard's film *Les Nuits fauves* (1992), which he directed and starred in as an HIV-positive film-maker, became something of a cult and won four César awards in 1993, three days after Collard's own death from AIDS.

6. Annie Ernaux's *Passion simple* (1991)

Ernaux's first works—*Les Armoires vides* (1974), *Ce qu'ils disent ou rien* (1977), and *La Femme gelée* (1981)—can be fairly unproblematically regarded as novels. The series of texts beginning with *La Place* (1984), including *Une femme* (1987), *Passion simple* (1991), *Journal du dehors* (1993), *La Honte* (1997) and *'Je ne suis pas sortie de ma nuit'* (1997), are more generically problematic, and explore in a variety of forms the experiences and memories of a narrator whom the reader is likely to be tempted to identify with Ernaux herself. As indicated in the chapter on Ernaux, in this and other respects the text which best complements *Passion simple* is Marguerite Duras's *L'Amant*. For introductions to recent fiction by women in France, see Elizabeth Fallaize, *French Women's Writing. Recent Fiction* (London: Macmillan, 1993); and on *écriture féminine* and French feminism, see Susan Sellers, *Language and Sexual Difference. Feminist Writing in France* (London: Macmillan, 1991).

Since the Second World War, film-makers have proved to be especially adept at exploring alternatives to simple 'boy-meets-girl' love stories. See for example François Truffaut's classic film of triangular love, *Jules et Jim* (1961). More recently, Coline Serreau's *Romuald et Juliette* (1989) and Leos Carax's *Les Amants du Pont Neuf* (1991) give new twists to familiar themes. Bertrand Blier's *Trop belle pour toi* (1989) is an unusual and cinematically stunning film about marital infidelity; and one of its stars, Josiane Balasko, went on to direct and star in the highly successful comedy about a lesbian affair, *Gazon maudit* (1995).

Chronology of the Mitterrand years

1981   May: François Mitterrand elected President.
       June: Socialist and Communist Parties win majority in legislative elections.
       September: Death penalty abolished.
       September: Jack Lang, Minister of Culture, refuses to attend the Deauville festival of American cinema.
       9 September: Death of Jacques Lacan.
       October: Nationalization of five key industrial groups and 36 private financial institutions.
       Mitterrand discovers he has cancer of the prostrate but keeps it secret.

1982   August: Terrorist attack on Jewish restaurant in Paris.
       October: Communiqué unveils the programme for the 'grands projets'.
       Decentralization reforms.
       Release of Wajda's film *Danton*.

1983   March: Austerity plan announced. Franc devalued.

1984   July: Laurent Fabius becomes Prime Minister.
       French Communist Party Ministers withdraw from government.
       November: First terrestrial pay-television channel Canal+ begins broadcasting.
       Death of Michel Foucault.
       France Telecom pioneers the Minitel.

1985   July: Greenpeace ship *Rainbow Warrior* protesting against French nuclear testing sunk by French intelligence service in Auckland harbour.
       Foundation of SOS Racisme and its slogan 'Touche pas à mon pote' (Hands off my mate).
       Release of Claude Lanzmann's *Shoah*.
       Release of Coline Serreau's *Trois hommes et un couffin*.

1986   February: Terrorist attacks in Paris.
       March: Right wins majority in legislative elections. Chirac becomes Prime Minister. First 'cohabitation'.
       Privatization programme begins, including the television channel TF1.
       14 April: Death of Simone de Beauvoir.
       September: Terrorist attacks in Paris.
       Mass protests against Devaquet bill to extend selection in Universities.
       Release of Claude Berri's film *Jean de Florette*.
       Erection of the Colonnes Buren in the Palais Royal courtyard.
       September: Loi Pasqua on immigration.
       Two new commercial tv channels launched, TV6 and La Cinq.

1987   Klaus Barbie trial for crimes against humanity.

1988   May: Mitterrand re-elected as President.
        Michel Rocard becomes Prime Minister.
    June: Socialist Party wins legislative elections but no overall majority.
    July: Mitterrand announces plans for new National Library.
    Release of Bruno Nuytten's *Camille Claudel*.
    Release of Etienne Chatiliez's *La Vie est un long fleuve tranquille*.

1989   February: Opening of Pyramide du Louvre.
    July: Celebration of bicentennial of French revolution. Grand opening of Opéra-Bastille, Pyramide and Arche de la Défense.
    Autumn: Affair of the Muslim headscarf.
    22 December: Death of Samuel Beckett.

1990   March: Release of Jean-Paul Rappenau's *Cyrano de Bergerac*.

1991   May: Edith Cresson becomes Prime Minister.
    Evin law restricts smoking in enclosed public spaces.
    October: Contaminated blood scandal breaks.

1992   March: Pierre Bérégovoy becomes Prime Minister.
    Mitterrand's cancer requires surgery and he announces his condition publicly.
    Trial of four doctors in the contaminated blood affair.

1993   March: Right-wing coalition wins legislative elections with large majority.
    Release of Claude Berri's *Germinal*.
    Release of Jean-Marie Poiré's *Les Visiteurs*.
    Edouard Balladur becomes Prime Minister, second period of cohabitation begins.
    René Bousquet assassinated ahead of his trial for crimes against humanity.

1994   May: Opening of the Eurotunnel.
    September: Mitterrand interviewed on television to answer allegations about his wartime record.
    November: Existence of Mitterrand's daughter becomes public knowledge.

1995   Release of Matthieu Kassovitz's *La Haine*.
    May: End of Mitterrand's presidential term and election of Jacques Chirac.

1996   8 January: Death of Mitterrand.

Index